OPEN UP THE
DOORS

Studies in Popular Music
Series Editors: Alyn Shipton, journalist, broadcaster and
former lecturer in music at Oxford Brookes University
and
Christopher Partridge, Professor of Contemporary Religion
and Co-Director of the Centre for Religion and Popular
Culture, University of Chester

From jazz to reggae, bhangra to heavy metal, electronica to qawwali,
and from production to consumption, *Studies in Popular Music* is a
multi-disciplinary series which aims to contribute to a comprehensive
understanding of popular music. It will provide analyses of theoretical
perspectives, a broad range of case studies, and discussion of key issues.

OPEN UP THE
DOORS

MUSIC IN THE MODERN CHURCH

MARK EVANS

LONDON   OAKVILLE

Published by

UK: Equinox Publishing Ltd
Unit 6, The Village
101 Amies St
London, SW11 2JW

US: DBBC
28 Main Street
Oakville, CT 06779

www.equinoxpub.com

First published 2006

© Mark Evans 2006

British Library Cataloguing-in-Publication Data

A catalogue record for this book is available from the British Library.

Library of Congress Cataloging-in-Publication Data

Evans, Mark.
  Open up the doors : music in the modern church / Mark Evans.
     p. cm.
  Includes bibliographical references and index.
  ISBN 1-84553-186-8 (hb) -- ISBN 1-84553-187-6 (pb) 1. Contemporary Christian music--History and criticism. 2. Music in churches. I. Title.
  ML3187.5.E9 2006
  264'.2--dc22

                         2006009194

ISBN-10 1 84553 186 8 (hardback)
ISBN-10 1 84553 187 6 (paperback)

ISBN-13 978 1 84553 186 7 (hardback)
ISBN-13 978 1 84553 187 4 (paperback)

Typeset by CA Typesetting, www.sheffieldtypesetting.com
Printed and bound in Great Britain by Lightning Source, Milton Keynes, UK and Lightning Source Inc., La Vergne, TN

For Mareta and Georgia,
may you both come to know the Spirit of the sound

Contents

Acknowledgements

The completion of this volume has been made possible by the kind contributions of many people. I am heavily indebted to all who have poured their time, spirit and wisdom into this project. Many thanks must go to Janet, Alyn, Val and the rest of the Equinox team who saw the worth of the project and made it happen. Liz Giuffre has worked tirelessly to secure copyright permissions – a thankless job that I thank you for. And special thanks to Sarah Norman, who has proven a most brilliant editor and improved the manuscript immeasurably.

My heartfelt thanks to Geoff Bullock, who shared his journey, and began my own. I am also grateful to Nikki Chiswell, Lucy Fischer, Mike Frost, Kirk Patston, Philip Percival, Rob Smith, Darlene Zschech and Phil Pringle, who all enhanced the project through their involvement. Support in various forms was also provided by Christine Carroll, Shane Homan, Sharon McDonald, The Cooma Crew, Tony Payne, Richard James, Ann Cole, Sally Craik and Tim Chavura. Many thanks to Vic and Jan Cole for making straight the path. To Megan, I pray that God blesses you as richly as you deserve, and that His grace does prove sufficient in all situations.

Thanks must go to my ministry partners St David's Forestville, Ryde Salvation Army and Soulfood Beacon Hill, who have all nurtured both my personal spirituality and my passion for congregational song. The constant support of the 'Lakoid' has been vital to this volume's completion. Not only was David Lakos consistently encouraging, he also proofread and indexed this work with great care (and joy!) – much to its benefit. Nat Wade and Phill Mudge have never wavered in their espousal of my work; support I cling to. Lauren Young has proven not only 'amazingly detailed' throughout the writing of this book, but also an amazing Joy.

I am deeply indebted to all my colleagues and friends in the Department of Contemporary Music Studies, Macquarie University; especially Denis Crowdy, and the technically gifted Dave Hackett. Valuable assistance has also come from Alex Mesker, David Blair, Mary Feely, Eric Damberg and Rebecca Coyle. I also applaud the patient endurance of my colleagues in IASPM – Australia/New Zealand branch who sat through developments in this research over many years.

Jeff Crabtree, Michelle Kay, Bruce Johnson and Robin Ryan have all pored over this manuscript numerous times, each time improving the material considerably. In all cases, your sincere friendship has underscored your critical involvement, and I thank you deeply for it. Phil Hayward, mentor and friend, has provided unceasing support from the outset of my research career many years ago. His professionalism, editorial ability, love of cricket and enthusiasm for research have all infected this book.

Finally to Julia, Ed, Matt and Katrina, thanks for all your support, understanding and encouragement over the years. Let the halcyon days begin!

Mark Evans

Permissions

The following copyright permissions were kindly granted for this publication. Every effort has been made to track down copyright holders where necessary. I would especially like to thank Parachute Music and Christian City Worships who licensed their music free of charge. Hillsong Publishing also made sections of their catalogue available at no cost. This kind of support will be crucial to the future of theomusicological studies, and is one area where administrators of congregational music can stand against the standard practices of the world.

'Ancient Of Days', by Harvill and Sadler © Integrity Media Australasia Pty Ltd. PO Box 1955, Toowoomba QLD 4350.

'Beautiful One', by Tim Hughes © 2002 Thankyou Music. Administered by worshiptogether.com songs excl. UK & Europe, administered by kingswaysongs. com, mail to tym@kingsway.co.uk. Used by permission.

'Blessed Be Your Name', by Beth and Matt Redman © 2002 Thankyou Music. Administered by worshiptogether.com songs excl. UK & Europe, administered by kingswaysongs.com, mail to tym@kingsway.co.uk. Used by permission.

'Can't Stop Talking' © 1996 Russell Fragar/Hillsong Publishing. All rights reserved. International copyright secured. Used by permission.

'Church On Fire' © 1997 Russell Fragar/Hillsong Publishing. All rights reserved. International copyright secured. Used by permission.

'Complete', by Andrew Ulugia © 2001 Parachute Music/Integrity Praise Music, www.parachutemusic.com

'Consuming Fire', by Tim Hughes © 2004 Thankyou Music. Administered by worshiptogether.com songs excl UK & Europe, administered by kingswaysongs. com, mail to tym@kingsway.co.uk. Used by permission.

'Days Of Latter Rain', by Geoff Bullock © Word Music LLC/Maranatha! Music. Administered by CopyCare Pacific Pty Ltd., PO Box 314, Ourimbah NSW 2258.

'Dwelling Places' © 1999 Miriam Webster/Hillsong Publishing. All rights reserved. International copyright secured. Used by permission.

'Gifted Response', by Matt Redman © 2004 Thankyou Music. Administered by worshiptogether.com songs excl. UK & Europe, administered by kingsway-songs.com, mail to tym@kingsway.co.uk. Used by permission.

'Give Thanks', by Henry Smith © Integrity Media Australasia Pty Ltd., PO Box 1955, Toowoomba QLD 4350.

'God He Reigns' © 2004 Marty Sampson/Hillsong Publishing. All rights reserved. International copyright secured. Used by permission.

'Hallelujah' © 2003 Jonas Myrin and Marty Sampson/Hillsong Publishing. All rights reserved. International copyright secured. Used by permission.

'Have Faith In God', by Geoff Bullock © Word Music LLC/Maranatha! Music. Administered by CopyCare Pacific Pty Ltd., PO Box 314, Ourimbah NSW 2258.

'Here I Am To Worship', by Tim Hughes © 2000 Thankyou Music. Administered by worshiptogether.com songs excl. UK & Europe, administered by kingsways-ongs.com, mail to tym@kingsway.co.uk. Used by permission.

'Hiding Place', by Ryan Smith and Jeff Crabtree © 2005 Christian City Wor-ships. Christian City Church Oxford Falls, Locked Bag 8, Dee Why NSW 2099. Used by permission.

'Holy One Of God', by Geoff Bullock © Word Music LLC/Maranatha! Music. Administered by CopyCare Pacific Pty Ltd., PO Box 314, Ourimbah NSW 2258.

'Holy Spirit Come', by Geoff Bullock © Word Music LLC/Maranatha! Music. Administered by CopyCare Pacific Pty Ltd., PO Box 314, Ourimbah NSW 2258.

'Holy Spirit Rain Down' © 1997 Russell Fragar/Hillsong Publishing. All rights reserved. International copyright secured. Used by permission.

'How Deep The Father's Love For Us', by Stuart Townend © 1995 Thankyou Music. Administered by worshiptogether.com songs excl. UK & Europe, administered by kingswaysongs.com, mail to tym@kingsway.co.uk. Used by permission.

Introduction

Personal Inductions

My initial involvement with contemporary congregational music came not long after my conversion to Christianity in 1990. While attending a traditional evangelical church in Sydney, Australia, my musical preconceptions about congregational music were confirmed by the strong reliance on the church organ, which was used in the (traditional) morning services and alternated with the piano in the (contemporary) evening service. I was invited to join the 'youth band' that played at the Sunday evening service once a month, as a pianist. The youth band had largely grown out of the Youth Minister's skills as a guitarist, and his interest in the new 'chorus' music that other youth leaders and musicians were becoming increasingly exposed to. This music had been sourced from David and Dale Garratt's *Scripture In Song*[1] series (late 1970s to early 1980s) and a more conservative collection, *Ring Of Praise* (1985), published by the Anglican Information Office. In the preface to the latter collection, editor Annie Judd noted that:

> The aim of the compilation has been to bring together a range of what we consider to be some of the better songs which have been written in the last two decades.

Such an aim brought the publication into line with material being offered in *Scripture In Song*, yet even at this early stage, ominous differences in opinions concerning the use of contemporary music in church contexts began to emerge. Judd continued:

> In most cases we see Ring of Praise *supplementing rather than replacing the best of the older hymns... We have attempted to include more of what we would call modern hymns than short choruses. While there is certainly a place for the latter, we have found that we tend to look for more 'substantial' content when choosing songs for services* (ibid.).

Herein lay the tension. While *Scripture In Song* was promoting – almost unreservedly – the latest congregational music being written, including contemporary chorus music,[2] others interested in Christian music were, at best, more hesitant about the new music's relevance, longevity, sense of reverence and theological content. Despite Judd's delineation of 'modern hymns' and choruses, such categorisation never took hold, and much of *Ring Of Praise* was grouped with the ever-growing body of contemporary chorus music. For a traditional evangelical church (or any other for that matter), introducing repertoire drawn from modern collections such as these immediately raised questions and created a sense of apprehension. For instance, were these new songbooks attempting to replace the traditional hymnals? Was the musical heritage of the church going to be lost forever? Would parishioners be driven away from churches by this new music? What kind of theological maturity would develop in churches that only sang the newer music?

Thus, as I took my place at the piano that first Sunday night, I found myself in the middle of a musical controversy. It was one that had equally passionate contributors, one that I would continue to be in the centre of for the next ten years, and one that would eventually accompany much of this book. Yet as I recollect that first evening, I realise now how blissfully unaware I was of the tension, the controversy and the debate. What struck me that night was that I was playing an old piano with a microphone lowered in it, taking my part in a musical bed that also held three electric guitars, a bass guitar and full drum kit, that was being led by a classical flautist and supported by two lead singers. The church that night was near full, largely attended by people under thirty, and the singing was robust. I recall glancing to my right as I played, at the old Conn organ that I had heard so often before. It had been unplugged to make way for the guitars. Something was definitely happening to contemporary congregational music, the effects of which were yet to be fully realised.

This book is written by, and from the viewpoint of, a committed Protestant Christian who is actively involved in performing, researching, teaching, writing and cogitating about music and worship. Such a disclaimer is important in theomusicological studies such as this, where too often material is disregarded on the basis of the author's affiliations – or lack of.

While I hold particular views about the nature of worship and debates within contemporary Christian circles I have – to the best of my ability – attempted to produce an academic overview and analysis of the issues that I survey and discuss. The concerns I identify, and the positions that I advocate in my conclusion, derive from my research and analysis, particularly from interviews with contemporary practitioners of congregational song, rather than being aspects of a preconstituted faith that I have set out to justify and/or bolster. Indeed, in researching and writing this book many of my former preconceptions and hypotheses concerning music and worship have been significantly modified and focused – illustrating the value and effectiveness of academic methods for those involved in religious practice. It is my hope that those reading this volume will also shelve their preconceptions about worship and congregational song in order to appreciate fully the scope and detail of this study.

Opening Up the Doors

> *Open up the doors and let the music play; let the streets resound with sing-ing...* ('Did You Feel The Mountains Tremble?' [M. Smith])

'Open up the doors' is a metaphor that works on many levels in relation to this book. It immediately predicates the biblical notion of opening the doors of heaven that the blessings of God may be abundantly poured out on his peo-ple (Psalm 78:19-25; Malachi 3:9-11). Yet metaphorically opening the heavenly doors also means that the praises and worship eternally taking place there might momentarily be revealed to all on earth. As Matt Redman reminds us, we witness the ultimate examples of corporate worship:

> *Through the open door*
> *Where the angels sing*
> *And the host of heaven are antheming...* (from 'Gifted Response').

In this sense the privilege of joining in the heavenly chorus should not, and can never be, underestimated. Our earthly worship is a mere shadow of the joy and intensity that true heavenly worship will be. But there is a further sense to the metaphor. Too long have our church doors been shut, the music inside insulated from the influence of the outside world, and more pointedly, bar-ricaded from influencing the world outside the doors. Christian music used to occupy a central place in the music culture of society. Now it has become a bottom-feeder in the near endless escalation of sub-genres and popular music forms. It is time to expose congregational song to outside forces. Not only am I speaking of the performance and dissemination of contemporary congre-gational song; it is time that the music also opens itself to academic critique and rigour. Our music has a spiritual purpose, to be sure, but that does not excuse mediocrity. To allow congregational song its rightful place within ver-nacular music studies, and more generally popular music studies, we need to expose it to the full rigours of critical analysis. But how will this help the Sunday night performance? It may not. But those of us involved in practising modern church music should be ever seeking to enhance and craft those gifts bestowed upon us; that our art be the best we can offer to the congregation, and to God. In that sense we '[f]ling wide [those] heavenly gates, [in order to] prepare the way of the risen Lord'.[3]

Partly, then, this book is about 'theomusicological' studies. It is about seeking to understand what they are, what might be included within the broad brushstroke that is theomusicology, and how we might go about performing them. This volume is therefore about progressing our discipline as well as our practice. There are many, many people the world over studying worship in colleges and seminaries, in universities and various tertiary education providers. Moreover, there are those practising worship leadership and ministry daily. I believe the time has come to move beyond more manuals and 'how tos'. We need critical examination, historical relevance, analysis, provocation and, dare I say it, some kind of theoretical approach towards contemporary congregational music. This may sound unnecessary, or downright boring, to some, yet the fact remains that in recent decades our discipline has lagged sadly behind the world of critical inquiry. This delay may mean that we have allowed our art to continue on, unchecked and unregulated by various tropes of analysis. This book does not seek to condemn or demolish existing musical practices. While my experience in assessing postgraduate students' research applications and examining research projects in theomusicology suggests that this is often a motivation for individual study, it is an unhelpful and divisive approach. Many mistakenly believe that somehow the Kingdom will be enhanced through systematic demolition of various churches or music producers. This is simply not the case. Our art, and thus our offering, ministry and outreach, will only be enhanced through critiquing what we do, in order to ascertain the various nuances of it. Not in order to dismiss, but to evolve and improve. To ensure our music bursts through the doors and onto the streets with relevance, impact and the gospel of Christ, our self-reflection needs to be honest, applicable and non-hysterical.

As a disclaimer it needs to be pointed out that *Open Up the Doors* is not, and for practical issues, simply cannot be, concerned with non-Western music. Or even, for that matter, the non-Protestant or missionary influenced music of various areas around the world (e.g. the Pacific islands). There is much more work to be done in these areas, and this volume aims to be an accompaniment to such important future studies. Likewise it also ignores Afro-American gospel and spiritual music. Not because this isn't a fertile ground for musical analysis and historical relevance; simply because the fence lines must necessarily be drawn somewhere lest the topic become unmanageable. Afro-American gospel is a music that skirts both congregational and secular settings, and is thus more appropriately studied in other contexts. Fortunately this work has already begun.[4]

The general aim of this book is to analyse elements of congregational song produced at the end of the twentieth century and beginning of the twenty-first in order to advance knowledge of the globalisation of popular music in regards to Christendom. More specific aims of this book, in conjunction with those outlined above, are:

   (i)   to examine the scriptural foundation for contemporary congregational music;
  (ii)   to investigate the culture of its transmission – particularly the extra-musical elements that enforce the vernacularism and associated community nature of the music;
 (iii)   to examine the depth and functionality of song lyrics;
 (iv)   to analyse musical elements of congregational song and how they evolved during the 1990s; and finally,
  (v)   to consider the influence of key music producers and publishers, such as Hillsong Church and Soul Survivor, on the culture of Christian music around the world.

Academic Inductions

My academic interest in contemporary Christian music developed through my studies in, and teaching of, contemporary music at Macquarie University, Sydney. Yet one of the most motivating sparks occurred not long after deciding to embark on this present research. In my initial investigation into contemporary Christian music I posted a call for information on the Pacific Music Research (PMR) email list[5] in September 1997. As with most calls on such lists this produced a wealth of useful information in private email and phone communications. What was unexpected, however, was the reaction of a minority of academics to the posting itself.[6] One particularly irate academic, Marcus Breen, posted a response indicating that he thought it inappropriate to discuss Christian music in an objective and secular forum. After others attempted to quell his angst, Breen responded:

> I am sorry...but I refuse to allow Christians to run the world. They have had a go at it for about 2000 years and continue to make a monumental mess of it. I am disinclined to create a space in the world of popular music for support of Christianity. I know we live in conservative times but whatever happened to critique? (PMR posting, 12 September 1997).

The problematic nature of this statement is quite apparent. For despite advocating an objective space for serious critique and analysis, Breen here enforced his own subjectivity into that space. As Trimillos noted in response:

> A scholar, because of his or her own cultural biases, may choose to ignore [the fact that Christian music is a] truly 'fundamental' aspect of most Pacific cultures in the twentieth century. Doesn't this represent another form of 'Western' domination, in which the biased scholar constructs the Pacific Other according to his or her notions of political (or in this case, religious) correctness? (PMR posting, 13 September 1997)

Trimillos identifies here the foundational aspect of Christian music in many Pacific cultures. To ignore such music, or dismiss it academically based on subjective ideologies, is to fly in the face of postmodern academic rigour. This clearly raises issues for the field of contemporary music studies generally, as noted by Niles:

> In general, I've found the subject of church music to be something most people have stayed far clear of, except to negatively cast it aside. Considering the importance of Christianity in PNG [Papua New Guinea] today, something very important is being overlooked (PMR posting, 10 September 1997).

Breen – and academics of a similar mindset – however, would have nothing of the 'importance' of Christian music. Breen noted:

> Surely there is a world of difference between analysis and critique of popular music recordings and what seems to be the uncritical engagement with the tools of western culture – Christian music making and values (PMR posting, 23 September 1997).

This book will directly confront Breen's assertion – by providing a detailed case study of popular congregational music. It builds on the work of Midian (1999), Zahn (1996), Corbitt (1998), Mansfield (1994) and Lawrence (2000) who, among others, have provided a wide range of academically incisive investigations into various guises of church music and history. Their collective academic writings have already proven Breen's statement naïve and unfounded. Yet Breen's opinions, and he is definitely not alone, are why more worship manuals and 'how tos' are not enough. What is required is a sustained, academically rigorous investigation of contemporary congregational music that considers all the permutations, ramifications and intricacies of the genre, and hopefully does so without prejudice.

The mere genesis of the above debate was enough to fuel my interest in critically pursuing the subject of congregational song, yet the passionate responses of those involved highlighted the fact that there were more issues at stake than I had previously realised. It became apparent that, while church music has long been a contentious issue amongst Christians, strong notions about the musical integrity and quality of Christian music also exist in the secular world. These opinions are no doubt heightened by the continuing commercial success of Christian music within the global music market. Statements like Breen's give credence to Johnson's assertion that we 'turn away in academic embarrassment from the everyday truth of music practices which deface our discourses of authenticity' (1998: 3). It has become apparent, therefore, that locating contemporary Christian music within the more general discourses of popular music is a necessary component of this present research. In understanding how the musically secular has been appropriated by the sacred, it is essential to situate the sacred within the secular. Chapter 1 broadly maps out the realm of contemporary music studies, placing contemporary Christian music within that map. Johnson's contentions regarding vernacular music are also explored in light of current trends and burgeoning manifestations of Christian congregational music.

1 Contextualising Contemporary Congregational Music

1. Contemporary Christian Music as Popular Music

The historical development of popular music studies has been thoroughly documented elsewhere, and need not be restated here.[1] What is relevant is to note the various points at which contemporary Christian music trends intersect with those of popular music generally, and more specifically, how they enhance and contribute to debates within the field of popular music studies. Recognition of these intersection points not only cements contemporary Christian music's place under the rubric of popular music studies, but also assists the evolution of the discipline of theomusicology by providing musical texts which offer alternate readings and positions in relation to current analytical understanding. For example, contemporary congregational music, as a musical form, has much to contribute to debates around lyrical analysis, performance contexts, production analysis, the role of audio-visuals and, of course, the notion of vernacular music. As Whiteley has noted:

> To theorise the significance of popular music...it is necessary to identify the interrelationships between musical sounds, lyrical texts and visual narratives... Musical meaning is thus located at various points (1997: xiv).

To these three elements it is necessary to add theological intent with regards to congregational music. Yet, as will be shown, each of these elements contains within it enough discursive information for a 'song' to be rejected or endorsed by the Christian community. Thus, the interrelationship between sound, text and ancillary visual elements is not always symbiotic. Indeed, one of the shortcomings of early contemporary congregational music was its dogged adherence to lyrical conservatism. In this sense, more than merely echoing the chronology of popular music studies, such reliance on the lyrical text directly parallels with early investigations into popular music. As McClary and Walser note:

> ...the verbal dimension of a song is much more readily grasped and discussed in terms of meaning [than the music]... The backbone of an analysis often is a discussion of the words – their versification, central images, and so on – and the music is dealt with only as

it serves to inflect the ambiguities left unresolved within the text itself
(1990: 285).

Christian choruses, for example, have often been dismissed by those responsible for planning and performing congregational music, because they contain considerably fewer lyrics than standard hymns and often revolve around one theological idea. The common complaint has been that choruses are 'doctrinally shallow and...redundant' (Basden, 1999: 86). Such criticisms have animated two distinct creative reactions from Christian songwriters. On the one hand many have sought to deepen the lyrical content of songs, often succumbing to non-musical prose structures in the process. Others have continued to strip back lyrical content to seemingly skeletal proportions. This type of lyrical reduction, and consequent increase in repetition, is also a feature of contemporary dance music forms. A key inquiry of this volume is to ascertain the spiritual depth and liturgical functionality of contemporary Christian lyrics. Yet as Whiteley (1997) notes, there is always a danger of focusing too intently on lyrical deconstruction at the expense of 'significant interpretation of the primary level, the musical text' (xv). She goes on to say that:

> ...analysis of musical parameters such as melodic, harmonic, timbral and textural entities, are largely ignored in comparison to the more accessible and easier to describe 'beat' (ibid.).

Whiteley's contention ignores recent scholarship directly devoted to timbral and, especially, textural nuances within popular music. Moore (1993) and Hayward (1998) both employ tropes aimed at – among other elements – the production discourse of a text. As Hayward acknowledges, 'traditional musicology regards the fixed notated score...as the central object of analysis' (1998: 9), yet 'the recorded version of a popular music track serves as a reference point for subsequent performances by the original or other artists – over and above any sheet music which might be available' (ibid.). This proves true for contemporary congregational song, where the CD version is quite often the first point of contact with a song, and certainly the reference point for subsequent reproduction in local congregational settings. Increasingly, the problem arises that the Christian music being recorded and released is often so highly produced that local parishes have little chance of closely emulating their favourite songs and artists. As will be seen, however, this quality is often limited to production value and definitely does not apply to the actual musicality of the piece.

Another factor validating Hayward's assertion that in popular music musicology it is the recording (e.g. CD) that is the central text (ibid.), lies in the acknowledgement that many congregational meetings, especially in rural or sparsely populated areas, rely solely on the recorded version of congregational song. That is, no musicians or band exist to perform the music so members sing along with the recorded version. To ignore the primacy of the recorded text, and its associated strands of texture (Moore, 1993: 106), is to miss a profusion of meanings that circulate throughout congregational music. What is also problematic about Whiteley's statement above is the notion that rhythmic analysis is easier to describe critically than other musicological elements. This may be true for some contemporary genres, though the Eurocentricism of the statement is embarrassingly clear – for example, how many African *djembe* drum patterns are initially easy to describe? Congregational song, whilst adhering to many western rhythmic stereotypes, does require subtle delineation of rhythmic inflections for these quite often dictate the use of the song. Indeed, many contemporary services are now planned around rhythmic distinctions (Basden, 1999; Liesch, 1996). Chapter 6 will provide a methodology for the musicological analysis that follows in subsequent chapters, involving a deconstruction of melodic, rhythmic, structural, harmonic, timbral and textural levels.

Consideration of the musical and lyrical construction of a text is no longer adequate in contemporary music studies. As Whiteley asserts:

> What is crucial to any musicological investigation are [sic] not simple or, for that matter, complex transcriptions of the musical content of a song, nor mere isolated semiotic analyses, but rather fresh analytical explorations of the ways in which musical discourses work in tandem with lyrics, performance styles, gendered identities and consumer positions (1997: xvi).

This is particularly pertinent to contemporary Christian music studies, with respect to performance styles directly affecting the consumption of (or participation in) the music, performance styles being subject to musical and/or lyrical content, increasingly prevalent issues of gender identification,[2] and the position of the consumer. Many of these concerns will be addressed, within the rubric of theorising contemporary music, in the following section, where the role of contemporary Christian music, as a form of vernacular music, will be explored. Of particular interest is the relationship between performance and participation within congregational settings.

2. Contemporary Christian Music as Vernacular Music

The following section is heavily indebted to Bruce Johnson's 'Watching the Watchers: Who do we think we are?',[3] a paper that insightfully calls for a redirection of scholarly focus away from mass-mediated foundations (namely genre and authenticity) towards music that would be 'fragmented into insignificance when approached generically' (1998: 8). Johnson terms this music 'vernacular music' (ibid.), noting that it is 'largely generated at the local level and expresses the sense of immediate, lived experience, of individual and collective regional identity. It includes ethnic, indigenous, folk, jazz, pub rock, and community and domestic music experience' (ibid.). Classic examples of this 'everyday music' (DeNora, 2000) abound, no more so than in places where the production and consumption of the music happens simultaneously. Many football games around the world involve such music production, where fans sing team songs and even counter the musical 'attacks' of opposition fans, and what's more, do so corporately. England's famous cricket fans, the 'Barmy Army', are another good example of this vernacular music production. More personally exclusive examples such as singing in the shower or singing lullabies to a restless infant exist, but remain even more disparaged by the contemporary music academy than those corporate examples (Mackinlay and Baker, 2005). For better or worse, contemporary congregational music obviously slots neatly into this framework, being generated at the local level by individual congregations, or else more regionally (e.g. by Sydney Anglicans).

With advances in the availability of 'home-recording' technology, and the ever-decreasing financial commitment involved, many churches are now producing (i.e. writing and recording) their own CDs for local production. Debates are now developing as to how relevant such music is on a larger, regional stage[4] and, as will be detailed later in this volume, whether the music being made locally is being produced solely for global transmission and reception, thus becoming stripped of any local identifiers or nuances. However, the fact remains that this music is essentially reflective of the immediate, lived experience of particular churches. Furthermore, congregational music is simultaneously individual and corporate. The vertical and horizontal operation of congregational song (that is, its vertical address to God and horizontal address to fellow participants) is further complicated by its ability to exist as individual representation, through identification with the personalised songwriter, or as communal response. Once again, the intersection of the study of congregational song with popular music scholarship provides an appealing juncture. Yet the notion of vernacular music itself arose, for Johnson at least, out of a dilemma, which he summarises thus:

> *Popular music and its generic multiplicity...seem to appear at the same time that mass mediations have robbed them of the foundations of their authenticity. These discursive constructs, based on generic and formalist distinctions and legitimated by criteria of authenticity, come into being*

> *even while the guarantees of their authenticity are dissolved by mass medi-*
> *ations. The classifications enter music discourse just as mass mediations*
> *abolish them, except in formal terms, in music practice. Furthermore, their*
> *proliferation is generated precisely by and through those mass mediations*
> (1998: 3).

Christian music – both product and victim of this generic multiplicity – finds itself stripped of all authenticity from secular perspectives (as highlighted by the PMR debate cited above). As the mass mediations become more intense, so too the scholarly leprosy. As Johnson states: 'we shy away in academic embarrassment from the everyday truth of music practices which deface our discourses of authenticity' (ibid.). As later discussion will show, contemporary congregational song has no authenticity to cling to. It is denied heritage by its divergence from traditional hymnody, whereby it is perceived to be produced in such a communal, homogenised way as to refute any suggestion of authenticity. Yet it remains the music of the everyday, 'the overwhelming majority of music experience' (ibid.: 4).

Johnson cites figures to show that, of all the arts in Australia, music is arguably the most pervasive, with more people attending formal musical performances than, for example, visual and performing arts.[5] He goes on to note that such formal musical events represent but a fraction of musical experience, and an even smaller amount of scholarly discourse. 'There are forums in which music is experienced in a way that generates collective and regional identities with profound intensity, but which receive little recognition in music studies: street marches, political rallies, sports stadiums, "ethnic" clubs, domestic celebrations' (ibid.), and of course, church services. Part of the reason for this appears to be our veneration of the 'Other', our longing to look beyond, often our own shores, to see that which may well be squeamish for the Others themselves. Hayward (1999) recalls such unease during a conversation about Hawaiian Exotica with Hawaiian-based ethnomusicologists:

> *I had not taken into account the element of embarrassment at examining*
> *styles which current tastes (until recently) deemed so irredeemably kitsch*
> *as to be one of the final frontiers of pop music study (3).*

There is a very real danger that we have allowed the current congregational music that proliferates in our churches, whether it be the compositions of Redman, Hughes, Zschech, Baloche or Tomlin, to become kitsch, to become the everyday music we are somehow embarrassed about analysing. This is not the fault of those outside the Church; it is the responsibility of those of us within the Church, who deal in researching and teaching about contemporary

Christian music, to not shy away from the everyday musical experiences of our local congregations. How easy it is to view the music of the emerging church in Africa or Korea as the new frontier of theomusicology. Indeed, we could even add the weight of ethnomusicology to such study and further validate our work. Johnson muses:

> The everyday music of Elsewhere is haloed with an aura of authenticity, and the dedicated study of ethnomusicologists and anthropologists. Everyday music in my own community remains unseen or so scorned that up to now our own music scholars, policy makers, historians scarcely even think of it. And because it remains officially invisible as such, we are scarcely aware of it even when we are experiencing it (1998: 5).

For Christians, the experience of congregational music is often crucial to their worship, to their response to God's character. Yet the 'awareness' of this experience has become the source of current debate. To what extent should the congregation be aware of the music around them, that is, focused on those creating it and the quality or attributes of it? Similarly, how does the music team of a church distinguish their functionality, being simultaneously performer desirous of quality, consumer of worship, and, ideally, humble servant leader of the congregation?

3. Participation or Performance: Unravelling the Roles of the Church Musician

In returning to Johnson's characterisation of vernacular music, one again finds a workable correlation with church music. He notes that:

> Vernacular music cannot be identified in terms of genre – pop, classical, jazz, folk, country. It refers to conditions of production and consumption, their relationship to the community that produces them. It is a category of music which...manifests itself through the tendency to close the gap between consumer and producer...where audiences participate in the production of the music by dancing, applause, dialogue with the musicians – all of these are more [or] less fulfilling the criterion of a musical activity distinguished by a narrowing of the distance between production and consumption (1998: 8).

Contemporary church services around the world (to a large extent irrespective of denomination but which fall within the broad Protestant rubric) simultaneously demonstrate the production and consumption of music. There are several manifestations of this, most notably the collective singing of songs, be they contemporary choruses or traditional hymns. Church members contribute to production by combining to sing, as one unit, songs 'to' God. He becomes the audience and recipient of their collective song. Following the theological doctrines of God's omnipresence (Psalm 139) and atonement access (Ephesians 2:18) the distance between production and consumption of this music is indeed minimal. On a more humanistic level, many congregational songs require members to individually address each other. In other words, the communal dimension, although always present in one sense, is surpassed by parishioners addressing each other – thereby nullifying the mediations between producer and consumer.

Clearly there are other levels at work, namely the mediation between songwriter and congregation, which is obviously reduced when the author is also a member of the congregation – as is the case with much music from Soul Survivor or Hillsong Church. This will not always be so, nor will the author always belong to that particular denomination, come from that congregation's city or country, or even be alive. Such mediations play a part in codifying the musical practices of various churches; however, the proportional distance between producer and consumer within congregational music is vastly different to that within contemporary secular music more generally. As such the effects on production become exaggerated. The influence of the congregation (read audience/performer), or more pointedly their expectation of influence, often outweighs their contribution to the creative process of music production. While collective ownership of the 'performance' is shared, the discrepancy between roles, specifically between those 'up-front' or 'on stage' and those 'in the pews', creates tensions that resound loudly in many churches. This is less evident in larger churches. Hillsong Church, for instance, exaggerates the space between those 'up-front' and those attending by various means of production – team membership, stage construction and design, lighting, video projection and stylistic uniformity. As a recent *Bulletin* article on the growth of Pentecostalism in Australia observed:

> *Instead of priests and altar boys,* the focus of attention *is a rock band, usually several musicians and singers who pump out music with the catchy rhythms and romantic tug of good pop* (Bagnall, 2000: 30, emphasis added).

Such a designation of attention, from a journalistic perspective, highlights the distance created in many of the larger, particularly Pentecostal, churches. This clearly demarcates the musicians as performers and the congregation as audience.[6] A commensurate argument by songwriter Nikki Chiswell notes that good performance breeds good participation:

> *The better the band is the more likely you will want to sing to it... People like to sing along to something rather than be the singer. We all sing along to the radio and, rather than knocking that, we should be thinking this is a good thing... The very best performers are the ones that get you so involved you are transported. Poor performance leads to people being left out. I work harder onstage at the front of church than I do at my gigs because* [you need] *all those techniques of audience connection, being truly yourself and becoming a magnet of what they want to do, rather than doing something that interferes with them* (interview with the author, 18 August 2000).

Liesch elaborates on the large church mentality: '[t]he larger the church, the higher the performance standard required. The larger the membership, the greater the need for a *great* ministry of music' (1996: 139). While there is no scriptural foundation for such a 'requirement', this type of expectation does manifest itself within current church culture, and with good reason. Those churches with large resources of people and equally, in many cases, large physical resources, have a responsibility to use such means for the advancement of Christian culture. While I would argue the actual 'performance standard' in regards to, say, 'entertainment value' is not particularly essential, the core areas of songwriting, instrumental (including voice) proficiency, musical leadership and production are vitally important in advancing the cause and discipline of contemporary congregational music. By default these larger (often Pentecostal) churches around the world are the ones linked into multinational distribution deals for their audio-visual product. In other words, these are the churches whose material is being sung and whose leaders are being aped all around the world. These churches have the capacity to raise the bar of congregational music that we might not have to shy away from it in embarrassment. This is not to say that smaller churches can't make their own impact. In the area of Sydney (Australia) where I live, a relatively small Uniting church at Pittwater has produced some of the most creative and skilfully constructed congregational music I have come across in my fifteen years of listening;[7] however, the impact of this church's music has been restricted to the local and regional levels. The danger for the large transglobally focused church is that, in their effort to appeal to every cultural and theological sensibility, their music is reduced to the lowest common denominator, stripped of its local vitality. The result is blandness and predictability, and a commercial imperative to keep producing more of the same. Analysis in later chapters will consider this phenomenon in more detail.

Returning to Liesch's challenge to large churches, he designates specialisation as the key tool in achieving great music from relatively large resources of people, perhaps ignoring various local social, ethnic and class issues. It is more important, however, to stress that this 'requirement' can be detrimental to the bigger picture:

> ...*it should be cautioned that* good music and a large music program *are not merely ends in themselves. The ultimate objectives of the church music program must always be to attract individuals to a saving knowledge of Jesus Christ and then to lead them to a fuller, more Spirit-filled Christian life. This is the ministry of music with which we must be earnestly concerned* (Osbeck, 1961: 32, emphasis added).

On the positive side, a reduction in consumer/producer mediations allows for spontaneous creative directions resulting in varied and, to a point, consumer-driven products. The discrepancy here with the popular music industry and its notions of star-text construction is glaring. Johnson points out how:

> *Especially in vernacular music, so often generated in the moments of performance, kinaesthetics rather than artistic logic is often the key to why the music sounds the way it does: that is, physical habits that take over during the moments of mental uncertainty – a particular movement of the fingers on valves or keys, a conditioned physical response to a particular harmonic challenge. The architectural acoustics, the weather, interaction with audiences – both who they are and what they are doing – all of these challenge the 'control' of the musician, and make nonsense of any reading of music in terms of formalist parameters also* (1998: 8).

Contemporary congregational song finds its relatives more among improvised music and various secular performance traditions than many might expect. Though this varies somewhat from church to church, the actual moment of musical production is ideally a fluid, liminal space. While some churches pride themselves on strict preparation and rehearsal of musical elements, philosophically at least, congregational music must remain relatively unscripted and improvisatory. Under direction from the worship leader, who (theoretically) responds to the congregation and the leading of the Holy Spirit, the creative outcome may take numerous paths. Primarily, the structure of the music is varied with repetition frequently employed as a major improvisational tool. As with improvised sections of traditional jazz tunes,[8] a single section of a song may be repeated until the creative and spiritual process has been exhausted. Quite regularly this will involve improvised (or rehearsed) instrumental sections, which obviously diminish congregational participation but nonetheless provide opportunities for personal reflection. If, at these times, the congregation is thought of as part of the musical collective then they can be viewed as enjoying the input of other colleagues; yet if thought of more as passive onlookers unable to participate then their purpose becomes less participatory. Either way the evolution of the performance is subject to variables, quite often kinaesthetic non-musical elements that enforce both the vernacularism and associated community nature of the music.

In *The New Worship: Straight Talk on Music and the Church*, Barry Liesch (1996) devotes much space to the issue of performance within church music. He finds the word 'performance' a hindrance in itself, arguing that performing, serving and ministering are practically interchangeable terms and should be referenced in conjunction with each other during public worship in order to build a healthy public perception of performance (ibid.: 127). The biblical foundation he offers for this suffers from a lack of contextualisation. For example, two passages (Numbers 4:26-27 and Exodus 35:30-33) fail to address the public worship of the people and are, in fact, directions for work required in preparation for this event. The Exodus passage actually called on the entire Israelite community to fulfil that which God requires (35:10), yet only those with God-given ability and desire were able to do so. The homiletic implications of this far outweigh definitions of performance. In citing Ezekiel 44:16, Liesch fails to record the full verse, let alone the full context, thereby reducing the value of his observations. He records: '[The levitical [*sic*] priests] are to come near my table to *minister* before me and *perform* my *service*' (1996: 126). In actuality, what should be noted is that only Levites[9] who were descendants of Zadok were called upon here, as Ezekiel 44:10-14 has clearly disqualified Levites generally, 'who went far from me when Israel went astray' (v. 10). The full verse then becomes increasingly curious in light of current worship performance tendencies: 'They alone [Levite descendants of Zadok] are to enter my sanctuary; they alone are to come near my table to minister before me and perform my service' (Ezekiel 44:16). God's pronouncement here that few are to perform ritual service to him surely traverses and negates focus on the ministry itself, instead centring all attention on God himself.

Liesch more insightfully cites Kierkegaard's (1958) three-point theology of:

- *the people should be the* performers *of worship*
- *the pastor and worship leader the* prompters *of worship*
- *God, the* audience (1996: 123).

The strength of Kierkegaard's notion is that God is the exclusive focus of corporate worship. Indeed, he is the initiator of it in that the participants respond to his character and deeds. However, as Liesch points out, there are in reality two audiences – God and the people (ibid.). As already noted there is a horizontal and vertical element to congregational singing. Woodhouse (1994: 19) summarises this diagrammatically:

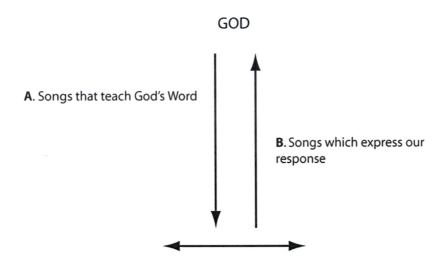

Figure 1.1. *The Dimensions of Corporate Worship*

In this diagram, 'A' represents God speaking to the congregation through songs or elements of worship that impart, or echo, the Bible directly. This is normally associated with readings of the Bible and exposition of it, though clearly songs that transcribe Bible passages (i.e. quote sections of scripture), or 'teach God's word', also fall into this realm.[10] In response to God's word the congregation often pray or sing their adoration, their confession, their dedication or the like, conceiving themselves to be in a process of dialogue with God. The majority of contemporary church songs reflect this responsive function. Curiously, not all accept that this basic interplay between God and congregants is a function of congregational song. John Woodhouse writes as the (now) Principal of Sydney's Moore Theological College, a seminary that exerts tremendous influence throughout evangelical circles. Yet Woodhouse's teachings were contradicted by the very music and worship conference that holds strong connections to the college – The Word In Song Together Music Ministry Conference (TWISTMMC). Here Director Philip Percival instructed delegates that 'singing is a "word" ministry... It's not a ministry of worship...teaching doesn't just [come from] the minister from the pulpit every week...singing is one of the prime ways it actually happens'[11] (Biblical Music Ministry notes, TWISTMMC, 2005). While this accords perfectly with Woodhouse's 'A' arrow, Percival went on to assert that congregational song is about receiving biblical instruction from God. As Tim Chavura has noted: 'Consequently, [in this model] congregational song should not be focused on giving something *to* God, but should be focused on receiving something *from* God'.[12] That such an approach is taught to a major conference with delegates who are already struggling to come to terms with congregational song's place within their particular liturgy is distressing, especially in light of the scholarship of Woodhouse (1994), Peterson (1996) and Carson (2002). What it does exhibit, however, are the vast differences in opinion that can exist side by side, within even relatively small communities of believers. The sooner some of these basic platforms are understood and accepted, the sooner some of the nervous mysticism surrounding congregational song can begin to dissipate. There *is* a responsive function of congregational song, and it is a key determinant in understanding the nature and applicability of modern song.

Returning to Woodhouse's framework (Figure 1.1), 'C' shows the horizontal level, where parishioners minister to each other by sharing communal statements, praying for each other, attending to the local parish concerns and singing to each other. It is this dimension that Kierkegaard fails to adequately acknowledge in his summary of corporate worship. Yet in both models the notion of 'performance' is greatly diminished, reduced to 'prompter'[13] by Kierkegaard (primarily for the God-to-congregation [A] dimension), and omitted entirely by Woodhouse. In discussing the multi-dimensionality of the Christian meeting, David Peterson (1992), one of the leading international evangelical scholars in the field of Christian worship, argues that the terminology of edification should replace the common language of worship in order to more accurately reflect New Testament (specifically Pauline) understanding of Christian gatherings. He notes that the apostle Paul 'employs the terminology of edification to oppose individualism, either in the ethical sphere or in the sphere of congregational ministry' (ibid.: 213). In practice such language enforces the person-to-person ministry between members of the congregation, rather than any top-down, performance-driven ceremony. Peterson also notes that:

> Paul expected that members of the congregation would come with some contribution prepared for the occasion or that individuals might be prompted by the Spirit to offer prayer or praise or some other ministry on the spot (ibid.: 214).

Spontaneous offering or sharing within the service abounds within many Pentecostal churches. Far greater reliance is placed on the gifts of the Spirit within public meetings than in traditional evangelical churches. Interestingly, the opportunity for spontaneous musical offerings is restricted in the majority of services to those confirmed in music ministry, thus intensifying their exclusivity and demarcating them further as performers. A concession to this is the notion of 'free worship' or 'singing in the Spirit' practised in some churches. During times of free worship the congregation are free to sing whatever they like – melodically, rhythmically and lyrically – while the band generally hovers between chords (I and IV, I and V, or ii-V-I, for example). These times tend to occur more frequently during slow, responsive songs, but this is not prescriptive. The worship leader or lead singer(s) facilitate the process, giving those unable to create their own tune the option of duplicating theirs. Quite often new tunes – or codas to existing songs – emerge during this time (usually at the prompting of the song leaders), and are picked up and extemporised upon by the entire congregation. Opinions about the place of free worship are strong, and not surprisingly, diametrically opposed. At one end of the spectrum are those who see no value in this form of expression: 'Religious verse that proceeds spontaneously, from the soul, as the private expression of the individual, is wholly inappropriate for congregational use' (Marshall and Todd, 1982: 1). This assertion is astonishing for its absolutism. When the apostle Paul acknowledged that believers bring to the corporate gathering with them 'a hymn, or a word of instruction, a revelation, a tongue or an interpretation' (1 Corinthians 14:26), are we to assume these had to be prepared, structured and ordered offerings? Clearly a cacophonous rabble, where all sing their own 'hymn' to God, is an unsustainable, and ultimately unfruitful, way to conduct corporate worship. Yet this is so rarely how these times are constructed. For one, they are led and controlled by the worship/music team. They are normally arranged so as to serve particular objectives within the service, and ultimately they offer participants, in the same way that corporate prayer might, an opportunity to respond to God; his character, Word, deeds, forgiveness, holiness etc., as best befits them at that specific moment.

One example amongst many is 'Hope Of Glory' (Hughes) from the live *Anthem Of The Free* (2003) CD. The song begins extremely atmospherically, with simple harmonic oscillation between chords I and $V^{6/4}$ (this progression allowing for the incorporation of chord ii substitutes in the dominant seventh, with common notes often held across the progression by the vocalists). The light texture remains rhythmically strong through quaver piano figures and later through the introduction of a basic rock drum rhythm. Singers extemporise various melodic figures that invariably refer to God's faithfulness, unchangeability, and subsequently the hope one can find in God. As the intensity of the song builds, it comes to focus on 'Christ in you, the hope in glory'. Electric guitar, piano and voices all take their turn at improvisation over these themes and the song's general timbral mood. Unlike standard practice, where songs continue to build to an inevitable climax, 'Hope Of Glory' features times of minimal fervour; allowing respite for the participant, or the chance to develop their own themes and offerings, based on their response to the particular message/circumstance. While congregational elaborations are not clear in this particular recording, the musical bed created for the track, and their emphatic focus on 'Christ in you', i.e. the participant, creates a suitable milieu for people to create their own responsive articulations. Times of free worship also provide musicians, for whom singing might be impossible, with a creative outlet for their praise and worship of God. This is exhibited clearly in 'Hope Of Glory' with long instrumental sections, which don't so much feature an instrumentalist – as we might expect in certain jazz genres – but rather allow the entire band freedom to develop their own melodic, rhythmic and timbral nuances.

All in all, free worship represents an excellent example of the vernacular improvisation alluded to earlier and is a contemporary example of the apostle Paul's expectation for a corporate gathering. While different congregational members may have various inhibitions about creating such spontaneous musical offerings, church music teams should be encouraging such times to have a role within team worship and, as a consequence, to become a natural part of the general church gathering. Not only do such times allow congregation members to choose their particular response to God at that moment, they further deconstruct the performative element of contemporary worship by allowing all participants to become involved as producers of the musical episode.

The Dangers of Performative Emphasis in Church Settings

> The choir and the worship team began to perform. The sound was good (but very loud). The choir robes were color coordinated, the band was in black, the platform lights were bright. The atmosphere was rockin' and hot. Four cameras on large platforms panned and arched in large circles, blocking the audience.

> The architecture, the activities, and the technology all told me a perverse truth: This event was designed primarily for those who would watch it through television screens later. All the real live people filling the auditorium were only part of the production; we were props for the real audience – the 'electronic audience' ... Is this what the Church has come to? I mumbled to myself. The Tonight Show! (Boschman, 1999: 50)

There is no doubt that performance-based worship does exist, and flourish, in contemporary churches. Boschman's account above pertains to one of the largest, and fastest-growing, churches in North America. In his scathing attack on performance-driven church services, Boschman traces the problem to the beginnings of electronic communication, from the first television evangelists through to the rise of 'electronic' Pentecostal worship. What electronic worship required were leaders and musicians who were 'dynamic and dramatic' (ibid.: 129), who were 'flamboyant and extravagant' (ibid.), and who – ultimately – were performers. Thus the focus of the church experience became 'the platform and the players of worship... [The] elite few [who] control the worship' (ibid.: 59). He goes on to note that the role of participant has been reduced to mere atmosphere:

> *What we are doing* [when we go to church] *is mostly applauding.*[14]
> *The focus is on the eye-ear-emotional stimuli, the electronic impact, the creation of a vicarious experience. There is so little for us to do, so we applaud* (ibid.: 130).

The ever-growing criticism of churches with an emphasis on performance, particularly that coming out of North America (Dawn, 1995; Boschman, 1999; Morgenthaler, 1995), has resonances in Australia, Canada and the United Kingdom, with respect to those churches that follow performative models of worship. Although performance-driven worship has often resulted in (numerical) church growth and revival in Christian experience, the perceived lack of a God-centred foundation ultimately provokes discontent. As Morgenthaler (1995) reports:

> *Many people have had enough. They have had their fill of superficial, human-centered services, and they simply are not going to take it anymore. Some may still come to church to hear the comedy routines and watch 'the show', but increasing numbers do not – they come to meet with God* (24).

As with much popular culture, performance-based worship appears to have a limited lifespan. Yet this is not a recent revelation, for C. S. Lewis raised objections to, and warnings about, similar facets of worship in 1963:

> *It looks as if* [the Anglican clergy] *believed people can be lured to go to church by incessant brightenings, lightenings, lengthenings, abridgments, simplifications, and complications of the service... Novelty, simply as such, can have only an entertainment value. And* [believers] *don't go to church to be entertained... The perfect church service would be one we were almost unaware of; our attention would have been on God* (Lewis, 1963: 4–5).

It would appear that balance between performance and participation within the contemporary church service is precariously poised. There are clearly advantageous elements emerging from the congregation's 'participatory performer' role, namely in the construction of relevant, specific vernacular music. To err on the side of performance, as many North American churches have done, is to risk alienating the congregation and secularising their experience of church. Furthermore, once the gulf between those performing and those being performed to becomes too broad, the fundamental characteristics of vernacular music (community, locality, immediacy, experience) are lost. The biblical mandate for a Christian musician is a call to look inward, reflecting the contention that there is no value in pure 'show'. If God is the primary audience for Christian music, then surely it is his appreciation that must be sought. As the Bible notes:

> But the LORD said to Samuel, 'Do not consider his appearance or his height, for I have rejected him. The LORD does not look at the things man looks at. Man looks at the outward appearance, but the LORD looks at the heart' (1 Samuel 16:7).

2 'Nothing New Under the Sun': Learning from History

1. Congregational Music: Historical Trajectories

Having considered the place of contemporary congregational music within the practice of popular music and popular music studies, it is important also to recognise the pivotal role Christian music has played throughout history. The history of Christian music necessarily traverses several domains: music history, Church history, the history of artistic endeavour and, of course, Christian music history, among other disciplines. The following is intended to highlight historical nuances that remain influential or informative today. As will become clear by the final chapter of this book, a good deal of contemporary debate revolves around issues already contested. By understanding the cyclical nature of congregational music and the various cultural reactions it exhibited at different points throughout history, we can come to a fuller appreciation of current music practice and purpose. Many of the fights have already been fought, the tears expended, the reactions faced and the petitions placed before God. To ignore the work of our musical forebears is to reinvent the wheel, when what we should be doing is testing how far and fast it can go.

The role of church music within western music history is generally well documented.[1] What these texts reveal is the entwining of western music history with Christian music history, to the point that the two become virtually inseparable. Indeed, to discuss the development of western music from the first century through the Middle Ages, as documented in popular Western music-history scholarship, is largely to discuss Christian music. Reasons for this will be elaborated below; suffice to say that the societal and cultural domination of the Church and its stringent governance were usually responsible. Given this connection, however, the following section traces the genesis and evolution of congregational music only.[2] The various historical fashions within congregational song offer much commentary on modern debates. Most curiously we can note that artistic trends tend to have kept pace with theological ones. This serves to raise questions about our current artistic climate, and more specifically, the theological directions that may be producing it. While acknowledging that other movements and secular avant gardes were indubitably occurring, less mention will be made of those artists from the fine music tradition who nonetheless contributed greatly to the canon of religious music.

The Early Church
Little is universally known of early church musical characteristics, though we can glean the following: music tended to be more spontaneous and (for a time at least) emotional than intellectual; it was not primarily for private worship but for the corporate community; and the music incorporated into early services was almost exclusively vocal. Faulkner notes:

> [e]*arly Christian worship adopted much of its form and its practice from the Jewish synagogue service, to which it then added its own representation of the disciples' last meal with Jesus. It thus inherited its cultic music and musical practice from Judaism, a matrix with an ancient, rich, and well-established musical heritage. The fundamental musical practice of the early apostolic church was thus Middle Eastern... Jewish* [and] *not Greek or Roman* (1996: 52–53).

Christianity developed, however, in a pagan Graeco-Roman environment whose ideas about music were very different from the early churches'. Andrews contends that the early source and inspiration for Christian music was in fact a popular Greek idiom that had developed in the fourth century BC (cited in Liesch, 1996: 35). This would accord with historical accounts which note the rapid growth of Christianity amongst the Hellenistic Jews:

> These were Jews who had come to Jerusalem from all parts of the Roman Empire to settle in the Holy City... The Hellenistic Jews were faithful to their religion, but in the world beyond Palestine – Egypt, Asia Minor, Europe – they had long been exposed to Greek culture. They mixed more easily with Gentiles and were more responsive to new ideas than were their Palestinian cousins (Shelley, 1995: 18).

It was inevitable then that tension developed between the 'sacred' music of Jewish Christians and the music that surrounded them. As a result Christian elders took a strong stand against pagan music culture,[3] despite the fact that culturally such a differentiation between secular and sacred music was, until then, quite unheard of (Lang, 1941: 32). As the Church developed, the denunciation of instrumental involvement became stronger. Instrumental music came to be seen as a sign of human weakness. Strong rhythm, hand-clapping and dancing were also condemned, yet the frequent admonitions against them in manuscripts from the period indicate that they were quite prevalent.

It was the famed St Augustine (354–430) who provided the Church with the first definition of a 'hymn', namely:

> *a song containing praise of God. If you praise God, but without song, you do not have a hymn. If you praise anything, which does not pertain to the glory of God, even if you sing it, you do not have a hymn. Hence a hymn contains the three elements: song and praise of God* (cited in Wilson-Dickson, 1992: 25).

And though Augustine's definition held with most churches until the fifth century, it was Ambrose (Bishop of Milan) who, having discovered a new type of liturgical song developed by Eastern Christians, wrote to the churches and encouraged the use of 'hymns' that no longer held to Augustine's description (ibid.: 35). The new music did not use the literal words of scripture, though it may have been based on them, and was more freely constructed than earlier hymns.[4]

Alongside the distinction between secular and sacred music came the classification between 'good' music and 'harmful' music during the fourth century. It is virtually impossible to ascertain what exactly was deemed harmful about or in the music, though what appears notable is that 'the distinction between bad/secular music and good/sacred music is one that goes back to a very early stage of Christianity' (Faulkner, 1996: 67). The Church's battle with the sensuality of music and its earthly attraction would be one that would continue through the ages. The early church attempted to wage war against the contaminating forces by restricting liturgical singing to psalm-based texts, and then only those that stirred the intellect rather than the emotions (Quasten, 1983). Two significant developments would ultimately arise out of this decree: only those ordained in the Church offices would be suitable for involvement in the liturgy, and a greater emphasis would be placed, for a time, on the spiritual character of the singer, their *compunctio cordis* (contrition of the heart).

The Middle Ages

Despite its early freedom and spontaneity, music of the early church became quite rigid, and almost entirely vocal with a limited emotional range. The songs were text-based, more often than not drawn from the Psalms of David. Rhythmically the music was quite subtle, offering participants minimal sensual pleasure and directing them more to spiritual devotion than corporate exhilaration. This musical environment of restriction would only intensify throughout the Middle Ages, giving rise to the evolution and proliferation of Gregorian chant. The monophonic syllabism of Gregorian chant was the antithesis of art music. Its beauty lay in simplicity, strength and purity, in its

ability to draw attention away from the self to God, the unison a capella[5] performance further enhancing the modal sound and the reverence the music
commanded. Gregorian chant was purely melodic, allowing great attention to
be devoted to its melodic construction: '[h]aving only one direction to travel
in, it went a long way' (Routley, 1977: 3).

Also significant in the history of church music is the place of music notation. It was an Italian monk, Guido D'Arezzo (995–1050), who did much to
advance the possibilities of notation. His work sought to uncover a method
of training singers to sing new songs from notation, rather than merely using
it as a means of recalling melodies they had already learnt. Once notational
systems began to establish themselves, the complexities of musical construction gained increasing fascination with composers. Such fascination,
along with technological advances and other factors, would ultimately lead
to a movement away from monodic musical structures, towards polyphony
and homophony. The ability to create with notation and directly compare
results assisted the rise of musical appreciation. By the tenth century the
clergy had long controlled the majority of liturgical music making, though
at this time the singing of the Ordinary of the Mass was assigned to the
schola, a choir consisting of clergy who had been trained in music. The establishment of the *schola* thereby replaced any form of singing by the people,
or even by the musically untrained. 'Perfect' execution of musical practice
began to overshadow the idea that congregational song was a matter of the
heart. Some writers began to report that God was praised through perfect
craftsmanship.

One of the earliest forms of polyphony, regularly used in religious ritual,[6]
was organum. Medieval polyphony consisted of relatively independent melody
lines, intended to be heard in a linear rather than vertical manner. (This lineal
polyphony is challenging to modern ears more accustomed to rich harmonies.) Parallel organum was composed by doubling the fourth or fifth interval
of a melody, and the practice eventually developed into counter-point. Some
composers, Perotin for example, did manage to compose elaborate organums
that stretched singer and listener alike, by drawing rhythmically distinct melodies in radically different directions. By the thirteenth century three- and four-
part compositions called motets were being written. Secular motets from this
period also survive, some of which mix secular and religious themes. Such was
the reception and zeal for new polyphonic forms that in 1325 it became necessary for Pope John XXII to issue a decree indicating the bounds beyond which
church composers could not go. The decree had no effect. Church music, after
the discovery of polyphony, has been described as a 'steady crescendo of complexity, ingenuity and ecstasy' (Routley, 1977: 5).

Somewhat puzzling in the development of polyphony is the departure from earlier thinking about the primacy of the lyrical text. By lengthening the notes, and incorporating elaborate melismatic elements in organums, for example, the text became increasingly difficult to comprehend as a linguistic communication. Instructional writing of the time appears to advocate a carelessness to lyrical detail:

> *After the music has been made and fixed, then take the words which are to go into the motet and divide them into four segments; and divide the music into four corresponding segments; and put the first segment of the words over the first segment of music as best you can, and proceed in this way all the way to the end. Sometimes it will be necessary to stretch many notes over few words in order to make the setting come out right, and sometimes many words must be squeezed into a small amount of time. Just fit it together any way you can* (Aegidius of Murino cited in Faulkner, 1996: 120–23, emphasis added).

Such techniques produced their share of criticisms, as one listener noted:

> *...when motets in the modern manner were being sung, I observed that the question was asked, what language such singers were using, whether Hebrew, Greek, Latin or other, because it could not be made out what they were saying. Thus, although the moderns compose good and beautiful texts for their songs, they lose them by their manner of singing, since they are not understood* (ibid.: 120).

What music survives from the Middle Ages is very professional, i.e. complicated and refined, music in which the congregation had no performative role.[7] It was music to be performed by trained clergy-musicians. There was nothing for the humble attendee to do in corporate worship other than to watch, listen and pray. At the end of the Middle Ages the Church had virtually banned all instruments, with some exceptions for the earliest organs. Fortunately there was enough instrumental music elsewhere in society for it not to be missed too much in church, nor to be disregarded altogether.

The Renaissance and Reformation
The humanism that developed throughout the Renaissance saw composers and artists draw upon secular as well as sacred texts. The new art desired works that were not only comprehensible to the audience but preferably exuded some form of artistic integrity as well (Grout, 1960: 173). While lyrics remained important, the new musical complexity allowed for sacred works that worked instrumentally as pieces in their own right. The music began to

reflect the imagery and intent of the lyrics, drawing upon the emotional capacity of melody and rhythm particularly. The Renaissance was the 'Golden Age of Polyphony' with church music leading the way, usually with a capella singing in newly favoured major and minor scales, rather than the previous modal impetus, though major and minor tonalities were not completely developed until the seventeenth century. Renaissance motets, though invariably religious and reverent, often exploited popular tunes already familiar to the congregations. Josquin des Prez (c. 1450s–1521), one of the most heralded composers of his generation, was dedicated to the motet form, viewing it as 'the most challenging and inviting genre of sacred composition' (Hanning, 2002: 117). What was important to Josquin was ensuring that the music conveyed the meaning of the texts used. To this extent, he carefully connected 'the musical stress to the accentuation of the words, whether Latin or vernacular, and wanted the words to be heard and understood' (ibid.).

After the discovery of polyphony, the interaction between secular and sacred music became increasingly symbiotic. Assisting this was the patronage of composers by the monarchy, and individual bodies other than the Church. Indeed, by the conclusion of the sixteenth century, 'the center of musical interest had shifted from sacred to secular composition' (Grout, 1960: 252).

Congregational music during this period was shaped by the attitudes that the church reformers held to music. The great Reformation is traditionally considered to have begun when Martin Luther (1483–1546) posted his 95 Theses on the door of the Castle Church in Wittenberg, 1517.[8] Luther represents not only a key theological figure, but also a crucial figure in church music evolution. Unlike some other reformers, Luther:

> *was a lover of music, a singer, a composer of some skill, and a great admirer of Netherlands polyphony and of the works of Josquin des Prez in particular; he believed strongly in the educational and ethical power of music and wanted all the congregation to take some part in music of the services* (ibid.: 253).

Luther himself wrote: '[After] the Word of God, the noble art of music is the greatest treasure in this world' (cited in Faulkner, 1996: 128). He suggested including German language songs at certain points in the service, to break from the traditional use of Latin, and set about translating Latin chants into German, incorporating his theological understanding. The result quite often made the music simpler and more powerful. Yet he also believed in retaining some Latin in the service (partly for the education of the young). The perceived inconsistencies in Luther's beliefs about music and the service led various local congregations to come up with assorted corporate worship practices.

Luther was a believer in hymnody that allowed the congregation to express their relationship with God. He is attributed with the composition of thirty-seven hymns, perhaps the most famous of which is 'A Mighty Fortress Is Our God',[9] first published in 1529. This strophic hymn, as a musical form of congregational song, also became known as the Lutheran Chorale, and is the most important musical contribution of the Lutheran Church.

> *Just as plainchant was the basis for musical expansion and elaboration for Catholic composers, so too the repertory of chorales became the starting point for a great deal of Lutheran church music from the sixteenth century until the time of Johann Sebastian Bach (1685–1750) and beyond* (Hanning, 2002: 153).

Lyrical texts, newly written or adapted from religious poems, were set in strophic form. Some had new melodies, others were adapted from popular tunes or Catholic Church music. They were predominantly sung by the congregation unaccompanied and in unison, though by the seventeenth century it was common for the organ[10] to play four-part harmonisation while the congregation sang the chorale melody. Four collections of chorales were published in 1524, with an important collection of 123 polyphonic chorales published by Georg Rhaw in 1544. Other volumes followed at frequent intervals; all were intended for congregational singing. In terms of performance, the choir, 'sometimes doubled by instruments, commonly alternated stanzas with the congregation, who sang in unison without accompaniment' (Hanning, 2002: 156). The participation of the congregation was paramount, and this example highlights a more dialogical aspect to the Lutheran liturgies.

As mentioned, many chorales were newly composed, but a great number were made up partially or entirely from existing songs. An important class of chorales were the *contrafacta* or 'parodies' of secular tunes. In this case the melody was retained, but the text altered or replaced entirely so as to give it a more appropriate spiritual meaning. Such adaptation of secular compositions for church purposes was common in the sixteenth century.[11] One of the most notable examples was the tune of Hassler's 'Mein Gmuth ist mir verwirret' (my peace of mind is shattered [by a tender maiden's charms]), which around 1600 was set to the sacred words 'My Heart Is Filled With Longing' and later altered to 'O Sacred Head Now Wounded'. This melody went on to influence Bach in two settings of the 'Passion According to St Matthew'. Thus one of the most loved and sung hymns in church history – as well as perhaps the greatest gospel inspired artwork of all time – find their genesis in the secular longings of a lovesick composer. The implications of such sacred exploitation of secular popularism continue to have resonance in contemporary congregational music.

The other renowned reformer was John Calvin (1509–1564), who was far more extreme (and suspicious) in his philosophy of art and artefact. Part-singing (harmony) and instruments were expressly forbidden, with Calvin insisting upon:

> ...*simple and pure singing of the divine praises* [psalms], *forasmuch as where there is no meaning there is no edification. Let them come from the heart and mouth, and in the vulgar tongue. Instrumental music was only tolerated in the time of the Law* [Old Testament] *because of the people's infancy* (Wilson-Dickson, 1992: 65).

Chorales had no place in Calvinistic services, replaced instead with the psalm tune, the 150 psalms in vernacular, metered rhyme. Calvin secured Louis Bourgeois, a superior music editor, to set the psalms (which had been accurately and readably translated) to music. This became commonly known as the *Genevan Psalter* of 1551 (ultimately finished in 1562) and the foundation of all English hymnody. Conversely the English Psalter, compiled by Thomas Sternhold (and also completed in 1562) was far less successful, with many of the lyrical texts seemingly forced into the composition.

Even more austere than Calvin was Ulrich Zwingli (1484–1531), leader of the Reformation in Switzerland. This fierce opponent of music in church was a gifted instrumentalist and vocalist, yet his zeal for reform and his particular understanding of the New Testament led him to the conviction that music should have no place in public worship. He banned the use of all instruments (indeed his teaching was responsible for the dismantling and removal of many organs), and singing (of any sort) in churches.

Needing a strong response to the passion and momentum of the Protestant reformers, the Catholic Church convened the Council of Trent. Largely known as the Counter-Reformation, the Council of Trent met intermittently between 1545 and 1563. Although music was not on the agenda long, when it was it raised vehement opinions. The use of secular material was opposed, seen as profaning, and polyphony was derided for confusing and complicating the portrayal of lyrical intent. What was sought was a return to simple plainsong forms, and the banishment of 'all music that contains, whether in the singing or in the organ playing, things that are lascivious or impure' (Council of Trent Recommendation, quoted in Hanning, 2002: 163). Fortunately for the Catholic Church they had the inimitably gifted composer Giovanni Pierluigi da Palestrina amongst their ranks. Apart from Bach, few composers of religious music are as well-known or revered today. His style, which came to be known as *stile antico* (the old style), was branded by some as the 'absolute perfection of church music' (ibid.: 171). Indeed, his compositional techniques were imitated, taught and modelled long after his death in 1594.

The effects of the Reformation quickly filtered through to England where King Edward VI proclaimed that, '[the choir] shall from henceforth sing or say no anthems of our Lady or other Saints, but only of our Lord, and them not in Latin; but choosing out the best and most sounding to Christian religion they shall turn the same into English, setting thereunto a plain and distinct note for every syllable one: they shall sing them and none other' (cited in Wilson-Dickson, 1992: 68). Later, Queen Elizabeth I (1599) would give the telling edict that there was to be:

> *a distinct modest song, so used in all parts of the common prayers in the church, that the same may be plainly understood, as if it were read without singing, and yet nevertheless, for the comforting of such as delight in music, it may be permitted that in the beginning, or in the end of common prayers either at morning or evening, there may be sung a Hymn, or such like song...* (cited in Routley, 1977: 20).

The concept of a 'distinct modest song' that was 'plainly understood' became the nucleus of much English church music throughout the seventeenth, eighteenth and nineteenth centuries. By the conclusion of the sixteenth century a new kind of thinking about the meaning and role of public worship had matured. Two streams of thought ran together: one noted that the Church at worship was the people of God at worship; the second noted that the Church was there to instruct the people. Worship was no longer to be viewed as theatre; it had begun instead to resemble a classroom.

The end of the sixteenth century also heralded the arrival of homophony, a musical texture that would dominate congregational song for the rest of the millennium. The spread of homophony is largely attributed to Basilica St Marco in Venice, during the late sixteenth and early seventeenth centuries:

> *In Venice...I heard the best music that ever I did in all my life...so good that I would willingly goe an hundred miles afoote at any time to heare the like... This feast consisted principally of Musicke, which was both vocall and instrumental, so good, so delectable, so rare, so admirable, that it did even ravishe and stupefie all those strangers that never heard the like... Sometimes there stand sixteen or twenty men together...and when they sung, the instrumental musicians played also. Sometimes sixteen played together upon their instruments...at every time that every severall musicke played, the organs...plaied with them* (Thomas Coryat (1611) cited in Wilson-Dickson, 1992: 84, original language preserved).

The architecture of St Mark's was designed in the shape of a cross, greatly affecting the music composed for performance in the cathedral. Quite often musicians (usually choirs but also instrumentalists) were spread throughout the cathedral, placed in the side galleries as well as front (and back). Coryat noted ten separate choirs joining concurrently (ibid.), an example of polychoral music, the rise of homophony and instrumental music, all of which would take their place prominently in the 'fine' church music that ensued, particularly that of the Baroque era. Perhaps no finer example of these exists than the religious compositions of J. S. Bach – though even his secular work was dedicated 'to the glory of God'. Bach's cantatas, largely composed during his employment at St Thomas's School at Leipzig, were designed to interpret and comment upon the Gospel message, powerfully impressing it to the congregation. Of these cantatas, the 'infinite variety and wealth of musical invention, technical mastery, and religious devotion' (Hanning, 2002: 277) cannot be understated. These qualities, in a song form that, each year, liturgical settings of the day required fifty-eight be composed – aside from special Easter and other festival needs – cast a serious shadow over modern songs delivered less frequently, and far less creatively. Although Bach was undoubtedly a master composer, there is much to be drawn from his attitude towards 'common' liturgical music.

The Renaissance period, and associated Reformation, brought major changes to church music philosophy and practice. They re-ignited the passion for music within worship that the Church had long sought to repress. Such was the power and legacy of the Reformers that their sentiments still echo through congregational practice today. Many 'current' debates, philosophies and attitudes have their origin in the Reformation. That the Church would still be struggling with ideas Luther doggedly defended or Calvin proved inaccurate may seem remarkable. Yet, as subsequent chapters will show, issues about instrumentation, corporate involvement, lyrical manipulation, adherence to scriptural texts, melodic complexity, rhythmic intensity and, of course, secularity, will play a role within the formation and consumption of contemporary congregational song.

The Hymn-writers

The eighteenth century saw the burgeoning of hymn-writing and singing in England, due chiefly to the work of Isaac Watts (1674–1748) and the Wesley brothers, John (1703–1791) and Charles (1707–1788). Their massive output, evangelical focus and theological influence helped ignite the new era of the Christian hymn. While there are distinct nuances to each of their hymns, and those of their colleagues, their hymns summarised Christian truths and experience, making them simple enough for the congregation to cope with and profound enough to have lasting spiritual value. This is evidenced by the proliferation of hymns from this period being sung regularly in churches today. As Marshall and Todd document, the crucial requirement of eighteenth-century hymns was that they:

> [t]ouch common experience, engaging their singers' attention and forcing them to recognize the poetry's truth to experience...hymns had to be vehicles for correct doctrine [remembering the Reformation climate from which they evolved] and had to teach attitudes that suited the particular sect or movement for which they were designed... These early hymn writers produced collections that covered every imaginable state of devotional mind, a comprehensiveness that complemented their orthodoxy (1982: 148–49).

Hymns of this period were constantly altered textually and musically, often being re-set to entirely different tunes. At least 250 different hymn books were published in the eighteenth century alone. John and Charles Wesley transformed church music. They delivered people from the tyranny of the metrical psalm. 'Watts taught his congregations to sing about Christ; the Wesleys taught the whole country to do so' (Routley, 1977: 44). They followed the notion that hymnody is church music for the ordinary person, not to listen to, but to actively engage in as a vehicle for learning and reminding one another of foundational Christian doctrine, as well as expressing corporately their individual experiences of being a Christian.

Charles Wesley is arguably the most influential figure in the history of hymnody, writing over six thousand hymns (Osbeck, 1982: 129), though obviously not all to different tunes; yet most were more musically challenging than those of Watts. Wesley's hymns came out of the Methodist revival led by his brother John, a movement 'involving enlightenment of the spirit and understanding, encompassing sense and poetry, and [using] hymns...as evangelical tools, performing the word of conversion essential to religious revival' (Marshall and Todd, 1982: 60). Subsequently, Wesley's hymns feature a profound subjective, individual emotionalism, born out of his own conversion experience.

> Wesley's purpose was not the expressive venting of feeling but rather the evangelical directing of feeling. Emotion, roused and controlled, would carry the singer to God. Passion was a means to a didactic end, and its expression was usually exemplary (ibid.: 79).

This subjectivity was not restricted to Wesley, and in fact would establish itself as a key feature of eighteenth-century hymnody. Such an individual focus, as with the music of today, was not without its fierce critics.

The evangelical hymn writers greatly increased the vocabulary of their congregations and their ability to cope with complex theological language and thought. This period also saw a radical development, that of large congregations meeting outside the established churches and chapels. As a precursor to contemporary worship, this period led to non-conformist modes of worship comparable to those practised by Pentecostal churches. Isaac Watts was an Independent preacher and educator, who operated out of the Mark Lane meeting. What perhaps characterised him most, given his lack of connection with established mainstream churches, was his personal piety and virtual ascetic commitment.

To focus exclusively on the accomplishments of Wesley, Watts and other hymn-writers from the period would be to ignore the larger picture. For the beginning of the eighteenth century was also the Age of the Enlightenment, a philosophical movement whose proponents promulgated particular views about music itself, thus dramatically affecting the composition and transmission of church music.

> Up to the Enlightenment, Christian ideas and attitudes had been major factors in determining the progress of music. As a result of the Enlightenment, leadership in musical creativity rapidly began to shift to the secular sphere (Faulkner, 1996: 171).

Faulkner goes on to describe facets of secular Enlightenment thinking that directly affected the function and quality of church music.[12] According to Enlightenment thinkers:

1. Music embodies, expresses and excites human emotion, feeling and passion.
2. Music provides entertainment and diversion.
3. The best music is characterised by constant variety.
4. Individuality and originality are virtues in musical composition and performance.
5. The gauge of music's excellence is popular acclaim; the public is the best judge of good music.
6. The best kind of music is natural and unlearned – an anti-intellectual attitude towards music.
7. Music is subject to examination by reason and science.
8. The social status of the musician was low.
   (Summarised from Faulkner, 1996: 172–79)

Contemporary congregational music, to varying degrees, bears the residue of these ideas. The emotion and sensuality of music (point 1) is heavily drawn on today for both spiritual and performative reasons. A swelling in musical intensity is often perceived to 'announce' the presence or anointing of the Holy Spirit, while the greater prominence of instrumental music allows for a more uninhibited response from the congregation by virtue of being less tied to lyrical involvement. A common failing of contemporary churches is an over-reliance on music as entertainment (point 2), particularly within the context of a seeker-service,[13] or, worse, to punctuate the elements of liturgy with music in order to give the congregation respite from more challenging and profound elements. The tendency for the audience to become the gauge of 'musical excellence' (point 5) has led to music being created for the public at large, with a resultant explosion in the popularity of specific songs. Nowhere is this more evident than in the Christian Copyright Licensing International (CCLI) Top 25 worship songs. This list, compiled on the basis of what songs are being photocopied for use in churches around the world, acts as a kind of Billboard chart for congregational song. A quick glance at the different national charts produced (with the possible exception of Sweden) highlights the marked similarities between the charts, a similarity that comes through the global adoption of specific songs. Thus the impact of these songs on the contemporary musical sensibility of the worldwide church cannot be underestimated, and is the reason these songs feature in the analysis sections of this book.

Due to modern church music's resemblance to Enlightenment thinking, questions arise regarding the musicality and theology of the music being produced. Are consumers concerned with beauty, quality and depth, or merely that which arouses emotional well-being? Such questions will be addressed throughout this book. Routley (1977) notes the damaging effects that resulted from consumer-driven popularity in the nineteenth century. He observes that, as the popularity of congregational music grew, the increase in people demanding enjoyment from music effectively narrowed the band of acceptable music. 'The most dangerous demand in any artistic field is a popular demand for "More of the same: as much as you can"' (ibid.: 66). The transglobalism of modern congregational song – and the attendant economic riches it can bring – risk making this statement the basis of all music composition and production around the world. This book will assess recent criticisms about the sameness of modern church music with regard to whether the music being produced results from a form of Enlightenment thinking.

The final element for consideration from the list above is the notion of anti-intellectual attitudes towards music (point 6). During the Enlightenment this attitude resulted in basic homophonic music, with memorable melodies being favoured above other musical elements. Also endorsed was the live performance of the text, beyond any philosophical understanding of theory or the text itself. At first glance a similar attitude appears prevalent in many contemporary churches where the 'live' environment is constantly enhanced through technology and performance standards, while the material itself is scarcely scrutinised. Ideally, both the text and the way it is communicated should receive equal attention.

Nineteenth- and Twentieth-Century Developments
Evangelical music history continued along the path set in place by Watts and firmly established itself in the USA. Evangelical hymns became the backbone of the two Great Awakenings in the nineteenth century. The Second Great Awakening introduced revivalist songs, while the rise in Methodism firmly entrenched the hymns of the Wesley brothers. Possibly the greatest contribution to the history of hymnody from the North American Church was the composition of 'gospel songs'. These have been defined as:

> *...sacred folk song*[s], *free in form, emotional in character, devout in attitude, evangelistic in purpose and spirit. The hymns are more or less subjective in their matter and develop a single thought, rather than a line of thought. That thought usually finds its supreme expression in the chorus or refrain which binds the stanzas together in a very close unity, just as it does in lyrical poetry where it is occasionally used* (Lorenz, 1923: 342).

Gospel songs took on real impetus in the evangelistic missions of Dwight Moody (1837–1899) and Ira Sankey (1840–1908) in the latter part of the nineteenth century, missions which 'returned' the music back to the United Kingdom. Fanny Crosby (1820–1915) was the most prolific contributor to the gospel song corpus. A blind composer, Crosby wrote over 8000 hymns including 'Blessed Assurance' and 'Jesus, Keep Me Near The Cross'. The relationship between gospel songs and evangelical missions continued throughout the twentieth century, especially via the crusades of American evangelist Billy Graham (b. 1918).

The nineteenth century in England saw the Victorian era of hymn writing (Queen Victoria ruling from 1837–1901). Osbeck (1961) distinguishes five categories of hymn written during this period: High Church Hymns; Evangelical or Low Church Hymns; Broad Church Hymns; Dissenting Hymns; and Post-Victorian Hymns (27). These classifications were largely the result of composers' incorporations of the culture that surrounded them, or their (quite often corrective) teaching on the 'health' of the Church.[14]

The nineteenth century also saw the emergence of feminine 'overtones of sexuality and sentimentality' (Balmer, 1999: 35) within evangelical music.

Songs such as 'Jesus, Lover Of My Soul', 'My Jesus I Love Thee' and 'Rock Of Ages, Cleft For Me' reflected this. Not surprisingly, the turn of the century also saw a predilection towards military hymns and those expressing a 'muscular Christianity' (ibid.), for example, 'Stand Up, Stand Up For Jesus (Ye Soldiers of the Cross)' and 'Onward Christian Soldiers'. In his telling conclusion on the hymns of the late nineteenth and twentieth centuries, Osbeck notes that hymn-writers were more concerned with 'the virtues, ethics and social implications of the Gospel rather than in expounding doctrinal truths' (1961: 31).

A revolution in Christian music took place in the second half of the twentieth century as the delineation between secular and sacred became increasingly blurred. The gospel music of Harlem had been segregated from the mainstream before 1935, but began to seep into secular culture. Traditional black worship comprised a style of preaching and singing called 'the frenzy'. Conversely, secular songs such as 'Higher And Higher' gained power as spirituals, a style that is now appropriated by Hillsong and others worldwide. Yet the revolution began in earnest with Geoffrey Beaumont's A Twentieth Century Folk Mass (1956). In the 1960s a significant rupture occurred within mainstream evangelical hymnody. The catalyst is believed by some to have been Ralph Carmichael,[15] an evangelical musician whose compositions 'He's Everything To Me' (1964) and 'Pass It On' (1969) – amongst others – suddenly permitted worshippers to choose between the historical hymns and newer, more culturally relevant pieces. Hamilton discerned another tributary running into contemporary evangelical hymnody. He argued that Carmichael and his peers were 'reformers' who 'began with church music forms and sought to incorporate baby-boom values' (1999: 32). He attributed the impetus for this movement to Eric Routley (1917–1982), hymnodist and Congregationalist minister, who in 1962 gathered some disenchanted British church musicians in Dunblane, Scotland to attempt to revitalise church singing (ibid.: 31). Their initial reformation then spread to the US, to Carmichael and others. The 'revolutionaries', on the other hand, began from 'outside' the church, amidst the secular world. Their starting place was secular rock and roll, resulting in congregational song driven by guitars and drums, featuring simple, accessible lyrics, and the adoption of other popular music conventions such as repetition and simple tonal-based harmonies (Hamilton, 1999).

Chuck Smith's Calvary Chapel in Costa Mesa, California, is widely accepted as the birthplace of this musical revolution. Smith's church recruited hundreds of hippies into their fold, the nucleus of the Jesus Movement that would powerfully exhibit their counter-cultural faith throughout the 1960s and 1970s. Free from any middle-class inhibitions, Calvary Chapel and its congregation was able to unleash a freedom of musical expression and creativity previously unknown in the Christian Church (Balmer, 1999: 35). Not surprisingly it was Calvary Chapel which launched the music publishing and recording company Maranatha! Music in 1973 to disseminate the 'new music' to other churches. This new music eventually came under the generic label of 'Praise and Worship'. What began as revolution has become big business; in fact praise and worship music is now a massive industry worldwide:

> The Contempery [sic] Christian Music company is now secular-owned and has become a billion dollar competitor, second only in America to country music as a profitable entertainment industry (J. Smith, 2000: 1).

Seen in this light, the twentieth century was a mix of reformation and revolution. The former has seen the composition of 'modern hymns', songs containing contemporary language and contemporary musical nuances, yet retaining basic principles and structures of traditional hymns. Similarly, many traditional hymns have been updated to incorporate new melodies and contemporary harmonies, with some minor modernisation of lyrics. These songs are quite often enormously popular within mainline evangelical churches as they bear witness to the traditional hymnody and history of the Church, simultaneously situating themselves comfortably within the current sounds of popular culture.

The revolution, largely propelled by the Pentecostal churches, has produced thousands of new congregational songs that – as a result of religious globalisation – are international and inter-denominational. Yet these songs of the revolution are yet to find a harmonious place within many mainline Protestant churches. Peterson makes the following observations about contemporary congregational song:

> Traditional metrical forms are not often followed. Sometimes the lyrics are confused and meandering, lacking theological depth and substance. Repetition is often used to create a mood...biblical verses and phrases are used extensively, but sometimes obscurely... There is a bright and vigorous note of celebration in much of this material but little to compare with the doctrinal strength of older hymns. Insufficient attention is given to the great gospel events and their meaning... Important biblical themes such as suffering and judgment are largely neglected... Modern music is not always easy to sing. Sometimes there are difficult time changes, syncopated sections or unusual intervals to be learned (1996: 147).

Clearly the revolution is not over, and what will help the revolutionaries is ensuring that they strive for quality in their congregational song and not just quantity. Also essential is an understanding of the biblical mandate for music within the Church.

2. The Biblical Basis for Music in the Church

*In the end we make music not simply because God gives us the capacity to
do so or appreciates our making it, but because God is inherently musical*
(Banks, 1992: 66).

By far the most salient qualification for church music's existence, irrespective
of its place within contemporary music studies or music history, is its basis
within the Bible. There are over 500 references to music, or associated activities, mentioned in the Bible, covering forty-four of the sixty-six books. Despite
this, however, the references are tantalisingly skeletal, often mentioned inci-
dentally rather than in detail. Nonetheless, '[i]t is as we study the Christian's
primary resource material, the Bible, that we can develop a theology or philosophy of church music that will be pleasing to God' (Thiessen, 1994: xi).

Old Testament References to Music
In the Old Testament (OT) Book of Zephaniah one of the more revealing and
somewhat startling references to music occurs: 'The LORD your God is with
you, he is mighty to save. He will take great delight in you, he will quiet you
with his love, he will rejoice over you with singing' (3:17). Apart from the comfort and hope extended throughout the verse, the noticeable detail is that
God himself sings. His method of rejoicing over his people is to overflow into
song. Three verses earlier God had given his faithful the instruction to 'Sing,
O Daughter of Zion; shout aloud, O Israel! Be glad and rejoice with all your
heart, O Daughter of Jerusalem!' (Zephaniah 3:14). Such joy and thankfulness
appears to find itself expressed more absolutely in music. Many Christians
believe that they sing in response to God because he first sang over them.

The first musical reference in the OT occurs in the fourth chapter of
Genesis.

*Lamech married two women, one named Adah and the other Zillah. Adah
gave birth to Jabal; he was the father of those who live in tents and raise
livestock. His brother's name was Jubal; he was the father of all who play
the harp and flute* (4:19-21).

This early genealogical account, by providing professional designations, indicates
the importance of music to God and his people. This is additionally gleaned
from the role music plays in accompanying momentous events throughout the
Bible. One notes the song of Miriam and Moses after the successful exodus from
Egypt (Exodus 15); the rejoicing of the people on David's return from victory over
the Philistines (1 Samuel 18:6-7); the fall of Jericho (Joshua 6); Solomon's coro-

nation (1 Kings 1:32-48); the return from exile and rebuilding of the temple (Ezra 2–3); the song of Mary (Luke 1:46-55); and the last supper (Matthew 26:26ff. and Mark 14:22-26). In stark contrast to music of the early church, music in the OT is repeatedly coupled with mention of instruments and dancing.

> *All the Levites who were musicians – Asaph, Heman, Jeduthun and their sons and relatives – stood on the east side of the altar, dressed in fine linen and playing cymbals, harps and lyres. They were accompanied by 120 priests sounding trumpets. The trumpeters and singers joined in unison, as with one voice, to give praise and thanks to the LORD. Accompanied by trumpets, cymbals and other instruments, they raised their voices in praise to the LORD and sang: 'He is good; his love endures forever.' Then the temple of the LORD was filled with a cloud, and the priests could not perform their service because of the cloud, for the glory of the LORD filled the temple of God* (2 Chronicles 5:12-14).

> *Praise the LORD. Praise God in his sanctuary; praise him in his mighty heavens. Praise him for his acts of power; praise him for his surpassing greatness. Praise him with the sounding of the trumpet, praise him with the harp and lyre, praise him with tambourine and dancing, praise him with the strings and flute, praise him with the clash of cymbals, praise him with resounding cymbals. Let everything that has breath praise the LORD. Praise the LORD* (Psalm 150).

Music is most often mentioned in the OT as an accompaniment to ritual practice, to the temple service. Although music had played a part in ritual practice for many years prior to the establishment of the temple (Faulkner, 1996), the musical structure, responsibility and personnel organisation that came with it heralded a new substance to temple worship. It was King David who organised the place of music in the temple, and the role of the Levites in administering it:

> *David told the leaders of the Levites to appoint their brothers as singers to sing joyful songs, accompanied by musical instruments: lyres, harps and cymbals. So the Levites appointed Heman son of Joel; from his brothers, Asaph son of Berekiah; and from their brothers the Merarites, Ethan son of Kushaiah; and with them their brothers next in rank: Zechariah, Jaaziel, Shemiramoth, Jehiel, Unni, Eliab, Benaiah, Maaseiah, Mattithiah, Eliphelehu, Mikneiah, Obed-Edom and Jeiel, the gatekeepers. The musicians Heman, Asaph and Ethan were to sound the bronze cymbals; Zechariah, Aziel, Shemiramoth, Jehiel, Unni, Eliab, Maaseiah and Benaiah were to play the lyres according to alamoth, and Mattithiah, Eliphelehu, Mikneiah, Obed-Edom, Jeiel and Azaziah were to play the harps, directing according to sheminith. Kenaniah the head Levite was in charge of the singing; that was his responsibility because he was skillful at it* (1 Chronicles 15:16-22).

> He [David] *appointed some of the Levites to minister before the ark of the* *LORD, to make petition, to give thanks, and to praise the LORD, the God* *of Israel: Asaph was the chief, Zechariah second, then Jeiel, Shemiramoth,* *Jehiel, Mattithiah, Eliab, Benaiah, Obed-Edom and Jeiel. They were to play* *the lyres and harps, Asaph was to sound the cymbals, and Benaiah and* *Jahaziel the priests were to blow the trumpets regularly before the ark of the* *covenant of God. That day David first committed to Asaph and his associ-* *ates this psalm of thanks to the LORD...* (1 Chronicles 16:4-7).

King David's greatest contribution to church music and liturgy was the com-position of the Psalms. While he was not the author of all the psalms,[16] he is credited with inspiring or commissioning many written by others. The psalms were written as Hebrew poetry and must be considered as such, 'with all the licences and all the formalities, the hyperboles, the emotional rather than logi-cal connections, which are proper to lyric poetry' (Lewis, 1961: 10). Being poetry they were invariably sung, as was the custom of cultic practice, and quite often accompanied instrumentally (predominantly with strings) by the Levites.[17] Although precise musical settings of the psalms will always remain somewhat speculative, Wilson-Dickson (1992) illustrates the depth of, and elaboration on, a number of musical responses within the psalms. Furthermore, due to the irregular metre of Hebraic poetry, the rhythm was probably 'dictated by the text, and not confined to a steady beat, while the melodic scheme would have [been] able to accommodate irregular verse-lengths' (ibid.: 21).

Of further relevance to contemporary congregational music are the the-matic and theological concerns of scriptural psalm songs. Following Hermann Gunkel's pioneering studies of the psalms, many commentators have sought to categorise them according to type or theme.[18] The following list of psalm types represents one, albeit convincing, categorisation of the psalms. Bearing in mind that the collected Psalms represented the earliest hymnbook of the Church, the list provides a valuable comparison point with the classification and quantifying of contemporary congregational song-types in this book.

1. Prayers of the individual (e.g. 3:7-8)
2. Praise from the individual for God's saving help (e.g. 30; 34)
3. Prayers of the community (e.g. 12; 44; 79)
4. Praise from the community for God's saving help (e.g. 66; 75)
5. Confessions of confidence in the Lord (e.g. 11; 16; 52)
6. Hymns in praise of God's majesty and virtues (e.g. 8; 19; 29)
7. Hymns celebrating God's universal reign (e.g. 47; 93–99)
8. Songs of Zion, the city of God (e.g. 46; 48; 76)
9. Royal psalms (e.g. 2; 18; 20)

10. Pilgrimage songs (e.g. 120–134)
11. Liturgical songs (e.g. 15; 24; 68)
12. Didactic (instructional) songs (e.g. 1; 37; 73)
    (Summarised from Stek, 1985: 782)

In his cataloguing of the psalms, Stek rightly notes the existence of crossover between labels. In the same way, Chapter 6 details the problems associated with categorising contemporary song into distinct groups. As with all art, as soon as you set up a boundary by which a text is to be confined you will discover the example that doesn't stay within the fence. Likewise there will always be those songs that could fall either way. At any rate, in regard to the health of a church's music roster, all attempts at classification and comparison will ultimately prove better than none.

New Testament References to Music
References to music in the New Testament (NT) are far more abstract than in the OT.[19] Not only are references less common, they also appear to echo the covenantal change, a movement from ritual to relationship, from practice to character. Though this over-simplifies the transformation somewhat, most NT references to music undeniably allude to character rather than performance or technique. Such a transition is echoed in the movement from temple worship to the synagogue, which had begun several centuries before Christ and would become of critical importance to Christians shortly after his death. Unlike the temple service with its rigid organisation, synagogue worship was planned and conducted by lay people. Services consisted of readings from the Law and from the Prophets, of psalmody, teaching, prayer and a final blessing (based on Wilson-Dickson, 1992: 22).

A seminal NT passage addressing music is Ephesians 5:17-21 and its companion passage in Colossians 3:16-17:

> *Therefore do not be foolish, but understand what the Lord's will is. Do not get drunk on wine, which leads to debauchery. Instead, be filled with the Spirit. Speak to one another with psalms, hymns and spiritual songs. Sing and make music in your heart to the Lord, always giving thanks to God the Father for everything, in the name of our Lord Jesus Christ. Submit to one another out of reverence for Christ* (Ephesians 5:17-21).

> *Let the word of Christ dwell in you richly as you teach and admonish one another with all wisdom, and as you sing psalms, hymns and spiritual songs with gratitude in your hearts to God. And whatever you do, whether in word or deed, do it all in the name of the Lord Jesus, giving thanks to God the Father through him* (Colossians 3:16-17).

Paul commanded the Ephesians to 'be filled with the Spirit', and to experience four beneficial consequences of such a life in speech, song, thankfulness and submission. Despite the efforts of some scholars (see Liesch, 1996 for examples), the differences between 'psalms, hymns and spiritual songs' of this era are not easily distinguishable. What is certain is Paul's desire that those filled with the Spirit should sing (the word 'psalm' implies musical accompaniment) to each other, exhorting one another on in the Christian faith (see also Hebrews 10:24). Following the dimensionality of worship mapped earlier in this chapter, this accords with the horizontal level of operation within corporate worship. Stott (1979) points out that singing and making music in one's heart (v. 19) refers to the vertical dimension of worship, singing *to* God. Here the emphasis on character is apparent, with sincerity and inwardness favoured over performance or ability – indeed the statement may even refer to music that has no audible qualities (i.e. purely mental or internalised singing). Internal worship transpires alongside thankfulness and submission, both pertinent to character. The Colossians passages make clear the foundation of these characteristics, for it is only as the word of Christ dwells richly within people that the Holy Spirit will fill them. Paul's concern then was to ensure that their 'psalms, hymns and spiritual songs' were consistent with the word of Christ, i.e. manifest according to a firm biblical basis (Lucas, 1980).

Given the Apostle's insistence on the word of God and his commandment to be Spirit-filled, it is appropriate that this volume examine both the scriptural foundation for contemporary congregational music and the character of its transmission. To separate one from the other is to deny the purpose and possibilities of congregational song. The ensuing chapters will seek to ascertain whether contemporary congregational music fulfils the dimensional requirements of public Christian gatherings, and, more importantly, whether it adheres to the scriptural, character and functional requirements detailed in the Bible.

3 Ending the Corporate Worship Wars

1. Music as Worship

While congregational song exists within the corporate worship environment, this is not a book about worship. Many publications on this topic have been published in recent years and the stream looks certain to continue. Confusion between the two derives from different understandings of the nature of congregational music and worship in general. As others have argued (Carson, 2002; Dearborn and Coil, 2004), efforts to crystallise an understanding of worship (and corporate worship in particular) can ease many of the tensions surrounding contemporary liturgy. Not everyone reads that bevy of worship books available in Christian bookshops today and not all of those books provide a clear definitional study of worship elements. For a book attempting to analyse the nature of contemporary congregational music, such a study is integral. What follows, therefore, is a consideration of the key terms utilised in worship practice and in the commercial aspect of congregational music. While no particular claim is made for originality, this overview serves to map the terrain, to clearly identify the fundamentals of worship and offer a common vocabulary for worship practice that will work across denominations, countries and markets, and enable empathic communication between 'warring' parties or misunderstood minorities.

Congregational song is one expression of the 'worship life' of the believer. Since the market-driven boom of this product in the 1980s, the commercial generic term for congregational song has been 'Praise and Worship' music. As the ensuing discussion will show, however, this term is even less useful than the all-encompassing 'world music' genre developed in the 1980s to classify music inflected with any form of non-Western sound.[1] It may appear pedantic to pursue such things as marketing labels but given their pervasive influence in shaping our understanding, perhaps only in subconscious ways, there is real value in arguing for a change in common descriptors. This chapter will argue that the terms *congregational song* and *congregational music* are far more accurate and useful terms for the modern church to adopt. This assertion is based on a biblical understanding of what praise and worship actually are.

A further problem relating to the lack of scriptural understanding of what the concepts of praise and worship represent is that congregational singing has, in some churches, *become* worship. Quite often our leaders inform us that we are going to have a 'time of praise and then some worship', or that we will sing 'some praise songs at the beginning before moving into a time of worship'. Such statements have taught church members, or at least let them believe, that singing congregational music is the act of worship. This has led to a large volume of instructional church music books being published under the banner of worship, and an ever-expanding body of work dedicated to unravelling the true scriptural meaning of the term. As a result, the proliferation of publications regarding worship is such that anyone concerned with, or employed in, the field has an alarming amount of material to digest. The following argument seeks to untangle the connotations of worship and present a framework by which the term 'worship' can be both understood and applied generally. It will also consider the various debates and stylistic variants that developed alongside the introduction of contemporary congregational music.

Defining Worship

The dilemma inherent in defining worship or relating an insight into worship is evidenced by the many and various attempts of others to do so:

> *Worship is living and orally communicating in song, sermon and sacrament, the story of the One who changed our story* (Boschman, 1999: 182).

> *Worship is a gift between lovers who keep on giving to each other* (Gaddy cited in Dawn, 1995: 76).

> [Worship is] *the submission of all our nature to God. It is the quickening of the conscience by His holiness; the nourishment of the mind with His truth; the purifying of imagination by His beauty; the opening of the heart to His love; the surrender of will to His purpose – and all of this gathered up in adoration, the most selfless emotion of which our nature is capable* (Temple cited in Dawn, 1995: 80).

> *Worship is not about great songs or great musicianship. It is about you, your heart and your relationship with God* (Zschech, 1996: ii).

> [W]*orship is an identification with brokenness, and* [a] *realisation that our strength comes not from what we have done but only* [from] *what God has done for us, and so we live our lives in response* (Bullock quoted in Evans, 1999b: 10).

> *Worship is our response to the overtures of love from the heart of the Father* (Foster, quoted on CD jacket for *The Father's Song* by Matt Redman [2000]).

> *Worship is the essential posture of man* (Boschman, 1999: 154).

A longer version of this list could have filled the chapter yet the examples provided give more than enough proof of the variance in attitude towards worship and its role in the life of the Christian. Is such variance really an issue? The
problem arises when the word 'worship' begins being employed to refer to a
section of a modern church service – as it does now – or to delineate a genre
of music – as it does now – or spawns a body of literature on a multitude
of different subjects – as is presently the case. In such cases the definitional
differences contribute to division, disagreement and confusion within the
church. As Carson notes, 'the construction of a theology of worship will not
be possible unless we come to reasonable agreement about what we mean
by *worship*' (2002: 19). Indeed, Carson's important definitional study of worship, from which this quote is taken, is a long overdue attempt to coalesce
the various interpretations of worship. In attempting to do so, Carson himself
constructs a 178-word definition. He acknowledges this is 'too long and complex' (ibid.: 26). Carson then spends a further thirty-odd pages deconstructing
his definition. As mentioned before, this is an important study that needed
to be written. However, I would contend that such a study remains outside
the purview of the general church worship director, music leader or ministry student. What follows is an attempt to further narrow our understanding of what worship means, how it is employed throughout the Bible, and
how a biblical knowledge of both praise and worship can assist us in, for the
purposes of this book at least, appraising the quality and function of modern
congregational music.

Definitional studies of worship usually begin by noting that the word 'wor-
ship' stems from an old Anglo-Saxon word, *weorthscipe*,[2] meaning 'worthiness'.
Given such a definition, to worship something is simply to declare its worth.
Yet Peterson (1992) argues that even this starting point is poorly positioned:

> *Worship defined in this way* [as attributing worth] *need not have any-
> thing at all to do with the particularity of biblical revelation. It leaves open
> the possibility of people making their own assessment of God's worth and
> the response which they consider to be adequate* (17).

More profitable is an understanding of the scriptural Greek and Hebrew words
involved in different expressions of worship, but often loosely translated into
English as 'worship'.[3] The most common Greek word translated as 'to worship'
in the Bible is *proskynein*. This term represents a bodily gesture towards a great
one. In early usage it commonly referred to bowing before a king or dignitary,
kissing their feet or the hem of their garment – a physical act of homage or
submission. It also came to represent the 'inward attitude of homage or respect

which the outward gesture represented' (Peterson, 1996: 11). Another key Greek verb used in the context of worship is *latreuein*, more accurately rendered as 'to serve'. This word is often connected to sacrificial or other ritual activities. It is best understood as daily service to God, involving the whole of a person's life, '[a] *total lifestyle* of allegiance to God' (ibid.).

Paul, writing to the believers in Rome, pleads: 'I urge you, brothers, in view of God's mercy, to offer your bodies as living sacrifices, holy and pleasing to God – this is your spiritual act of worship' (Romans 12:1). In response to what God has done through Christ, believers are to present themselves to him as living sacrifices; this is their spiritual *latreuein* (worship/service). It is through total life experience that they express obedience towards God. The service (*latreuein*) Paul calls for is obedience motivated by Christ, his life, death and resurrection. Acceptable worship (*latreuein*) is the service (*latreuein*) rendered by those who truly understand the gospel and desire to live out its implications in every sphere of life. Peterson (1992) illustrates how the chapters following Romans 12:1 (namely 12–15) portray acceptable worship as:

> *...effective ministry to one another within the body of Christ, maintaining love and forgiveness towards those outside the Christian community, expressing right relationships with ruling authorities, living expectantly in the light of Christ's imminent return, and demonstrating love especially towards those with different opinions within the congregation of Christ's people* (178).

This clearly illustrates the total lifestyle of obedience encapsulated by the term *latreuein*, a point also important throughout Carson's (2002) study. The final Greek word[4] for consideration is *sebomai*, though this is but one of the *phoboun* word-group used to render the various meanings of the Hebrew text[5] in the Septuagint (Greek translation of the OT). *Sebomai*, and similar root derivatives, are used to 'indicate the fear, reverence or respect due to a God' (Peterson, 1996: 12). *Sebomai* was reflected by the obedience of the subject, though again the emphasis is on total lifestyle commitment, rather than any particular ritual practice. In light of this, it is important to note that not all worship is acceptable to God. Amos records one example of God condemning the Israelites, and their worship, for their lack of morality, and obedient, heartfelt cultic practice:

> *I hate, I despise your religious feasts; I cannot stand your assemblies. Even though you bring me burnt offerings and grain offerings, I will not accept them. Though you bring choice fellowship offerings, I will have no regard for them. Away with the noise of your songs! I will not listen to the music of your harps. But let justice roll on like a river, righteousness like a never-failing stream!* (Amos 5:21-24, emphasis added).

Drawing on all of the above scholarship, Peterson concludes that 'acceptable worship in Old Testament terms involves homage, service and reverence, demonstrated in the whole of life' (1992: 73). He highlights the interconnectedness of these terms and their relationship to ritual practice through the following diagram (ibid.: 74 – diagram adapted):

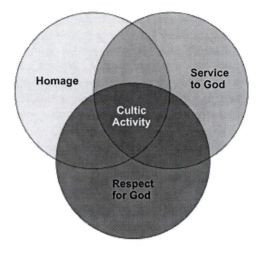

Figure 3.1: *Old Testament Worship*

In Figure 3.1 above, note that the cultic activity or ritual practice of the believer represents the intersection point of all worship responses. This 'cultic activity' represents the church, or temple, experience of the people. It is important to realise that this is by no means the only point of intersection for the three worship responses. The believer is called to service, homage and respect for God throughout his or her life, all three of which will intersect independently of any official ritual practice. Such an understanding of OT worship provides the basis for comprehending the teaching of Christ on worship, which forms the foundation of contemporary worship practices.

The NT heralded a change in worship practices and understanding. While Christ did not replace or make OT ideas about worship obsolete, he certainly transformed conceptualisations about worship. Christ sought to refocus believers on the relational nature of worshipping God. He moved them away from thinking about worship as a set of specific and rigid cultic activities. A most pointed example comes from Christ's meeting with a Samaritan woman:[6]

> *The Pharisees heard that Jesus was gaining and baptizing more disciples than John, although in fact it was not Jesus who baptized, but his disciples. When the Lord learned of this, he left Judea and went back once more to*

Galilee. Now he had to go through Samaria. So he came to a town in Samaria called Sychar, near the plot of ground Jacob had given to his son Joseph. Jacob's well was there, and Jesus, tired as he was from the journey, sat down by the well. It was about the sixth hour. When a Samaritan woman came to draw water, Jesus said to her, 'Will you give me a drink?' (His disciples had gone into the town to buy food.) The Samaritan woman said to him, 'You are a Jew and I am a Samaritan woman. How can you ask me for a drink?' (For Jews do not associate with Samaritans.) Jesus answered her, 'If you knew the gift of God and who it is that asks you for a drink, you would have asked him and he would have given you living water.' 'Sir,' the woman said, 'you have nothing to draw with and the well is deep. Where can you get this living water? Are you greater than our father Jacob, who gave us the well and drank from it himself, as did also his sons and his flocks and herds?' Jesus answered, 'Everyone who drinks this water will be thirsty again, but whoever drinks the water I give him will never thirst. Indeed, the water I give him will become in him a spring of water welling up to eternal life.' The woman said to him, 'Sir, give me this water so that I won't get thirsty and have to keep coming here to draw water.' He told her, 'Go, call your husband and come back.' 'I have no husband,' she replied. Jesus said to her, 'You are right when you say you have no husband. The fact is, you have had five husbands, and the man you now have is not your husband. What you have just said is quite true.' 'Sir,' the woman said, 'I can see that you are a prophet. Our fathers worshiped on this mountain, but you Jews claim that the place where we must worship is in Jerusalem.' Jesus declared, 'Believe me, woman, a time is coming when you will worship the Father neither on this mountain nor in Jerusalem. You Samaritans worship what you do not know; we worship what we do know, for salvation is from the Jews. Yet a time is coming and has now come when the true worshipers will worship the Father in spirit and truth, for they are the kind of worshipers the Father seeks. God is spirit, and his worshipers must worship in spirit and in truth.' The woman said, 'I know that Messiah (called Christ) is coming. When he comes, he will explain everything to us.' Then Jesus declared, 'I who speak to you am he' (John 4:1-26).

While verse 24 is often cited in worship studies and church services alike, consideration of the full passage provides a more complete picture of the transformation of believers' worship that came through Jesus. As a personal ministry, the dialogue of Christ in this passage 'initiates a totally different way of relating to God' (Peterson, 1992: 98). He moves the woman away from believing that worship only takes place at the temple, boldly claiming to be the temple himself. In this he is moving worship from an explicitly outward cultic experience (in Jewish understanding), to a more inward, spiritual relationship. Christ also claims that, with his coming, believers will be able to worship in spirit and in truth (John 4:24). Christ referred to himself as the 'truth'

(John 14:6), in that he was the true revelation of the character and purpose of God. Likewise the spirit referred to here is the Spirit of Christ, of God. '[T]o worship God "in spirit and in truth" is first and foremost a way of saying that we must worship God *by means of Christ*' (Carson, 2002: 37). Jesus goes to great length to explain to his disciples that he is sending his Spirit to them, that they might understand the 'mysteries' of God, and indeed, that they might be able to worship him more completely (John 14–17).

> *Fundamentally, then, worship in the New Testament means believing the gospel and responding with one's whole life and being to the person and work of God's Son, in the power of the Holy Spirit* (Peterson, 1992: 286).[7]

The NT spells out for Christians the dominant place worship should have in their lives. The Romans 12 passage analysed above indicates plainly that a Christian's whole life should be presented to God as a living sacrifice, or living worship. It is not a single act, it is not a strictly musical notion; the entire life of the believer is to be lived in worship to God. Worship is living a life in response to what God has done through Christ. As Peterson notes, worship:

> *...involves honouring, serving and respecting him* [God], *abandoning any loyalty or devotion that hinders an exclusive relationship with him. Although some of Scripture's terms for worship may refer to specific gestures of homage, rituals or priestly ministrations, worship is more fundamentally faith expressing itself in obedience and adoration* (ibid.: 283).

Defining Praise
As noted above, the generic label for congregational song, largely used for commercial marketing purposes, is now 'Praise and Worship'. It is necessary, therefore, to consider not only the biblical notion of worship but also that of praise, and its role in defining congregational song. To praise God is to declare his character and deeds. From a study of Hebrew and Greek words used to denote praise in the OT and NT respectively, Harding concludes that praise is 'to make known, to acclaim, the deeds and qualities of another...to praise God means to respond to his favour...for all the world to acknowledge the marvellous deeds and character of the God who speaks and saves'[8] (1987: 42). Drawing on Harding, Payne (1996) goes on to compare praise to advertising, noting that to declare the merit of someone's character or actions is to boast about them, to advertise them to others.[9] He makes the interesting observation that:

> *Music is to praise as the jingle is to advertising. It can make it effective, memorable, even grand, but unless the product is actually described and promoted, the music is of little use* (ibid.: 4).

Such a contextualisation posits music as the mere accompaniment to praise, rather than the act itself. While it is clearly possible to praise God through music, by singing about him and his works, Payne shows that it is incongruous to view the musical event solely as praise. Keck (1992) highlights another issue in contemporary congregational music – the insertion of the participant's role into praise. This is reflected in many songs that move lyrically from discussing the attributes of God, to incorporating human experience within that expression.[10]

> [A]*uthentic praise of God acknowledges what is true about God; it responds to qualities that are 'there' and not simply 'there for me'... God is to be praised because God is God, because of what God is and does, quite apart from what God is and does for me* (1168).

To this end, Keck identifies and posits a particular function for language address in praise:

> *Using the second person, speaking to the one praised, establishes or maintains a relationship; using the third person, speaking about the praised, invites others to share in the praise, and so generate and maintain community* (ibid.: 1167).

This latter idea, of speaking about the praised, is one fleshed out in the NT as being of primary importance to the Christian. NT passages that discuss praise expand the concept somewhat, to include the believers' declaration of the gospel:

> *Through Jesus, therefore, let us continually offer to God a sacrifice of praise – the fruit of lips that confess his name. And do not forget to do good and to share with others, for with such sacrifices God is pleased* (Hebrews 13:15-16).

In this passage the Christian's sacrifice of praise is to declare the gospel of Christ to others. Evidently this can occur outside of music, indeed, outside of the church. This further negates the argument of those who claim music to be the primary component of praise, and emphasises instead the third person narrative of praise. In the lyrical analysis of contemporary congregational music that is the subject of succeeding chapters, attention will be paid to both the objective/subjective nature of lyrics and the terms of address utilised. This is essential to any study seeking to gauge the efficacy of contemporary praise music to inform, encourage and edify the congregation, independent of any Christian narcissism and self-preoccupation that may also be present. As Keck contends, '[u]nless purposeless praise of God is restored to its central place in worship, mainline Protestantism will not be renewed' (1992: 1170).

One contemporary song that encapsulates the biblical notion of praising God, and even explains somewhat the justification of it during the course of the song, is Tommy Walker's 'That's Why We Praise Him' (1998).

> *He came to live, live a perfect life*
> *He came to be, the living word our light*
> *He came to die, so we'd be reconciled*
> *He came to rise, to show His pow'r and might and*
>
> *That's why we praise Him*
> *That's why we sing...*

Congregational Song Versus 'Praise and Worship'

Given the above preamble on biblical concepts of worship and praise, it is plainly evident that the generic 'Praise and Worship' tag for contemporary congregational music is misleading. What would appear more accurate and relevant is the label *congregational song*. Fundamental to this label are three distinct but related elements.

Firstly, the term congregational song reflects the corporate nature of contemporary church music, that is, it highlights the communal element of production and consumption, again reflecting its vernacular music status. The performance context, of pivotal importance in understanding and appreciating congregational music, is also implied in the label yet it remains free of denominational references which may otherwise cloud objective categorisation.

Given the current penchant for live recordings of congregational song, this label is equally disposed to discussion of the physical product and its poietic level of operation (see below).

Secondly, the word *song* is a practical reference to the predominant character of the music. '[S]ong is the expressive, lyric, and symbolic language of people who live in communities of like people' (Corbitt, 1998: 39). It is vital to observe, however, that the term *song* remains, in relation to contemporary music studies, rather problematic. McIntyre (2000) discusses various definitions of 'song', noting the disparity between individual scholars, legal representatives, musicians and the audience of popular music. What he does confirm is the historical notion that a song must contain a vocal element – typically melodic. In a similar fashion to Hayward (1998), McIntyre argues that the primary reference point for popular music is the recorded, produced version of the song, rather than traditional sheet music summaries of the performance. Subsequently:

> ...the component parts of songs in this latter part of the century are per-
> ceived by the audience as being much more than simply melody and lyric or
> even, following the legal framework, melody and musical work. They now
> can include the patterns of the song form, such as verse/chorus or ternary
> forms, as well as arrangement, production values and even the projected
> media image of the person or persons performing the song. This is in addi-
> tion to melody, lyric and harmony (2000: 321).

This expanded definition suits congregational song agreeably, given the performative emphasis placed on structure, the weighty value now attached to production and arrangement, and the growing 'mediaisation' of congregational song composers and performers. Nonetheless, the key constituents of melody, harmony and, in particular, lyric, still apply. Congregational song is founded on lyric, thus to fulfil this categorisation the music must be lyrical as opposed to purely instrumental, notwithstanding the fact that some congregational song albums contain instrumental tracks. Instrumental music designed or used within the corporate worship environment would better be delineated as congregational music. Indeed the function and operations of such music within corporate worship is an area in need of academic attention. Corbitt rightly argued that:

> The music of the kingdom...includes more than congregational song.
> Within the worship context, instrumental music is used to bond segments
> of worship together (1998: 265).

While the 'music of the kingdom' does indeed extend further than congregational song, to include Christian rock, reggae, rap, dance, jazz, non-Western church music and much more, the music of the 'worship context' of corporate worship (see below) is predominantly lyrical. As Corbitt notes, instrumental music is often the 'glue' that seams elements of the church service together, and although examples of instrumental music written for use within the service do exist and are increasing in number, more often than not 'instrumentals' are presently:

(i)   extended introductions or codas to congregational songs being *sung* in the service;

(ii)   a single verse/chorus rendition of a song;

(iii)   a complete instrumental rendition of a song played as a 'filler', for example, at the end of Holy Communion;

(iv)   an opportunity to give vocalists a rest and/or be ministered to; or

(v)   instrumental commercial CDs[11] of well-known contemporary congregational song played before or after the corporate worship service.

Instrumental music enhances and supports congregational song, but does not replace it as the object to be participated in. Furthermore, the communalism of congregational song, its joint production/consumption aspect alluded to earlier, eliminates the inclusion of instrumental music in its definition due to the often performative nature of instrumental music and the distance, or mediation, involved between performer and congregation.

The third and final element impacting on the classification of congregational song is its scriptural foundation. As discussed in Chapter 1, the passages in Ephesians 5 and Colossians 3 relating to music offer a seminal indication of the place of music within the Christian gathering:

> *Let the word of Christ dwell in you richly as you teach and admonish one another with all wisdom, and as you sing psalms, hymns and spiritual songs with gratitude in your hearts to God* (Colossians 3:16).

In seeking to understand this passage, some traditionalists may modify this to, 'as you sing psalms, hymns *and choruses* etc.' Pentecostals, on the other hand, argue that singing in the Spirit, a form of spontaneous composition or Spirit-led improvisation, constitutes 'spiritual songs'. However, given the ambiguity of the words 'psalms, hymns and spiritual songs', and despite the vigorous efforts of many to definitively explain them, it is most productive to categorise all three as congregational song. Support for this conviction can be found in their scriptural, and it could be argued, lyrical basis – 'Let the *word* of Christ dwell in you richly' – as well as their involvement in the vertical and horizontal dimensions of worship. The music is to be used to sing to God, as well as for the congregation to teach and admonish one another. This, then, is the character of congregational song: it is lyrical music based on the word of God, music that can be sung to or about God, and/or music that can be utilised during the gathering of Christians for mutual edification.[12]

Corporate Worship

Just as a misuse of the term worship has impacted on Christian music, so too the general application of the term to the weekly gathering of Christians has caused confusion and division. Worship is clearly not restricted to congregational liturgy, but can and should be reflected individually through thought, word and deed of the believer. Yet, as Carson notes, 'there is a narrower sense of worship, it appears; and this narrower sense is bound up with corporate worship, with what the assembled church does in the pages of the New Testament' (2002: 49). The church service, or community gathering of believers, becomes the corporate form of worship where people gather to honour God because of what he has rendered in their lives, 'to encourage one another to live out in everyday life the obedience that glorifies God and furthers his saving purposes in the world' (Peterson, 1992: 287). Corporate worship,[13] then, is the collective celebration and response of Christians who have actively been worshipping God – in many guises – throughout the week. In this sense, corporate worship can only be performed by those who believe in God's promises to them and live their lives in response. Corporate worship allows Christians the opportunity to collectively declare their knowledge of God, thereby encouraging each other with the truth they believe and bolstering unity;[14] to collectively respond to God; to serve each other; and to present to God their needs:

> [T]he purpose of our gatherings is not to do what we could do on our own at home (spend time in private reflection and prayer), but to build or edify each other, to admonish and encourage one another, to corporately draw near to God in prayer and praise, and together to be involved in the giving and receiving of the ministry of the Word of God (R. Smith, 2000: 5).

The NT speaks of the distinctiveness of such events (Acts 2) and calls Christians to maintain recurrent assembly (Hebrews 10). To distinguish between 'worship' and 'corporate worship' is to acknowledge worship as a lifestyle allegiance to God, while simultaneously advocating the uniqueness and indispensableness of Christians gathering together. Keller feels this is an old debate within Protestantism (2002: 203) yet, amidst some generalisations about the modern church, goes on to document Calvin's adherence to such a distinction.[15] Furthermore, corporate worship, minus the overtones of liturgy and history, covers those Christian gatherings distinct from a church service, yet within the rubric of NT gatherings.

Just as worship in and of itself contains virtually endless scope for the Christian, so too corporate worship across denominations and congregations would appear to involve a huge variety of ingredients. Corporate worship is certainly not uniform and may involve such things as music, singing, praying, dancing, reading from the Bible, teaching, responding to God, responding to others and ministering to people in the congregation. 'There is no single passage in the New Testament that establishes a paradigm for corporate worship' (Carson, 2002: 55), yet there are numerous passages that speak of elements integral to meetings of the early church. Edmund Clowney (1992) has produced a very helpful list of the elements of corporate worship present in the NT. Interestingly this list excludes many features of the contemporary church service that we have become accustomed to experiencing: drama, musical items, choirs and the like (Carson, 2002: 52). While 'there is no explicit mandate or model of a particular order or arrangement' (ibid.: 51) of corporate worship elements dictated by the passages Clowney cites, several ingredients of worship – joyful praise, prayer, thanksgiving, and hearing the Bible read, expounded and applied – are all featured heavily (1 Thessalonians 5:16-22, 27). Other elements are elucidated throughout the NT, especially those concerning the ministry of believers to each other during times of gathering (1 Corinthians 12; Romans 12).

'Determining the nature of true worship is much more important than exploring the ways humans can bring novelty to worship' (Gaddy quoted in Dawn, 1995: 94), and it has been the intention of this chapter to do exactly that. However, it must be acknowledged that:

> It is an age of novelty in congregational life. Whether we like it or not both minister and people are willing, on the whole, to break with the past and to experiment with the way in which they meet as God's people... In particular there is a widespread lack of confidence in ordered liturgy as a sufficient vehicle to express the worship of a congregation (Jensen, 1987: 111).

The proliferation of new corporate worship styles, and the endless instructional volumes produced to accompany them, showcase this 'age of novelty'. It is true that many amendments, enhancements and general re-considerations of corporate worship have produced practices that would appear to honour God and further edify his people. However, the overwhelming result of this change has been a growing tension between denominations, congregations and even sections of congregations. It is this tension that is most often referred to as the 'worship wars' (Dawn, 1995: 177).

2. Corporate Worship Wars

If any single topic dominates 'worship theology' in contemporary times, it is the notion that Christians from many denominations are currently in the middle of a worship war. Current scholarship and magazine articles often reference, and thereby further, these 'wars'. A recent cover story for *Christianity Today* contained the following stereotypical title, 'The Triumph of the Praise Songs: How guitars beat out the organ in the worship wars' (Hamilton, 1999). The epicentre of the war is focused around worship styles within churches and denominations, and, in particular, contemporary worship styles as opposed to traditional worship liturgy. Dawn begins her volume on worship with the following question:

> I am worried about the Church. The 'worship wars' that rage in so many congregations are preventing us from truly being the Church. Can we find some way to prevent discussions about worship styles from becoming fierce and bitter battles waged between two entrenched camps? (Dawn, 1995: 3)

Dawn's contention here is that the church is effectively disarmed by remaining factionalised in regard to worship. Instead of the centralising, grounding unity that Christians are called to, current worship wars fragment the church into ineffective pockets of spirituality. The aim of the following section is to explore the territory and content of these 'fierce and bitter battles', which rage over many fronts. These fronts are all encapsulated within corporate worship and that necessarily forms the framework within which they are considered, but once again the focus here is particularly concerned with the role contemporary music plays within these battles.

'Contemporary' Versus 'Traditional'

> Years ago, it would have been unthinkable that two adjectives, contemporary and traditional, would so thoroughly captivate the imagination of the church... No other words dominate the worship landscape like contemporary and traditional (Marty, 1998: 284).

Even the words 'contemporary' and 'traditional' are in themselves inappropriate terms for classification. Marty goes on to note that they may be:

> useful concepts for making wallpaper and china choices, but they are of little help in expressing the magnificent breadth of praise that has formed the Christian community. Both words encourage [liturgical] formats that answer largely to the feelings of the worshipper. The adoration of God gets lost in a bog of subjective tastes (ibid.).

This is evident in the claims of both parties. Proponents adhering to, and exalting, traditional worship insist on the historical foundation of 'their' liturgical style.[16] They fear that homogenised contemporary worship styles, and particularly the music that accompanies them, lose the reverence and majesty they feel God deserves, but their views may also reflect a natural human tendency to elevate and defend the musical tradition that they grew up with. Meanwhile, proponents of contemporary worship argue they are using formats and music that are relevant to the cultural norms around them.[17] The only way to reach their contemporaries, they argue, is to embrace the culture in which they are submerged. They argue that traditional styles of worship are formal and rigid, no longer relevant in a postmodern society. In an intriguing twist, Gilbert states that '[s]ecularisation has contributed to the polarisation of people into traditional and progressive *or* contemporary' (1980: 156; emphasis added). In other words, the very espousal of secular culture has caused this previously unknown division. A clear distinction now prevails between those who embrace the secular world and its culture and those who do not. Dawn sees value in the stance of both groups, arguing that:

Only in a dialectical tension of tradition and reformation can we ask better questions to insure that worship is consistent with the nature of God as revealed in the Scriptures and in the person of Jesus Christ (1995: 93).

This may appear commendable, although it ignores her earlier contention that the 'bitter war between "traditional" and "contemporary" styles...can easily become idolatrous' (ibid.). It becomes idolatrous because the 'dialectical tension' she advocates quickly disintegrates into self-serving factionalism. That is, because God is no longer the subject and object of worship, the style of worship and those who advocate it have become the subject and object, removing the transcendence and holiness of God from the experience of corporate worship. Marty notes that the function of a pastor, or anyone who plans and facilitates corporate worship, is to keep *God* 'as the subject in the grammar of worship' (1998: 285).

The pivotal element on which most debates concerning corporate worship hinge is music. In fact, Dawn distinguishes between contemporary and traditional styles largely on the basis of music alone:

> [t]*he term* traditional [signifies] *music in the standard denominational hymnals – that is, music in the memory of a particular faith persuasion. The word* contemporary *indicates attempts to utilise music that will appeal to younger people, who often have not been actively involved in congregations* (1995: 168).

In his discussion on the development of contemporary congregational song, Hamilton agrees that musical distinctions now mark the church: 'American churchgoers no longer sort themselves out by denomination so much as by musical preference' (1999: 29). Indeed, 'the kind of music a church offers increasingly defines the kind of person who will attend' (ibid.: 30). Hamilton attributes much of this to the baby boomers' predilection for allowing music to become the cultural marker of style. This generation, and the ones that followed, choose music in order to state their cultural affiliations and, necessarily, their individual identity. Hamilton sees the deepening differences over worship, and particularly musical style, as the new sectarianism. He notes:

> But at bottom we [Christians] *are all still sectarians; we still prefer to congregate with the likeminded. Our new sectarianism is a sectarianism of worship style. The new sectarian creeds are dogmas of music. Worship seminars are the seminaries of the new sectarianism; their directors are its theologians. The ministers of the new sectarianism are our church worship leaders* (ibid.).

In an effort to curb sectarian factions, and retain membership, many churches are now adopting separate services to accommodate various corporate worship styles. And although church gatherings have long been differentiated via liturgical style, it is now common for the musical style to be determined first, and the target audience duly invoked. Some, like Dawn, see such fencing as ultimately destructive to the unity of the church, yet churches involved in these non-blended[18] services argue that attendance is retained and often increased when worshippers choose their attendance stylistically. It is customary in many evangelical churches worldwide that morning services are often dedicated to traditional musical and liturgical forms – usually involving some form of prayer book and the denominational hymnal – while evening church services (or those later in the day) are devoted to contemporary stylings, i.e. a looser liturgical form, featuring the latest congregational songs projected on walls or screens. Such peculiarity is less noticeable in Pentecostal churches which, by and large, adhere to contemporary popular music in all their meetings. However, the establishment of services based on worship style and music has led to a proliferation of options for the contemporary church, and an industry of instructional and developmental aids.

Other Styles of Corporate Worship

> *Today, worship is too often a cacophonous, raucous, aerobic dance class. People stand on platforms and command you to do stuff you would never do in any rational moment of your life...like turning to the total stranger next to you and screaming, MY NAME IS BRADLEY AND I'M A JESUS POWER RANGER!* (Boschman, 1999: 42).

Boschman's somewhat amusing description represents one extreme of the worship spectrum. It is not only the extremes of the spectrum that cause concern. Boschman notes that the abundance of church models and paradigms,[19] to Christian observers, is evidence of a 'declining era' in the Church's worship (ibid.: 27). Basden's investigation and cataloguing of worship styles is predictably more tolerant of the differentiation. He notes:

> *...worship has differed significantly from century to century, from tradition to tradition and from denomination to denomination. Worship is more dynamic than static, more fluid than fixed, more developmental than determinative* (1999: 34).

On this point of the fluidity of corporate worship styles, Boschman and Basden, and others, would agree.[20]

In speaking of the contemporary culture of worship, Basden makes the observation that '[d]iversity in worship styles is here to stay, and no amount of wishful thinking or biblical arguing is going to change that reality'[21] (1999: 35). Such a contention is not absolute, indeed some would view it as simply the product of today's relativist, pluralist, postmodern society. In light of his contention, however, Basden (ibid.: 36) provides a spectrum by which the majority of worship styles currently employed (in western churches at least) can be classified. He identifies five unique worship styles, which vary from extremely formal and traditional (on the left) to extremely non-formal and contemporary (on the right).

Liturgical	Traditional	Revivalist	Praise & Worship	Seeker

In this model the (again misleading) title 'Praise and Worship' is attributed to services that are considered contemporary. While there is validity to Basden's justification for these categories, problems arise in generalising about movements along the spectrum. For example, to claim 'popular music is replacing classical music as worship styles move from left to right' (ibid.: 102) is naïve on several fronts. Firstly, hymnody (as proven above) should not be associated with the fine music tradition. Secondly, the elimination of hymnody from the right of the spectrum is not a given.[22] Finally, 'popular music' is unsuitable as a stand-alone term of reference given the many connotations it may invoke. The value of Basden's model lies in the recognition of various forms within the 'contemporary' banner and, even more pointedly, within the 'traditional' banner. Similarly, Keller (2002) documents new worship models that combine different elements from contemporary and historical camps, or at the very least contain an understanding of the alternate positions.

A liturgical style of worship is based on the ancient and medieval Church's emphasis on the reverence of the believer and the transcendence of God. Biblically, Basden argues, it finds its root in Isaiah 6:1-9 where the prophet Isaiah has a vision of God in his temple and subsequently commits himself to the call of God. Reflecting Isaiah's encounter with God, liturgical services move from 'adoration to confession to absolution to commission' (1999: 42). The main adherents to this style of service are the Roman Catholic Church and many mainline Protestant churches. For the latter, the involvement of Thomas Cranmer, and his *Book of Common Prayer* (1552), is pivotal to the development and institutionalisation of the style. Yet even those within the liturgical practice are beginning to lament the loss of reverence creeping into corporate worship. Jensen, commenting on the Australian milieu, has noted:

> *...emphasis has now come to be placed on fellowship rather than worship, on encounter with the brother rather than encounter with the Lord. A deliberate 'chattiness' and informality has become part of liturgical style* (1987: 112).

'Traditional' worship, according to Basden, is less formal than liturgical. Its biblical basis is attributed to the Ephesians and Colossians passages exegeted in Chapter 2. Historically it would appear to have arisen as a corrective to medieval worship, largely enforced by the Reformers of the sixteenth century. Today, traditional worship is quite segmented, with clear delineation between elements within the service, in contrast to the apparent seamlessness of worship manifest in popular musical styles.

Liesch (1996) offers a similar, though contracted, classification of worship styles. His paradigm contains three separate styles, each of which can incorporate different elements and, to a degree, sequencing options. He cites the Liturgical Service, Thematic Service, and Flowing Praise Service as representative of modern worship styles. Again the Liturgical style is modelled after Isaiah's encounter with God in Isaiah 6, while the Flowing Praise Service, common amongst Pentecostal churches, is based on Psalm 95:

> *(1) Come, let us sing for joy to the LORD; let us shout aloud to the Rock of our salvation. (2) Let us come before him with thanksgiving and extol him with music and song. (3) For the LORD is the great God, the great King above all gods. (4) In his hand are the depths of the earth, and the mountain peaks belong to him. (5) The sea is his, for he made it, and his hands formed the dry land. (6) Come, let us bow down in worship, let us kneel before the LORD our Maker; (7) for he is our God and we are the people of his pasture, the flock under his care* (Psalm 95:1-7).

This style comprises five discrete stages of worship 'experience', each supposedly derived from the Psalm: invitation (v. 1), engagement (v. 2), exaltation (vv. 3-5), adoration (v. 6) and intimacy (v. 7). The aim is to move the congregation smoothly through these stages, such that participants are unaware of the process. The basic premise is to move people from an invitation to worship to an intimate encounter with God. Such is the pattern repeatedly observed in the OT, particularly the Psalms. A major problem with the model lies in this fact alone – that emphasis is placed on an OT, i.e. pre-Christ, style of worship. The other danger is that worshippers can be manipulated psychologically into the various stages, largely through the intensity of the music employed. The psychological intensity of the worship journey is mapped by Liesch (1996: 48) as follows:

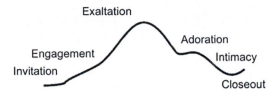

Figure 3.2: *Psychological Dimensions of the Flowing Praise Service*

Clearly Liesch's diagram lacks crucial axis information indicating exactly what is being measured in the graph. There is no mention as to why the curve bends and kinks as it does. Liesch's graph does little to alleviate any anxiety surrounding possible psychological manipulation in corporate worship.

The Thematic service specified by Liesch, although contemporary in concept and practice, represents a partial marriage of Liturgical and Flowing Praise elements. In this style, which Liesch nominates as the favoured design for the majority of evangelical churches, the entire service is centred on the topic or object lesson of the sermon. Various elements may be incorporated (prayers, drama, a children's spot, solo songs, audio-visual materials, dance, readings, etc.), and congregational song or hymns from any tradition employed; yet all should be thematically related to the sermon. The basic idea is one of preparing the people to hear the word of God. In this sense it is similar to the Flowing Praise service, in that all elements lead to the sermon. The major difference is that the elements in a Flowing Praise service do not necessary dovetail with the concerns or scripture of the sermon. In the Thematic service the topic is constantly evoked and expounded through all elements of the service.

Musically the three styles of service can be quite different. Liturgical services predominantly draw on hymns, especially those from the relevant denominational hymnal. Thematic services can rely on either contemporary or traditional music, with intermingling of the two quite common. The Flowing Praise service is almost exclusively based on contemporary congregational song, and to work effectively requires relatively advanced musicianship and preparation due to the sheer number of songs involved and their interconnectedness. Liesch (1996: 81) provides a generalised but useful diagrammatic comparison of the three styles which would prove especially useful to those corporate worship leaders and practitioners seeking to clarify their church's corporate worship model and preferences. The diagrams also beg further analysis and deconstruction from those interested in mapping the form of contemporary corporate worship.

Changes in Technology and Performing Media

> *Worship is enduring, but the styles of worship are ever changing. Culture,*
> *training, religious restraints, and even technology have formed, reformed,*
> *and transformed the way we worship* (Cornwall in Boschman, 1999: 13).

In comparing various corporate worship styles it is important to pause and reflect on the effect that technology has played in their growth. For technology not only impacts upon the performing media of the music, but also upon the way worship is disseminated and consumed.

The performing media for congregational music changed dramatically in the second half of the twentieth century. The instrumentation present in services, long the sole domain of the church organ, today resembles a popular music concert in many churches. The move away from the organ was, in some cases, treated with suspicion and disdain – similar, of course, to its introduction into the church. The initial change saw many churches move first to the piano as their primary instrument, and later to the electric piano and keyboards. This latter move coincided with the introduction of the acoustic guitar, followed by its electric counterpart. The rest of the ensemble, namely bass guitar and drums, quickly fell into place, completing the archetypal pop/rock group formation. Other instruments were added at the discretion of the music director and according to parishioner availability, but commonly included flutes, saxophones, and various stringed instruments. A complete brass section is now a customary feature of most larger churches.

Other technology-based developments were the replacement of hymn books by overhead projectors in the first instance, and later, from the mid-1990s, computerised lyrical projection. The projection of lyrics onto screens or walls freed participants to move physically during congregational singing. Clapping, raising hands and dance movements accompanied this technological revolution. Projection also enabled the congregation to be led in corporate worship more easily. Songs could flow effortlessly into each other, without the need to turn to a new page in a hymn book. Musical interludes, often used by worship leaders to explain songs or invoke specific spiritual responses such as repentance, forgiveness etc., were easily incorporated into the song by simply ceasing the projection of lyrics. In more recent times, the projection of lyrics has been layered with accompanying images in the background – images that reinforce the message, set a responsive tone, or generally complement the intention of the lyric. Conversely, technology has made it possible to project a video of the music team underneath the lyrics. This allows congregants to feel greater relationship with those leading them, particularly in large churches, but also has the negative effect of creating a more pronounced performative element to the corporate worship. Projection of lyrics has also contributed to denominational syncretism. In the absence of an *Anglican Hymn Book* or *Australian Hymn Book*, for example, Anglican churches were more disposed to use non-Anglican music simply by buying the overhead transparencies. Many people privately view such musical syncretism as antithetical to their denominational sensibilities – and some churches have enforced a blanket refusal to sing songs that emanate from certain other churches, no matter how important that song may be to the body of Christ at that time. Unfortunately such dogmatism has a strong heritage in the Western church.

Not all churches have been affected identically by technological change, yet the cultural change to church music has been widespread. These changes have particularly affected contemporary forms of worship, which will foreseeably continue to adapt to technological advancement. Boschman (1999) argues that unless the Church embraces technological – especially digital – advancement it will become increasingly irrelevant to the culture it is trying to reach. By the same token, if the Church chooses not to stay abreast of contemporary culture then it can hardly be considered 'active' in reaching out to the non-churched. Churches in this category risk existing solely for themselves, and dying out as a result.

4 Resistance or Accommodation: The 'World' of Quality

One of the great plagues on modern church music has been its designation as a music that merely apes the culture around it and thus subsumes the sanctity of the gospel through dilution with the evils of the world. This is not to deny that modern congregational song bears witness to the influences and stylistic sensibilities of popular music. Yet it also bears witness to the fact that:

> Church congregations often respond to the arts outside the four walls of the church with ignorance and resistance. They appear to be caught between praise and paranoia when considering the arts of contemporary culture that knock at their door (Corbitt and Nix-Early, 2003: 16–17).

This paranoia sees much art, let alone music, shunned by the Church in favour of safer, more historically 'sacred' creativity. What is far more instructive is an appreciation of how modern music is incorporating aspects of the culture in which it is produced, how those modifications are affecting the message of the music, and how those stylistic changes are being received by the people who actually sing and respond to the music.

One of the most common binaries used to classify, denigrate or describe congregational song is the secular/sacred polemic. Corbitt notes that:

> We often use the term 'sacred' to define music of Christians and the term 'secular' to define the music of nonbelievers. These terms, however, do not accurately describe the situation because some music has a way of being 'sacred' to a particular group of believers, and at the same time, 'secular' to others (1998: 36).

Frost and Hirsch (2003) usefully identify that '[t]here is no distinction in the New Testament between priest and laity, the sacred and the secular, the religious and the everyday' (68). Taking this further they declare that the schism between secular and sacred is unbiblical (127). Such a contention is decidedly beneficial in moving debates beyond standard parameters, and seeking more useful outcomes than the traditional acceptance or rejection.

In attempting to not propagate further a false dichotomy, this volume restricts the terminology of secular music and sacred music to indicate the distinction between music that is produced by and for the popular music industry, and that produced by, and for use within, the Church. The nature of congregational song makes this application easier than, for instance, Christian rock, which is at once music for Christians and non-Christians, music for the world and for the church, and music that takes its place within the global music market.[1] It is ultimately the 'function of the music and meaning in the text' (Corbitt, 1998: 37) that becomes the focal point of congregational song.

There has been a tendency within worship scholarship to associate the terms secular and sacred with popular/low culture and elite/high culture respectively. These terms themselves are inherently problematic and complicated[2] and often lead to unsustainable binary polemics. Drawing on Myers, Dawn (1995: 188) provides a table juxtaposing the form and content of popular culture with that of high culture, intensifying the strain by myopically associating contemporary congregational song with the former, and traditional church music (including hymns) with the latter.

popular culture	traditional/folk and high culture
Focuses on the new	Focuses on the timeless
Discourages reflection	Encourages reflection
Pursued casually to "kill time"	Pursued with deliberation
Gives us what we want, tells us what we already know	Offers us what we could not have imagined
Relies on instant accessibility; encourages impatience	Requires training; encourages patience
Emphasizes information and trivia	Emphasizes knowledge and wisdom
Encourages quantitative concerns	Encourages qualitative concerns
Celebrates fame	Celebrates ability
Appeals to sentimentality	Appeals to appropriate, proportioned emotions
Content and form governed by requirements of the market	Content and form governed by requirements of created order
Formulas are the substance	Formulas are the tools
Relies on spectacle, tending to violence and prurience (including language)	Relies on formal dynamics and the power of symbols
Aesthetic power in reminding of something else	Aesthetic power in intrinsic attributes
Individualistic	Communal
Leaves us where it found us	Transforms sensibilities
Incapable of deep or sustained attention	Capable of repeated, careful attention
Lacks ambiguity	Allusive, suggests the transcendent
No discontinuity between life and art	Relies on "Secondary World" conventions
Reflects the desires of the self	Encourages understanding of others
Tends toward relativism	Tends toward submission to standards
Used	Received

Figure 4.1. *Popular Versus High Culture*

Faulkner too falls victim to the idealisation of traditional culture and the church music 'contained' within it:

> *The resulting music* [from the current popular/consumerist environment] *perfectly constitutes the musical pole opposite that of earlier church music: it is fundamentally popular, almost entirely sensual in its appeal, and it possesses a minimum of intellectual content. Propelled by self-conscious humanity's apparently insatiable appetite for being entertained, it has produced ever more intense forms of emotional expression, with a corresponding increase in the illusion of sincerity... It is marked to an increasing degree by mechanization: drum machines, accompanimental sound tracks replacing live musical accompaniment, electronic amplification, electronically produced imitations of the sounds of acoustical instruments, and the rise of recordings and tapes... it has had the unfortunate effect of obliterating folk music and inhibiting community singing in general wherever the mass media are easily accessible, and of transforming music into a vicarious, consumer-orientated, and nonparticipatory experience* (Faulkner, 1996: 194).

Apart from ignoring the popularist history of hymnody, the coalescing of popular culture with contemporary congregational song ignores many song forms existent within the modern church. Furthermore, it affords traditional hymnody a classification never intended by its composers. To associate the traditional with high culture immediately enforces generational stereotypes as well as implying a degree of opaqueness, more appropriately viewed in terms of cultural idiosyncrasies. Thus restricting classification to secular and sacred, devoid of cultural connotations, allows more objective and comparative analysis to occur.

Secularisation and Church Music

> [C]*hurch music is on the fringe of modern musical creativity. It sets no trends; it only follows trends established by the surrounding culture* (Faulkner, 1996: 192).

To the casual observer Faulkner is exactly right. Surely there are subtle nuances and devices particular to church music, but generally the modern sound echoes the culture encompassing it. As we well know, this was not always the case. Church music has, in the past, held sway at the forefront of musical creativity and ingenuity. But today: 'Who would deny our near desperate need to recover the distinctly artistic element – that ingredient of surprise – in our worship, discipleship, mission and community life together?' (Frost and Hirsch, 2003: 186).

Returning to the binary established earlier between the secular and sacred, it is imperative to come to an understanding of the role secularisation has played, and continues to play, within the Church generally. That is not to say that all 'sacred' music, i.e. music produced for application within the boundaries of the church, is the only music suitable for the church context. Nor is it to rule out secular music as being irrevocably opposed to the artistic needs of a church. Indeed, as Corbitt and Nix-Early point out: 'We believe that all art – sacred and secular – is potentially redemptive' (2003: 24).

This section is heavily indebted to Alan Gilbert's (1980) work into the historical growth of secularisation, contained in *The Making of Post-Christian Britain*. Through adoption and extension of Gilbert's theses, it is possible to formulate parameters by which secularisation within contemporary congregational music can be assessed. To begin with, Gilbert offers the following definition (albeit protracted) of secularisation:

> *A thoroughly secular culture would be one in which norms, values, and modes of interpreting reality, together with the symbols and rituals which express and reinforce them, have been emancipated entirely from assumptions of human dependence on supernatural agencies or influences. In it the natural world would be regarded as autonomous, and knowledge, values and social structures would be ordered upon purely mundane principles. 'Secularization' describes the social and cultural processes tending to produce such a secular milieu. It includes, historically, all those developments and influences within any society which have been antithetical towards 'religious' assumptions, values, practices and institutions; and where successful, its effect has been gradually to transform more or less religious cultures into increasingly secular ones* (Gilbert, 1980: 9).

It is this gradual transformation that many see undermining the faculty of sacred music to enrich the spiritual experience of believers. As such it becomes a metamorphosis of religion, rather than a direct decline in the significance of religion (ibid.: 3). Either way, the capacity for Christians to be the salt of the earth (Matthew 5:13), to remain *in* the world but not be *of* the world, has been eroded. As Gilbert notes:

> *...Christian history has illustrated in numerous ways that the cost to the Church of shaping the wide culture is to be itself shaped and re-shaped by a myriad of inescapable involvements* (1980: xiii).

Indeed, as detailed earlier, it was the early church's distinction between the sacred and the secular that 'established an intellectual framework within which secularisation was almost bound to occur' (ibid.: 18). Gilbert goes on to map the expansion of secularisation from the Middle Ages, when the influence of the secular was lowest, through the formative Renaissance and Reformation, to the fertilisation of the Enlightenment. All the while secularism had been in progress, gradually surpassing the religious mindset and corroding traditional church power-bases (e.g. the State).

In terms of the arts, Gilbert surmises that:

> *Any cultural development tending to preoccupy people with ideas, interest and knowledge bereft of supernatural, metaphysical, other-worldly assumptions, tends inevitably towards secularization* (ibid.: 63).

In the case of church music one is immediately drawn towards lyrics at this point. A shift in the facility of Christian lyrics to express interest in, and knowledge of, the supernatural (i.e. the spiritual), is symptomatic of escalating secularism. The lyrical analysis provided in the ensuing chapters will verify this phenomenon within congregational song, where the diminishing personal reference to the Godhead is indicative of secular encroachment. While there is nothing intrinsically wrong with songs that express deep emotional sentiments (remembering that God himself is love – 1 John 4:8), an exclusive trend towards this style of writing could ultimately transfigure congregational song into love poetry, attractive to the secular surrounds but devoid of deeper spiritual benefit.

Gilbert views the Church's response to this creeping secularisation as falling into two polemics: accommodation on the one hand and resistance on the other. With accommodation '[s]ynthesis is the aim, even when the result gets perilously close to capitulation...[whereas] resistance co-exists with the hope that by refusal to compromise Christianity will increase, not relinquish, its capacity for influencing the "world"' (ibid.: 133). Frost and Hirsch argue that contextualisation is what is important, not only in a musical sense, but for the entire western church:

> *The missional-incarnational church must contextualize its language, worship, symbols, rituals, and communal life in such ways as to be sensitive to and impactful in a particular cultural context* (2003: 81).

In this sense 'Contextualisation...can be defined as the dynamic process whereby the constant message of the gospel interacts with specific, relative human situations' (ibid.: 83). This contextualisation clearly has overtones of accommodation inherent within it, yet by stressing the constancy and permanence of the gospel message, it reminds those involved of the core ideology they are promoting. Still, there can be little doubt that the dominant discourse permeating the Christian music scene involves issues of accommodation and resistance.

A form of such polarisation has occurred in the domain of contemporary congregational music, between songwriters from mainstream (often traditional) churches and Pentecostal songwriters, most pointedly during the 1990s. The burgeoning success of Pentecostal music was in part due to the growing similitude that the music bore to the world around it. Many Hillsong writers, for example, have sought to imitate the sound of popular music in vogue at the time, 'accommodating' the current secular sound.[3] Songwriter Reuben Morgan has noted:

> When listening to other people's material, Christian or secular, analyse the grooves and harmonies and work out why the songs are so popular and memorable. There is no shame in copying a groove and adapting it to your own ideas... Some of my songs were written in exactly this way (Song-writing workshop, Hillsong Conference, 2000).

Other songwriters reacted against accommodation by resisting the sound of the world, and calling for more traditionally-based congregational songs to be written. This resistance alienated evangelical and Pentecostal songwriters into 'labelled camps' and musical styles that they were increasingly bound to.[4] Such constriction ultimately realised songs that were considered musically uninteresting on the one hand, though irrepressibly religious,[5] and thoroughly worldly on the other.[6] In seeking to ascertain the roots of this secularisation, it is important to show how Christian music may remain both *of* the (secular) world but not *in* the world. To erode this distinction is to deny the holiness, the 'set apartness', to which Christians are called. Yet the process of secularisation is often so gradual, and comfortable, that this danger is ignored. For this reason alone, Gilbert rightly asserts that: '[s]ecularization is a much deadlier foe than any previous counter-religious force in human experience' (1980: 153).

Keck extends the trepidation surrounding secularisation past musical nuances to the contemporary culture of worship itself:

> ...far too often the 'mainline' churches are...engaged in worship which is thoroughly secularized. I recall an occasion when the traditional invocation was replaced with the rousing cheers for God: 'Gimme a G; gimme an O; gimme a D!' ... There will be no renewal of mainline Protestantism until its worship of God is redeemed from such silliness and the secularization it reflects...what is [lost] in the secularisation of worship [is] the identity and integrity of the church as church, that is, whether the church stands faithfully in the presence of the One who is both the object and the source of faith. And the antidote to this secularization is restoring the integrity of the center of worship – the praise of God (1992: 1167).

Writing from a North American perspective, Keck is observing a corporate worship culture that, in many respects, developed ahead of Canada, South Africa, Australia and the United Kingdom, among other places. The warnings for these countries are clear, particularly those chasing after worship styles that positively reflect the secular culture in which they were produced. Common to this thinking is the notion that the object of worship, God, has been replaced by Christian self-preoccupation, a mirroring of the self-interest and individualism of contemporary culture:

> If praise extols the excellence of another, and if praise is the heart of Christian worship, then worship is secularised when the focus shifts from the character of God to the enhancement of ourselves, when theocentrism is replaced by anthropocentrism, however much talk of God remains. In fact, the secularised character of worship is manifest precisely in the ways that God continues to be talked about, as well as in the ways that God is hardly talked about at all (ibid.: 1169).

Stripped of theocentric objectivity, the corporate worship service merely becomes an example of the 'secularity that marks the world we live in' (ibid.: 1170), rather than a spiritually grounded alternative. Quite often elements of secular culture (movies, games, etc.) are incorporated to make interaction with a simultaneously judgmental and gracious God more palatable. Problems with this arise when the ornamental secularisation obscures the object it was designed to enhance:

> To be sure, there have been many attempts to make the worship of God more joyous...we have blown up balloons, danced in the aisles, marched behind banners; we have turned to jazz and we have sung ditties whose theological content makes a nursery rhyme sound like Thomas Aquinas. But it is not enough to make things livelier, or set to music our aspirations and agendas. We can do better than that, and we must, for when the truth of God as made actual in Christ and attested in the gospel evokes the truthful praise of God, Christian worship enacts an alternative to the secularism which otherwise deludes us with its promises (ibid.: 1171).

Thus the primary aspect to investigating the secularisation of congregational song is examining the manifestation of 'truthful praise of God'. Such manifestations transpire in the lyrical content, yet are assisted by the musical construction of songs and the mediation of the music through the modern worship culture.

Criteria for Determining Quality in Congregational Song
Criteria for, and opinions about, what represents quality within congregational song are almost as numerous as the songs themselves. Within the definition and

parameters of congregational song outlined in Chapter 3, however, it is possible to set certain benchmarks by which the music can be analysed and compared:

> *Like many of the biblical psalms,* good *Christian hymns or songs tell us what God is like and what he has done. They encourage us to respond to him with faith, repentance, love, hope, obedience or gratitude* (Peterson, 1996: 139, emphasis added).

For this to happen in congregational song, R. Smith writes that the primary arbiter is necessarily lyrical. He goes on to say that the words of a song must be:

> *...true and helpfully expressed. That a song has a good tune is not enough. If the words are erroneous, incomprehensible or easily open to misunderstanding, then it is more of a hindrance to the work of God than a help* (2000: 4).

At no point does Smith offer any musical or intellectual trope by which the term 'good' can be understood. With regard to the sense in which Smith uses 'true', lyrics need to be theologically sound, that is, biblically based and contextually relevant. Indeed, such is the weight of lyrical intent within the purpose of congregational song that, should the lyric be theologically misleading, the song may have little place in corporate use. Drawing on Gieschen (1986), Dawn identifies several theological flaws often encountered in contemporary congregational music:[7]

1. Songs that add our efforts to God's saving work. These are songs which include human endeavour in the process of salvation. As such they are at odds with Bible passages such as Ephesians 2:8-9;
2. Songs consisting of sub-Christian texts that are theologically correct but shallow. Gawronski argues that this type of song has been:

    > *Written, no doubt, within the past 20 years,* [and] *is a piece of that resigned sentimentality that is characteristic of 'easy listening music'. Although pleasant enough, it is spiritual Wonder Bread: It utterly lacks roots, depth, sustenance. It is alright as a starter, to open the heart to prayer. But unless fed by some solid food...serious seekers will turn elsewhere* (cited in Dawn, 1995: 172).

3. Songs characterised by disinformation (e.g. songs that reiterate the call to praise God but never actually do);
4. Songs that muddle Christian doctrine (e.g. ascribing attributes to the Godhead not justified through scripture); and
5. Camp songs,[8] which may be doctrinally true but carelessly expressed. (List summarised from Dawn, 1995: 171–74)

Both Smith and Dawn draw attention to those lyrics that are 'carefully' or 'helpfully' expressed. They argue that the language, poetry and metaphors should be such that they resonate with the local congregation (and hopefully the wider denomination). Many contemporary songwriters agree:

> We have to reach for this in our music subculture, not just theology in music but also poetry. This is my big thing. This is where we [evangelical songwriters] all fall down, we are writing stuff that is not lyric... We are so frightened of getting it wrong that we are afraid to use our imagination. That's where we can be set free – to use our imagination in lyric...let's be courageous with the words we use in our songs. If we really understand the truth we'll write much more imaginative lyrics (Chiswell, interview with the author, 2000).

To this end, it is virtually impossible, except in the most fanciful imagination, to conceive of a book on the poetry of modern church music. While such volumes exist with reference to the great hymn canon, and even specific composers within it, there would be little by way of colourful prose to include in a volume on modern texts. This is a real deficiency that needs addressing in modern song. Moving away from formulaic lyrical expression, however meaningfully presented, will enhance the artistic qualities of congregational song and therefore the identificatory possibilities for the participants.

The other dominant criterion in assessing quality within congregational song is the musicality of the piece. R. Smith notes that the best music is 'appropriate, enjoyable, memorable and singable' (2000: 4), to which Corbitt adds 'danceable that is [it] has enough rhythm to catch the attention, movement, and structure a congregation needs to sing together' (1998: 285). Clearly these terms in and of themselves are incredibly broad. The analysis that follows will elucidate the elements of melody, rhythm, texture and timbre (among others) commonly held to possess the positive attributes identified above. Only in this manner can the level of musical construction in congregational song be accurately ascertained. The current desire for musical quality in congregational song is reflected in the copious volumes released to instruct and assist the development of 'successful' church music programs.[9] Gieschen (1986) probably takes this to the extreme, calling for congregational song that exudes *excellence* and *greatness*. This he defines as:

> Skillfulness, expertness, competence, aptness, consistency of style, clarity of basic intent, adroitness, inventiveness, and craftsmanship. Pieces which contain these qualities of excellence in sufficient amounts would be accepted for use; those deficient would be rejected. It is on this basis that we exclude music with forced or awkward harmonies; music that is too repetitive and

> *boring; phrases that don't seem to be going anywhere; music that is so pre-*
> *dictable and full of clichés; clumsy part-writing; music that lacks any sense*
> *of freshness or newness; music whose discourse is so rapid that its experience*
> *seems empty; pieces that don't engage your interest* (quoted in Dawn, 1995:
> 198).

While there is much unsubstantiated subjectivity and general terms in this definition, there are nonetheless useful components in considering effective song. Especially we would do well to take note of Gieschen's admonitions against clichéd, predictable music. Quite often modern song is guilty of drawing on well-worn phrases and constructions, and then repeating them more than their originality allows. Yet Gieschen appears focused on the evils of particular genres, perhaps without reasonable justification:

> *If music of excellence can be written in all styles, then all styles can also*
> *come up against these criteria and fail. And Pop music, since it has not*
> *been screened by history, should be expected to fail rather frequently*
> (ibid.).

Dawn's summary is far less judgemental, yet more penetrating:

> *The secret to greatness in* [congregational song] *is that the emotions and*
> *insights* [that the music] *evokes thoroughly match those roused by the*
> *theological content and that both music and text speak fully and honestly*
> *of that which really matters* (ibid.: 201).

Both these views will be scrutinised in the following chapters, in order to discover whether contemporary congregational song is 'failing' in purpose compared with hymns, for example: those which have been screened by history. Furthermore, the debate within the evangelical church community as to whether major music producers throughout the world speak 'fully and honestly of that which really matters' will be explored. Although theology and musicology are key disciplines for assessing congregational song (and indeed underscore the analysis presented throughout this book), other considerations are necessarily involved:

(i)   Does a particular song suit corporate worship or fulfil a role within it?
(ii) Does the song promote negative or positive performance practice by way of congregational involvement and/or musical difficulty?
(iii) Is the song applicable to the wider church body (outside of the local congregation)?
(iv) Do other cultural or secular associations need to be considered?

Hymns Versus Choruses

One of the most hotly contended battles in corporate worship worldwide is the debate over the respective merits of hymns and choruses. For better or worse this debate is played out in church elderships, music teams and in the pews on a weekly basis. Those endorsing traditional worship advocate the continued use of (largely canonised) hymns – drawn predominantly from the eighteenth, nineteenth and twentieth centuries. In the other camp, many of those advocating contemporary worship styles promote near exclusive use of contemporary congregational song. The following sections address the contentions of both groups, beginning with the proponents of traditional hymnody within corporate worship.

Mark Noll's (1999) passionate defence of evangelicalism places great credence on the role of evangelical hymnody throughout history. 'The classic evangelical hymns contain the clearest, most memorable, cohesive, and widely repeated expressions of what it has meant to be an evangelical' (37). He notes:

> Whatever their many differences of theology, ethnicity, denomination, class, taste, politics, or churchmanship, evangelical hymn-writers and hymn-singers pointed to a relatively cohesive religious vision (ibid.: 39).

This vision contained three fundamental elements. Firstly, a clear picture of redemption relying on the death of Christ upon the cross. Second, the curiously broad, ecumenical use of the hymns. Finally, the social vision and concern portrayed in many of the hymns (ibid.: 39). Noll provides useful examples of each element, though the basis of his argument rests heavily on the ecumenicalism of the hymns. Not only were the hymns sung in a large assortment of churches, but moreover, they were written by composers from many denominational backgrounds and theological positions thereby securing a large ecumenical platform. Indeed, Noll claims that some of the more revered hymn-writers would not be awarded positions of leadership in today's evangelical church due to their shallow theological acumen. Evangelical hymns, says Noll, do not offend because they do not promote the particular concern of any distinct faction within the Church (ibid.). As noted above, many contemporary songs fall into the same classification yet have been thrown out of churches due to their origin. Here in Australia many churches purposely refuse to sing music from Hillsong Church, while boisterously ignoring the Moravian influences heard in the music of the Welseys. That said, one of the dominant features of – particularly Pentecostally produced – music has been its growing ecumenical appeal. There would be few churches in Australia, of any denomination or persuasion, unaffected by the music of Hillsong Music Australia (HMA). Though some Christians told me they would never set foot in Hillsong Church due to theological differences, they were more than happy to sing music written and produced there. Later analysis will show that the doctrinal peculiarities of Hillsong Church are by and large suppressed in their music. Should a lack of denominational 'politics' be considered a marker of 'quality' within hymnody, then both hymn and chorus advocates will need to find different areas of polemical engagement. Rather than politics, the case for traditional hymnody would benefit from concentrating on the grounded Christology explicitly detailed in many evangelical hymns.

Due to their structure and length, Peterson argues that traditional hymns are superior to choruses in that they:

a. Provide a more extensive treatment of a biblical passage (over a number of verses);
b. Develop a biblical theme (by considering various points of view in different verses);
c. Tell the story of someone else's spiritual pilgrimage (in order that other Christians might identify with it);
d. Paint a picture of some biblical scene (to encourage appropriate response);
e. Explore the different dimensions of the response we should make to God.
(Adapted from 1996: 142–43)

Clearly the weight rests firmly on lyrical length here, an element of congregational song under direct scrutiny in subsequent chapters. The inadequacy of this list lies in its reliance on generalised assumptions about contemporary choruses. Should analysis prove the existence of widespread lyrical obscurity and brevity then Peterson's contentions hold valid. Thus the need for sustained critical and purposeful analysis of congregational song, if nothing else, to finally endorse or deny the plethora of assumptions that circulate regarding it.

Dawn cites Greg Asimakoupoulos in noting the lyrical importance of hymns: 'My hymnal increased my vocabulary of praise. Reading the lyricist's words was like learning a new language' (1995: 200), though she additionally argues that hymns should be subject to the same 'selection grid' of greatness discussed above for congregational song. For Dawn, to reject the traditional music of church history is to:

> ...lose the opportunity to learn not only from its text but also about its musical form, and thus we will miss the opportunity to gain sensibilities that great art can teach us (ibid.: 201).

In this statement Dawn moves past the conventional lyrical forte of hymns, to focus on the music itself. Unfortunately this contention is not corroborated by any form of empirical evidence or analysis.

A typical hymn-versus-chorus contemplation is provided in M. Fischer's (1999a) comparison of Charles Wesley's 'Jesus, Lover Of My Soul' (1740) with the chorus of the same name by Daniel Grul, John Ezzy and Stephen McPherson (1992). Fischer notes:

> Both songs start with the same line, alright, but really that's where the similarities end. The chorus is focused on our response to God, which would be fine were it not for the fact that it puts an awful amount of confidence in our ability to hang on to God.

> > Jesus, lover of my soul
> > Jesus, I will never let you go...
> > I love you, I need you
> > Though my world may fall apart [sic],
> > I will never let you go...

> That might be fine as an expression of gratitude to God, but in the end it's right out of touch with the Bible's view of our abilities. According to the Bible, we dare not trust our ability to hang on to God – that's the whole point behind trusting him instead (n.p.).

He goes on to quote sections of Wesley's hymn in order to highlight the disparity between the two songs:

> Other refuge have I none,
> Hangs my helpless soul on Thee...
> All my trust on Thee is stayed;
> All my help from Thee I bring;
> Cover my defenceless head
> With the shadow of Thy wing.

His conclusion is somewhat ironic – given that this form of public critique is exactly the type of catalyst that fuels the hymn/chorus debate – and tinged with ingenuousness:

> The last thing I want to do is weigh into the ever-simmering 'Hymns versus Choruses' debate – far be it from me to reignite a fire which is best left to die out. What I'm saying is that whatever the form of songs we choose to sing, it is the CONTENT which is the critical thing (ibid.).

Such a critique reflects the underlying struggles that contemporary corporate worship leaders face in structuring services and pooling music repertoires. First there is the battle with literalism. In discussing the above chorus, Fischer focuses on the songwriter claiming a believer's 'ability' to hang on to God, that is, a mere mortal is conceptualised as being able to control his or her relationship with the supernatural Creator. Such a notion is clearly absurd. Yet taken as a figurative expression of life dedication and commitment to the will of God, the songwriter's intent is perfectly justified. This literal interpretation is rampant amongst those arguing against contemporary congregational song. In part it represents a failure to distinguish between the figurative, experiential domain and the literal, objective domain within contemporary song. Interestingly, in the example cited, there is no mention of Wesley's second line, 'Let me to Thy bosom fly' which, if scrutinised with the same literalism as the chorus, might well raise some complex theological issues.[10] Another ever-pressing issue within the debate is contextualisation. This applies in many areas, be they lyrical, musical, performative or historical, and, as with the one-line quotation above, allow arguments to foment over meanings never intended. Fischer exhibits this phenomenon by his selective quotation of both hymn and chorus. The complete contemporary version of the song reads:

> *Jesus, lover of my soul,*
> *Jesus, I will never let you go;*
> *You've taken me from the miry clay,*
> *You've set my feet upon the rock and now I know.*
>
> *I love you, I need you,*
> *Though my world may fall, I'll never let you go.*
> *My Saviour, my closest friend,*
> *I will worship you until the very end.*

The lines omitted by Fischer refer to Christ's saving work, reflected in the language of the psalmist David (Psalm 40). Seen contextually it is the love of Christ that has saved the writers (from their sin) and set them on a solid foundation (in relationship with God through Christ). In *response* to the work of Christ the protagonist declares his or her love and *dependence* on him, vowing to worship (i.e. serve, respect and fear) Christ until the very end (of life). In this light Fischer is correct, *content* is important, but only if it is appropriately contextualised.

One of the most balanced critiques concerning hymns and choruses is provided by Liesch (1996), who devotes the early chapters of his book to exploring the issues at stake. In discussing hymns he notes that they have stood the test of time, that is, they have proven their value to the people of God in a variety of personal and cultural situations. The longevity of hymns is largely attributed to their lyrical messages rather than musical attributes, for hymns 'underscore denominational distinctives, communicate the profundities of faith, and offer a thoughtful exposition of church doctrines' (22). While upholding the historical significance of hymns, Liesch is sceptical about the number of choruses that will be 'canonised' in 30 years' time, let alone 200 years. Liesch also advocates the scriptural foundation of hymns, proving that many are merely transcriptions of Bible passages. While this is true, he ignores contemporary songs that fulfil identical criteria. Of more value is his contention that hymns are quite often deeply instructive and helpful to the congregation due to the extraordinary circumstances in which they were written.[11] Thus the stories behind hymns can also be used to encourage and edify the congregation. Although a fierce advocate for contemporary congregational song, Liesch provides the following summary of inherent shortcomings within this modern tradition:

> In general, choruses lack intellectual rigour and fail to offer a mature exposition of biblical doctrines. Choruses bracket the cross and resurrection together in their lyrics but shortchange the full reality of sin and human weakness and fail to capture adequately the agony and suffering of Christ on the cross. They put the weight on sin defeated and therefore gloss over persistent sin in our lives. There's very little emphasis on corporate confession or repentance. And the cost of discipleship and need for endurance and perseverance in the Christian life get scant attention (1996: 20).

He reasons that hymns can address these insufficiencies, and thus what is beneficial in the contemporary church is a blend of hymns and choruses. This blend need not be fifty/fifty, and should rather reflect the demographic of the congregation. Furthermore, hymns can be adapted for contemporary cultural nuances, in the same way they have been continually adapted, updated, edited and contemporised throughout history:

> If we become the victims of any particular musical trend we will soon be out of date. If we simply respond to the latest fads we will provide people with nothing of permanent value and contribute to the spread of secularism, with its insistence that only 'now' matters. In particular, contemporary Christians need to be put in touch with the contributions and insights of former generations of believers. There is a rich treasury of hymns from across the centuries that can minister to our needs today and provide what is lacking in modern songs or choruses. Of course, the reverse is also true: some modern music expresses biblical truth that is hardly emphasised in older material (Peterson, 1996: 141–42).

Liesch (1996: 30) provides the table below to highlight the strengths of both musical traditions and, while subsequent analysis will prove that some of the binaries are misleading, the general premise – that each tradition holds a positive function within the church – can be observed.

Hymns and Choruses Edify Differently

Hymns	Choruses
enduring 'stars'	momentary 'fireworks'
historic, classic	contemporary, popular
lengthy, developed	short, repetitious
numerous thoughts	one general thought
transcendent	intimate
more intellectual	more emotional
appealing to mature believers	appealing to mature believers, children, and the unchurched
full of content	minimal content
require attention to text	free attention to God
lyrics dated	lyrics contemporary
vocally demanding	vocally easy
rhythmically stiff	rhythmically freer
medium for specific doctrines	medium for basic character of God

Figure 4.2: *The Strengths of Hymns and Choruses*

Given the strengths of both musical traditions it appears unnecessary and problematic to continue their polarisation within the Christian community. Many factors must be taken into account prior to determining the musical complexion of corporate worship, yet the most edifying and effective outcome would appear somewhat inevitable. As Peterson bluntly observes:

> ...it would be foolish to sing only modern songs and abandon some of the riches we have inherited. Church services should regularly contain a couple of traditional hymns as well as a mix of contemporary songs (1996: 148).

There are two modern musical forms that can assist churches in developing a balance of musical styles that may placate and indeed encourage various quarters of the congregation. The first is to perform modern songs written in hymn-like fashion, what one might call 'modern hymns'. That is, songs containing contemporary language and contemporary musical nuances, yet retaining basic principles and structures of traditional hymns. The second is to utilise traditional hymns that have had their music re-written or re-arranged into a contemporary style. To deal with the former first, one of the most highly regarded composers of modern hymns is Stuart Townend. Writing out of the UK, Townend has produced many songs that have captured the excitement of various generations of believers, the most notable of which is 'How Deep The Father's Love For Us'.[12]

'How Deep' appeals to many for a variety of reasons, most remarkably for its combination of traditionally developing, strophic-form lyrics, and its blend of hymn-like melody and modern rhythmic inflections. The song alternates between simple quadruple and 6/4 measures. This metric oscillation is not only rare within modern song, but also allows the lyric a lilting feel despite its relatively straight crochet dominant rhythm. Syncopation is used routinely in the piece, with a dotted-crochet quaver pattern announcing the start of every second bar. The consistency of this pattern allows participants a relaxed and easy performance, one akin to the syllabic timing used in most hymns. To avoid this becoming mundane, Townend incorporates a melodic lift to raise the intensity of the song. He lifts the melody a third, to begin on the fifth of the scale. This gentle rise is enough to promote energy and passion in the song despite the rhythm and melodic construct remaining the same. As mentioned, the song is in strophic form with three verses of text. Adding to the universal appeal of the song is the strong Christology developed in the verses, which portrays the saving work of Jesus with a good deal of powerful imagery. Adding to the climax of the song is a personal identification with mystery revealed:

> *Why should I gain from his reward?*
> *I cannot give an answer,*
> *But this I know with all my heart,*
> *His wounds have paid my ransom.*

Another song to draw on hymn-like practices is 'Oh The Mercy Of God' (Bullock). Unlike the seemingly formulaic forms carried through into the majority of contemporary congregational song releases, 'Oh The Mercy' is a flowing, slow-paced, simple triple-metre song. The song features strong Holiness and Salvation song-type characteristics, with ideas drawn largely from Ephesians 1. The song incorporates verbatim scriptural quotes that reinforce the density of the theology: 'to the praise of his glorious grace' (Ephesians 1:6). Furthermore, the lyrics alternate between second and third person address, which, in combination with the plural point of view, renders the song more powerful and unifying.

The hymn-like qualities of the composition are governed by a simple crochet-based melodic rhythm that extends over the range of a ninth and ascends steadily towards the climax of the chorus. It is extremely conjunctive and balanced, not dissimilar in character to the bulk of melodies contained in traditional hymn books such as *The Anglican Hymn Book*, *The Hymnal*, and *Mission Praise*. The words (136 of them) have prominence, and elaborate rhythmic construction is abandoned in favour of textural colour. The sound of 'Oh The Mercy' along with its hymn-like construction (as with 'How Deep'), might lead to speculation that these types of songs appeal more to an older age demographic, or at the very least, to a predominantly easy listening audience. Such factors might also contribute to their versatility within modern liturgical settings.

As mentioned, another type of song useful for appeasing different musical interest groups within a church are re-written hymns. Many traditional hymns have been updated to incorporate new melodies and contemporary harmonies, with some minor modernisation of the lyrics. These songs are quite often enormously popular within mainline evangelical churches as they bear witness to the traditional hymnody of the Church, simultaneously situating themselves comfortably within the current sounds of popular culture. Often entire albums are devoted to such re-arrangements; for example those by Ruth Buchanan. Arrangements such as these exist throughout the world, with multiple versions of classic hymns now available to music directors. What is most integral is choosing the version of a hymn that most suits a particular local congregation. Examples that have flourished in the Australian scene include 'My Hope Is Built' (1998) by Nikki Chiswell, and 'May The Mind Of Christ' (1994) by Mark Peterson.

A related type of song is that which uses most of the words from a traditional hymn, with entirely new musical settings. Often these songs abandon the common strophic form of hymns and rework lyrics in standard binary forms. 'You Are My King' (Foote) is such a song. Drawing heavily from the hymn 'And Can It Be', 'You Are My King' forms a recognisable connection with the hymn, both melodically and lyrically, in its chorus: 'Amazing love, how can it be/ that You, my King, would die for me?' Both the hymn and Foote's new song reveal strong Testimony and Christological themes. Thus, even though an entirely new song creation, 'You Are My King' exhibits a strong lineage to the former 'canon' and again represents a useful bridge between disparate congregation demographics.

The various human 'battle fronts' outlined above contribute extensively to the overall worship milieu and it is in the context of these battles that contemporary congregational song exists. The theories elaborated above inform the analysis provided in subsequent chapters, and in some cases will provide the lens through which the music must necessarily be seen. Many wars are noted historically for the technology and weaponry with which they were fought. It may well turn out that current worship wars are remembered not for the battles themselves, but for the congregational song and performance media produced by them.

Song Canonisation
Most health professionals acknowledge that a balanced diet is essential to the well-being of any person. To achieve this we are encouraged to include foods from the five basic food groups in our diet everyday. It would seem to me that a similar philosophy would be helpfully applied to the musical diet of our modern churches. Due to the denominational branding of churches, or even the specificity of individual churches and their musical needs, some churches are effectively restricting their diet to one food group. Often this food is the music produced from their particular church or denomination. For example, Christian City Church (CCC) used to pride itself on only using its own music in its corporate gatherings around the world. Most CCC music is produced from their Sydney homechurch, so even at a base level this music is going to be less localised and distinct to congregants in the Vancouver CCC church, for example. This is not to single out CCC by any means. Indeed they represent an interesting case study exactly because they have changed their position on the matter, with Senior Pastor Phil Pringle recognising the need for diversification in the worship diet of the congregation:

> *The need to hear what the Spirit is saying to the Church is imperative. The Holy Spirit brings the current message of God and colour of what he is doing in a major way through the worship expressions of the Church both locally and universally. Thus we* [at CCC] *recognise our own worship leaders as bringing a constancy of fresh life as well as keeping our congregation in connection with the Church at large around the world. We recognise other song writers are bringing what the Lord is saying to the Body of Christ, so we will incorporate them as well* (personal communication with the author, 2006).

Such a diversification is even more indispensable in smaller churches where there may only be two to three main songwriters. In such cases limiting the catalogue to songs from these writers inhibits the breadth of Christian experience being sung about, and experienced.

Many of the large music producing churches around the world restrict the use of other people's songs during their gathering. Certainly, they argue that they have enough good songs to satisfy a meeting of believers – no matter the thematic concerns of the service. Yet the point remains: they are only consuming one kind of song, their musical diet is one-dimensional. A cynical observer might conclude that the reasoning for such a policy is strictly commercial – that is, we sing only 'our' songs so people will only buy 'our' albums. Advocates will argue this, saying that they only use their own music because that is the church's 'brand name', that is, the language and experience they understand. The real travesty of this thinking comes when one reflects on the vast volume of contemporary song being produced around the world. There is now so much quality congregational song being written around the world, which is easily accessible through CDs, music books and the internet, that there can be no excuse for using material of an inferior standard. How refreshing it was to hear Darlene Zschech invite members of the Hillsong Conference evening rally in 2005 to join in singing 'How Great Is Our God' (Cash/Reeves/Tomlin) in whatever language they were used to singing it. It is simple logic that using music only from one source will not always yield the optimum results. A diet of only one food will make you sick – no matter how good that food is.

One offspring of this unfortunate tendency is that the constant turnover of contemporary songs means very few songs are being retained around the world as some form of modern canon. Now all those involved in popular music studies realise the inherent dangers in promoting a canon, a list of songs valorised and applauded exclusively. Yet perhaps these pedagogical problems are lessened somewhat in the context of the Christian faith. As people age they often return to the music of their youth, music they grew up with, music that was special to them at important moments. Indeed, oftentimes particular artists are lauded throughout their career by fans for exactly those reasons. Does this have even greater resonance in the life of Christians? Songs important in the formative stages of their Christianity, or as a response to significant periods in their life, remain integral to the faith life of the believer. This is one of the reasons why classic hymns remain revered by older members of congregations. This is their music. They identify with and draw strength from those songs. The question for us becomes: what will happen to our currently popular congregational song given its place within a throw-away pop culture society? With the constant turnover of albums every year, a new hit-list of must-use songs, the facility to retain a catalogue of tried and tested songs soon disappears. The album-a-year policy of Hillsong is testimony to this. Many of the great songs recorded on previous albums are never to be sung again, such is the requirement that new songs be adopted, tested, recorded and sold. But this is true virtually across the board. Will it be enough in thirty years that Christians constantly sing new songs, and have no history of hymnody which to draw? I know there are those who say 'yes'. But I want to question such a mentality. If we are producing congregational song which we consider to be disposable, fleeting and of little long-term worth, then what does that say for the quality of the text to begin with? As noted above, Liesch remains sceptical about the number of contemporary songs we will still be singing in thirty years. Yet a time will come as current congregations age that a yearning to find comfort and encouragement from the songs of the past will emerge. Will the songs still be in current rotation, or will we have replaced them with last year's 'best of'? Certainly, songs like 'Shout To The Lord' (Zschech) may continue on into the future, but will it take a song of such universal acceptance to make the next congregational song canon? We do risk becoming a victim of a musical trend (Peterson, 1996), more a cultural trend, that praises the immediate, the successful and the popular. Yet we need to ensure that the congregational song of today leaves a lasting value to the Christians of tomorrow.

5 The Rise and Rise of Pentecostal Music: History, Hillsong and Star Texts

The growth in contemporary forms of congregational song can be directly linked to the proliferation and increased influence of Pentecostal churches worldwide. Pentecostal churches are by far the dominant producers of contemporary congregational music, and often have the larger congregation sizes and matrixes of ideologically aligned networks to support flourishing production centres. Because of this, the religio-cultural forces brought to bear on congregational song are quite specific. Many trends, styles, and corporate worship practices have the stamp of some form of Pentecostal beginning. Understanding these tributaries and their outworking in the music of today is crucial to a full contextualisation of the current sound. Grasping the forces that produce modern church music – the institutions, apparatuses and people involved – realises a greater discernment when actual texts are under consideration.

The following case study traces the evolution of the major Pentecostal churches in Australia. While Hillsong Church has become one of the world leaders in congregational song, the development and artistic prominence of Pentecostal churches in Australia can be viewed as an illustration of similar developments already taking place in Canada, New Zealand, South Africa and parts of the United Kingdom – all of which have evolved in the shadow of North American Pentecostalism. What is most pertinent about the Australian example is that it represents an entirely different model to that established in North America. In Australia the paradigm was based around churches producing congregational music, rather than individuals. In the US (and UK) it was more often than not the individual, usually the worship leader, being marketed as artist. The contemporary Christian music phenomenon of star creation was basically placed atop congregational song. Thus Kevin Prosch, Don Moen, Graham Kendrick, Keith Green and Ron Kenoly became household names in the congregational music scene. In Australia it has been Hillsong Church, CCC and Planet Shakers that have dominated.

Analysis of the denominational traits that have directly influenced corporate worship practice will enable a more thorough contextualisation of congregational song, given that it remains a domain of operation peculiar to culture of contemporary Christian music (see Csikszentmihalyi, 1996). As in Chapter 2, the historical background surrounding the evolution of Pentecostalism in Australia provides curious insights into modern debates and stylistic uprisings. The music, and controversies, of yesteryear constantly supply important perspectives on supposedly modern ailments.

History and Antecedents

Early Congregational Song in Australia

The tributaries of modern congregational song and liturgy in Australia can be traced back to the early to mid-nineteenth century. During colonial settlement in Australia, church music became:

> ...a potent reminder of the worship of the traditions from which colonial churches derived,[1] one proof of identity and of the 'differentness' of one denomination from another (Mansfield, 1994: 131).

In mapping the impetus for, and influence of, congregational song in early Australian churches, Mansfield delineates denominational differences that developed following the Church of England's early monopoly of worship. Carey, however, seems unaware that a monopoly existed:

> In practical terms, there were three main Christian traditions carried to the early colony: the established churches whose values were represented by the governors and military authorities; evangelical Protestantism, represented by most of the early clergy and missionaries; and Catholicism, represented by between one-quarter and one-third of the convict and free settlers and the clergy they gathered to serve their community (1996: 2).[2]

In terms of the established churches, Church of England liturgy was dominated by reliance on the Word of God; any singing of hymns was restricted to metrical psalms and hymns corporately sung by repeating the line read or sung by the precentor (Mansfield, 1994: 132). As the Church developed in the early nineteenth century, an organ was introduced to corporate worship, but not without its share of controversy and enemies. 'Singing psalms is generally intended as a help to devotion, but in the Sydney churches it inspires nothing but disgust, weariness, and even ridicule' (unattributed letter to the *Sydney Gazette* [1824], cited in Mansfield: ibid.). Not until the middle of the century did various alternative patterns of worship establish themselves, heralding a new era of denominationalism.

During this time the Catholic music scene, centred around St Mary's Cathedral, Sydney, had regular programs of public performance, specialising in religious music stemming from the fine music tradition. Presbyterian worship, on the other hand, was devoid of choirs and instruments, consisting only of 'metrical psalms and paraphrases led by a precentor whose only aids were voice and tuning-fork' (ibid.: 134). Presbyterians, like Anglicans, remained highly suspicious of congregational hymnody, with its potential to invoke 'irrational emotionalism'. The other prevailing denomination at this time was the Wesleyan Methodists. Mansfield notes that they:

> ...could not do without their hymns, handed down in the great collections of John and Charles Wesley... Methodists gloried in their reputation as a singing people... Singing typically was from the heart, fervent, loud and very slow, as was the custom of the time ... [which] as the partner of uninhibited preaching and earnest prayer, could become rowdy (ibid.: 134–35).

Methodist and Presbyterian worship in the early Australian church included congregational involvement, although Presbyterians maintained the centrality of God's Word[3] while Methodists promoted hymnody that reflected the life experience of the Christian. Either way it was these evangelical Protestant churches that flourished in the colonial church:

> The absence of an official established church left an open field for the fervent missionaries of reformed Protestantism and a steady stream of Methodists, Congregationalists and Baptists...to convert and reform convicts, Aborigines and other heathens of the South Seas (Carey, 1996: 10).

As the twentieth century approached, large changes in denominational liturgy, particularly musical, occurred within a relatively short time frame. Presbyterians saw the introduction of the choir, then hymns, and finally, the organ, each meeting 'dogged resistance from a minority' (Mansfield, 1994: 140). Wesleyan Methodists embraced choirs and organs, and architecturally reflected their importance in the design of their churches. Although Anglican and Catholic churches were characterised by dignified yet restrained worship, where congregational singing was subordinate to more formal musical involvement (ibid.: 136), Anglicans finally adopted hymns as a regular feature of congregational worship[4] in Australia. Another prominent change, which first took hold in the Methodist and Presbyterian churches, was the cessation of precentor leadership, allowing instead the giving of the entire hymn to the congregation. Mansfield reports that new tunes were beginning to emerge at the end of the century, replacing the well-loved hymn tunes, with somewhat predictable opposition (ibid.: 141).

A further development was the establishment of evangelistic song, powerfully brought to the non-church community by the Salvation Army – who established operations in Australia from 1880. Such a commitment to the unchurched presented a challenge for mainline churches, one which many faced proactively. Enhancing this was the popularisation of the music flowing from (largely North American) evangelical missions. The missions of Dwight Moody, and his music director, Ira Sankey, saw American gospel songs flow powerfully into Australian church life[5] (ibid.: 148) at the end of the nineteenth century. Sankey's *Sacred Songs And Solos* became a much revered songbook throughout the USA, Britain and Australia. Sankey's collection gathered together:

> *...a style of song characterised by direct appeals to Christian decision and commitment, unashamed tugging on heart-strings, and simple tunes, which...bore strong resemblances to the music of popular theatre* (ibid.).

As the Christian community in Australia developed, music became an integral factor in fashioning denominational identity and differing perceptions of worship. Such was the scope of liturgical variety that, post-Federation, there was a decline in the number of people who affiliated themselves with one of the major denominational traditions (Carey, 1996: 114). Christian plurality was one thing, but after both world wars – particularly World War II – there was also a massive influx of migrants. These new settlers brought their own religions, sects and spiritual ideas with them. Australia, without the long-established baggage of a historical church tradition, had proven itself open to various worldviews and many new religious groups found fertile soil in which to sow their ideas/ beliefs (e.g. Greek Orthodox, Russian Orthodox and Coptic churches). At the same time, a transformation – that had begun early in the colonial churches' history – was taking place. For the first time, non-Anglican Protestant evangelicalism had become the majority faith of active Christians (ibid.: 87–88).

In summarising the condition of Australian spirituality at the end of the twentieth century, Carey notes that there have been four major changes to the pattern of religious belief in Australia:

1. The emergence of a truly secular society;
2. The proliferation of New Age belief systems and para-religious activity (e.g. environmental and human rights groups);
3. The strengthening of actively proselytising Christian sects (e.g. Jehovah's Witnesses, Mormons, Seventh Day Adventists);
4. The rise of the de-institutionalised [in that it is not run from any 'central' bureaucracy] form of Christianity known as Pentecostalism,

which is now the fastest growing religious movement in Australia. (Adapted from Carey, 1996: 172–73)

Such a list rings true for many Western countries around the world. In the light of these (changing) religious beliefs, current congregational song has developed and, in terms of the final point at least, has flourished. The following section extrapolates on this final point, regarding the (relative) explosion of Pentecostalism, and again, represents an example of similar phenomena across the globe.

Pentecostalism in Australia
Pentecostalism is not in itself a denomination but rather a brand of Christianity. It was originally considered a sect by most mainstream Christians but is now 'a recognised group of Christian denominations whose major identifying mark is the practice of glossolalia'[6] (Chant, 2000: n.p.). Glossolalia,[7] or 'speaking in tongues', appears in the Bible as a gift of the Holy Spirit sent upon the early church shortly after Christ's ascension (Acts 2). Theological debate continues as to whether these 'tongues' were pre-existent earthly languages or a new heavenly language (i.e. some form of 'love language' with God) – and to whether such gifts were restricted to the early apostolic Church or are still freely given and received today – but Pentecostals stringently maintain the centrality of glossolalia to Christian experience. The gift of glossolalia is normally associated with a highly charged experience known as 'Baptism in the Holy Spirit'. 'Pentecostals believe that being baptised in the Spirit is an experience discrete from conversion[,] accompanied by glossolalia' (Chant, 2000: 42 n. 25).[8] Aside from this insistence on baptism of the Spirit, Pentecostalism on the whole was, and remains, strongly evangelical.

The Pentecostal movement is commonly thought to have begun in Azusa Street, Los Angeles, under the leadership of William Seymour – an Afro-American with little formal education – between April 1906 and 1909 (ibid.: 43). Seymour held public meetings day and night for three years, in which vibrant worship, spontaneous preaching and gifts of the Spirit were manifested. There had been other Pentecostal gatherings recorded prior to 1906, 'but none captured the [public] imagination in the same way' (ibid.).

In Australia Pentecostalism began as a rural phenomenon, with largely middle-class constituents. While there are accounts of Pentecostal style services occurring in rural Victoria during the late nineteenth century, the movement is recognised as beginning in Melbourne's Good News Hall in 1909, under the direction of Mrs Janet Lancaster. In New South Wales, 'the first purpose-built Pentecostal building was erected in 1919 near Parkes, a community approaching 5000 people' (ibid.: 65). Chant points out the importance of Australian Pentecostalism's rural beginnings, as opposed to its urban evolution in the USA. Furthermore, he notes that Australian Pentecostalism's first leaders were largely Australian, not American, and indeed, that the movement has a closer lineage to European Wesleyanism, Evangelicalism and 'Dowieism'[9] than to any North American sources (ibid.: 39–40, 543). Pentecostalism is unique in this sense, in that it is the only religious group to have developed in the last two centuries that has not been brought to Australia by immigrants (Hughes, 1996: xi). Since its recognised inception in 1909, Pentecostalism has risen to become the fastest growing Christian movement in Australia (Kaldor *et al.*, 1999: 21–27). Carey (1996) notes the universality of this phenomenon:

> [Pentecostals] *burst into international prominence in the 70s during the so-called charismatic renewal...by the mid 80s large numbers of churchgoers were spilling out of old churches and into new ones in a massive shift in the Protestant landscape that some have compared to the Reformation of the 16th century* (189).

Figures from the National Church Life Survey (NCLS) 1996 revealed the continued growth in Pentecostal denominations (Kaldor *et al.*, 1999; Kaldor, Dixon and Powell, 1999). From less than 200 congregations in 1958, there were over 1600 Pentecostal congregations in Australia in 1998 (Carey, 1996: 44). Most revealing was the statistic indicating that more Pentecostals now attend church weekly than do Anglicans. Most commentators (including the NCLS researchers) attribute these burgeoning numbers to the worship style of Pentecostal churches:

> ...*Pentecostalism is a true child of the twentieth century... The most distinctive feature of Pentecostals is their mode of worship, which includes praying with the hands outstretched, dancing, speaking in tongues, faith healing, cheery singing and other exuberant practices led by a preacher. They are anti-intellectual to the extent that they stress inherent spiritual authority rather than mastery of theology or any formal ritual. This formula has proved incredibly successful in recent times to the continued bemusement of outsiders* (Carey, 1996: 188).

Although Carey cites some vague generalisations such as 'cheery singing', she nonetheless highlights those aspects of corporate worship which are overtly Pentecostal. Rightly noting Pentecostals' penchant for embracing the tools of the twentieth century, Carey is alluding to their desire to utilise all the tools of modern communication and technology. To this end Pentecostal churches often look and feel different to traditional churches, further enhancing the sensate nature of the church experience that many are drawn to. It is this primacy of spiritual encounter, this focus on 'an experiential and sensate encounter with God' (Chant, 2000: 41) which has attracted so many. Rather than demonstrating 'continued bemusement', non-Pentecostal churches have long been aware, and wary, of this experiential focus. Nowhere has this been more true than in regards to congregational song. At the same time, however, they have become alert to the fact that congregations appear to have a predilection towards contemporary styles of worship that allow them to interact with God in more tangible ways. A consequence of this awareness has been a degree of 'Pentecostalisation' of traditional mainline denominations. It is common for Pentecostal styles of worship to exist within mainstream Protestant churches even though Pentecostal doctrines are not observed, or even approved (Hughes, 1996: 105). This is especially the case in the domain of congregational song (Chant, 2000: 46). Not only has the ecumenicalism of congregational song allowed the music to seep into mainstream Protestant churches, but also the mannerisms and experiential behaviour that accompany them.[10] For example, body movements and dance moves featured on Hillsong Church music videos are often incorporated into Protestant airings of the same song(s). This adoption has contributed to the globalisation of congregational song, with such wholesale, international uses of stylistic nuances creating a similitude of experience, and inviting future texts to copy the success achieved prior. Whether this dramatically decreases the creativity of international congregational song remains to be seen.

Having discussed the influence of the Pentecostal movement, it is pertinent now to shift attention to two of the most significant Pentecostal churches in Australia, namely Hillsong Church and Christian City Church (CCC). These churches[11] have been largely responsible for the widespread dissemination of Pentecostal-style congregational song throughout the Australian Christian community. While the two churches share many similarities, 'there are crucial differences in structure and ethos, not readily apparent to the external observer' (Crabtree, interview with the author, 2005). Both churches are also prominent in the international market, producing music that is sung throughout their churches worldwide, and also by traditional mainstream churches that have no connection to them. Nationally, it could be argued that the music of Hillsong Church, from the end of the twentieth century through to today, largely represents the sound of Australian Christianity. Indeed, one of Australia's leading figures in congregational music, Jeff Crabtree, has argued that:

> Hillsong music is so widespread and influential in Australian contemporary churches, particularly in terms of the similarity of music written and recorded by other churches in response to it, that I would argue that it is effectively a new genre of music (2006: 24).

The juggernaut that is Hillsong is definitely due to the music's international distribution and popularity, but also to Hillsong Church's vision and progress.

Hillsong Church (Hills Christian Life Centre)

Hillsong Church began its life in August 1983 as the Hills Christian Life Centre, located in Castle Hill, part of Sydney's developing north-west suburban district, as an outreach from Christian Life Centre Sydney. The church was founded by Brian and Bobbie Houston who had moved to Australia from their native New Zealand in 1978, a year after Brian's pastor parents, Frank and Hazel Houston, had moved to Australia to found Christian Life Centre (CLC).[12] Hills CLC initially met in Baulkham Hills High School Hall, in an industrial area of Castle Hill, with a congregation of seventy, but which reduced in number during the first few weeks. Brian Houston was associated with the 'mainstream' Pentecostal denomination Assemblies of God, thus tying Hills to that denominational affiliation.

Assemblies of God (AOG) is the largest Pentecostal denomination in Australia. It can be traced back to Melbourne's Good News Hall, although it was Queensland Pentecostals in the 1930s who took up the name AOG in earnest.[13] The first national conference of AOG was held in Sydney in 1937. AOG churches grew dramatically, in number and size, throughout the 1980s and 1990s, making them one of the most significant denominations in Australia. In 1997 Brian Houston became the president of Australian AOG churches.[14]

Since its inception, Hillsong Church has held firmly to the vision Houston had for the church:

> Hillsong mission: *to reach and influence the world by building a large bible based church, changing mindsets and empowering people to lead and impact every sphere of life* (www.hillsclc.org.au).

It was not long before Houston's grander vision for the church began to take hold. In 1985 the church moved from the school hall to a warehouse in the industrial area of Castle Hill. Over the next two years, more warehouse space was leased to accommodate the growth of the church. In 1991 the church moved out of the warehouse into the Hills Centre – a multipurpose public auditorium with a 1550 person capacity. As former Hillsong worship leader Geoff Bullock recalled:

> Houston wanted to have something that was a greater advertisement for the culture. So we moved out of the warehouse and into the Hills Centre, and it was a fundamental watershed. We became far more market orientated (interview with the author, 1998).

In 1987 the contemporary Australian Christian music scene was dominated by David and Rosanna Palmer operating out of Harvard Christian Life Centre in Melbourne, the pioneer Australian Christian rock band Rosanna's Raiders, and 'Power Praise' material emerging from Melbourne. In Sydney the major player was the newly developing (and flourishing) Christian City Church[15] (CCC), founded in 1980 by Phil Pringle – another New Zealander – in the North Shore suburb of Brookvale. Phil and Christine Pringle were the primary song-writers along with a small number of others. Christine Pringle had already released a pioneering worship-styled album in the 1980s. In 1990 CCC released their first live congregational album, *Stand*, the first live congregational album ever recorded in Australia. Bullock described the album as being 'all very Dire Straits, [with a] whole new contemporary edge which no one had ever seen before in Sydney' (interview with the author, 1998).

In comparison to CCC, Hills CLC had a more conservative edge than their North Shore counterparts. As a result, Bullock and Houston set about creating a music culture that reflected that difference, yet still managed to clutch onto the music-driven, church growth bandwagon. At a simplistic level, perhaps the initial distinction came from Hillsong producing piano-based music (under the influence of Bullock) while CCC was ostensibly guitar-based.

In 1988 Hills recorded their first – now largely forgotten – album of congregational song, *Spirit And Truth*. This was followed by *Show Your Glory* in 1991, which, along with its predecessor, was a studio album rather than a live congregational recording. *Spirit And Truth* was distributed only amongst the church and those close to it. *Show Your Glory* was the first Hillsong album to be marketed, albeit limitedly, outside of Australia. With the church still establishing itself these albums were free of any distinctive Hillsong ethos, which would become institutionalised from the next album, *The Power Of Your Love* (1992). Bullock noted:

> in the early to mid-90s...everything that was coming out of the church needed to reflect its methodology and its ethos – so you wrote [music] to the vision. You wrote to the ministry. And everything you did supported the vision of the leadership (interview with the author, 1998).

With the move to the Hills Centre, church services increased in size, volume and vibrancy. At the same time as the church service was escalating in popularity and influence, the youth arm of New South Wales AOG, 'Christ's Ambassadors', came under the direction of Pat Mesiti, one of the Hillsong pastors. Renamed 'Youth Alive', and remodelled into event-style evangelism, a youth band was formed from the Hillsong music team and CCC musicians,[16] which took what was happening in the church musically, and played it louder and 'rockier', appealing directly to a youth demographic. Despite its growing freedom of worship, Hills CLC 'still had borders which made it difficult to play rhythm and blues – loud, triumphant music – especially in a venue that was built for vocal performance without amplification' (ibid.). The Youth Alive concept helped to circumvent these borders, furthering the influence of Hillsong music outside of the church itself by staging events in the Sydney Entertainment Centre and other venues. Youth Alive was marketed interdenominationally, thus exposing a wider range of people (especially the influential youth who were often involved in church music teams) to the music of Hills CLC. Such publicity allowed the music to penetrate other churches, and other denominations, more readily than if they had merely released their congregational CDs.

Houston's motivational, and often sloganistic, vision for Hillsong Church infuses much of the church's public output and is particularly prominent throughout their website. Part of this vision can be glimpsed in the excerpt below:

> The Church that I see is a Church of influence. A Church so large in size that the cities and nations cannot ignore it. A Church with a message so clear that lives are changed forever. A Church growing so quickly that buildings struggle to contain the increase.
>
> I see a Church whose heartfelt praise and worship touches heaven and changes earth. With worship that exalts Jesus Christ through powerful songs of faith and hope. I see a Church whose altars are constantly filled with repentant sinners responding to His call to salvation.
>
> Yes, the Church that I see is so dependent on the Holy Spirit that nothing will stop it nor stand against it. A Church whose people are unified, praying and full of Spirit-filled believers.
>
> Yes, the Church that I see could well be our church, Hillsong Church (Houston, www.hillsclc.org.au, accessed 5 April 2001).

The quantitative dimension of Houston's vision has certainly been realised. Hillsong Church is one of Australia's largest churches, with a current congregation in excess of 17,000 people on any given Sunday. They moved from the Hills Centre to a new building in the midst of Norwest Business Park, Castle Hill, before officially opening their new, purpose-built building and office complex on 19 October, 2002. The new building stands next to the existing premises and includes a 3500-seat auditorium. Houston's vision is seemingly interminable: 'Most people here think it is too small' (Houston, quoted in Bagnall, 2000: 29).

While Hillsong now represents one of the Western world's mega churches, the process of development and influence has nonetheless been more gradual. Pastor Brian Houston noted, 'I think [most] Australians know of Hillsong Church, it seems to have really come up above the radar in the last two or three years, but the growth has been progressive over more than 20 years' (ibid.). Tied into that progressive (albeit rather rapid progress) development has been the insistence on contemporary models of corporate worship and song. And this model has been repeated in Pentecostal churches around the world. The classic example of this being Australia's Planet Shakers Church. Originally a youth conference/event organised out of Adelaide's Paradise AOG church, Planet Shakers was based around the music performed there and initially attracted youth delegates from South Australia. As the event grew in popularity, attendees would come from all over Australia, and ultimately, from overseas. Such was the momentum and impact of Planet Shakers that the decision was made to form a church of the same name, and relocate to Melbourne. This shows the intrinsic relationship between notions of identity, church growth and influence, and congregational song. At their first service in Melbourne, Planet Shakers attracted 600 people.

In one sense, congregational song has responded to the desires of the people over a period of time, yet in another it has pushed forward, dragging congregational song into the culture that surrounds it. It has been subject to generic trends within the music industry at large, and simultaneously subject to the baggage of liturgical tradition. Still relatively young in terms of larger music histories, it has nonetheless begun to evolve, to be shaped by generations and movements. It has definitely begun to show signs of its dominance. Perhaps the level of evolution is what is at stake. Has the music simmered into the richest quality attainable? As the rest of the book teases out this question, we continue here investigating more of the apparatus of congregational song, those elements and people that have been instrumental in the evolutionary process.

Hillsong Music Australia
It is not surprising that Houston's vision for Hillsong involves a significant role for congregational song, given that Hillsong Music Australia (HMA) claims annual worldwide sales in excess of two million albums. HMA recognises its pivotal role within Hillsong Church, its website claiming:

> *Hillsong Music Australia was birthed from the vision God gave for Hillsong Church. Hillsong Music plays an integral part in that overall vision and it's* [sic] *growth over the past few years reveals God's blessing and provision for Hillsong Church in so many ways* (http://www1.hillsong.com/store/document.cfm?content&code=aboutus).

This style of language, enforcing the divine endorsement of Hillsong Music, runs throughout promotional material for the group. Clearly Houston's church vision and teaching focus has permeated the operation of HMA – the resource arm of Hillsong Church. HMA begin their 'purpose' statement with another reference to divine initiative:

> Hillsong Music is a vital component in the ministry that God has entrusted to Hillsong Church, its primary function being to resource the church world-wide.
>
> To enable people to enter into an atmosphere of worshipping the Lord by providing resources that help churches break into another dimension of worship.
>
> To empower people, ministries and churches through teaching, leadership and of course, praise and worship.
>
> To take the blessing and anointing God has placed on Hillsong Church beyond our walls to the nation of Australia and the nations of the world (ibid.).

Resourcing the Christian Church worldwide is a formidable goal, but not one without large financial reward in this case. Yet such a goal is not exclusive to Hillsong. Whether stated or not, many of the key congregational song producers around the world distribute and market their product on such a scale that smaller independent releases often go unnoticed. As the twenty-first century progresses this phenomenon is becoming even more pronounced. While more attention will be paid to this facet of congregational music later, it is worth noting here that this tendency to support the highly visual and well-recognised producers and publishers is creating a sameness within congregational song that is fast becoming malignant. Unlike the secular music industry where smaller markets are encouraging independent talents through industry awards programmes, private gig sales and internet delivery systems (see Evans and Crowdy, 2005), congregational song runs the risk of alienating emergent artists to the point where the genre itself will become stale and irrelevant.

The final line of the HMA purpose statement explicitly confirms God's 'anointing' of Hillsong Church, and the church's desire to share that blessing with others, not only nationally but internationally. This is the heart of HMA's ethos; that they have been anointed to bring Australia and the world 'a new song' (Psalm 96 among others), that God has blessed them in a way unknown to other churches. They therefore wish to assist or 'enable' other churches to 'break into another dimension of worship'. Ignoring the problematic use of the term 'worship', this idea unmistakably posits Hillsong Church as 'that to be aspired to'. They know the new dimension of worship, they are in step with God's Spirit, and long for other churches to 'experience' this new worship life as they do. Once again this is not unique to Hillsong. Other large churches throughout the world claim similar experiential authorities, and often these churches endorse each other through conference programs and schedules, and guest teaching appointments. In this culture of self-projection, HMA has presented a musical product that is unique within the Australian market. Despite the fact that other large Pentecostal churches such as CCC also release large amounts of congregational song into the market, Hillsong clearly represents itself as the one church anointed by God to bring 'a new song' to the world:

> In the end [the Hillsong] fundamental is that the church is anointed, therefore all those people who come to the church are anointed by association...whatever success [those people] have is because of their association, not because of their own doing (Bullock, interview with the author, 1998).

Given that the philosophy of Hillsong Church sees the revelation of God's blessing in their success, there certainly is some justification for their brashness. HMA began with one casual staff member and occupied a one-room office for the early years of its existence. In 2001, HMA employed twelve full-time staff and 10 per cent of the church's staff resources (Hillsong Annual Report, 2004) and accounted for 27 per cent of the total income of the church (ibid.).

As HMA began to grow, the marketing and distribution of the music was assumed by Christian Marketing Australasia. HMA was originally given the name 'Power Ministries International':

> the incorporation of the word 'International' was ridiculed in some circles with many not believing that this little local church from 'Down Under' could amount to anything of international proportion (http://www1. hillsong.com/store/document.cfm?content&code=aboutus).

In July 1997, Hillsong Australia took over all the Australian marketing and distribution responsibilities for HMA. The music is currently distributed to over eighty-seven countries worldwide and lyrics have been translated into numerous languages. HMA distribute directly to all Christian retail stores Australia-wide and in recent years have begun to distribute a number of other products including albums from the Parachute Band in New Zealand. In January 1999, Hillsong products were released into the secular Australian music market by Warner Music Australia (ibid.).

HMA have released congregational CDs annually since *The Power Of Your Love*, producing a new CD for each Hillsong Conference (held annually in July). The church has diversified its catalogue to include other compilation and speciality CDs including the *Hillsong Worship Series*, *Hillsong Instrumental Series*, *Millennium: The Story So Far*, *Jesus: Christmas Worship Down Under*, *Hills Praise*, the *United – Live* series, as well as a variety of compilations, songwriter discs and miscellaneous products. Integrity Music USA have recorded two live albums at Hillsong Church. The first, *Shout To The Lord*, has currently sold more than five hundred thousand units worldwide, and the second, *Shout To The Lord 2000*, has reached number two on the US Christian charts and also registered on the *Billboard* charts. In 2005, Hillsong released an album in collaboration with internationally renowned Christian band Delirious.

Given this phenomenal success, and the fact that the live congregational CDs of HMA now achieve gold status (35,000 units in Australia) within weeks of release, it is not surprising that the website concludes with the following affirmation: 'Hillsong Music is at the forefront of Christian Music throughout the world' (http://www1.hillsong.com/store/document.cfm?content&code=aboutus). This level of market dominance brings with it both enormous influence on other producers and a responsibility to produce congregational song which enhances and advances the genre. The pressure surrounding such facets, not to mention the commercial imperatives, faces all major congregational music producers throughout the world.

The Hillsong Anointing

Part of the Hillsong ethos states that the church itself has been chosen by God to produce new congregational song. As Zschech noted:

> Our church [Hillsong]...[has] *an anointing for a new song. We have tried other things, but we have an anointing for a new song. We still sing hymns, we sing them often... We haven't thrown out the old, but we understand the anointing on our house. Now that is going to be different from the anointing on your house. Once you understand the direction of your leadership* [then] *operate out of that in strength... We have so many songwriters coming through, but that is the anointing of our house* (Hillsong Conference, panel discussion, 15 July 1999).

The theological concept of anointing has its origin in the OT where people or things were often anointed to signify holiness; that is, they were set apart for God and his work. In the book of 1 Samuel, Saul is anointed by God to become the first king of Israel. Even though he ultimately ends up pursuing his successor to the throne in order to kill him, Saul is deemed 'untouchable', despite his flagrant wickedness, because he is anointed of God (1 Samuel 26). The *Illustrated Bible Dictionary* notes that the term 'anointed' was 'used metaphorically to mean the bestowal of divine favour or appointment to a special place or function in the purpose of God'[17] (Douglas *et al.*, 1980: 68–69). Indeed the Hebrew word for 'anointed one' is *meshiach*, from which we get the English translation 'Messiah', and the Greek translation, 'Christ' (Nelson, 1989: 64). Also carried into the NT understanding of 'anointing' was an association with the outpouring of the Holy Spirit (Douglas *et al.*, 1980: 68–69):

> *You know what has happened throughout Judea, beginning in Galilee after the baptism that John preached – how God anointed Jesus of Nazareth with the Holy Spirit and power, and how he went around doing good and healing all who were under the power of the devil, because God was with him* (Acts 10:37-38).

The contemporary anointing is believed to be the same anointing Christ had, since the Holy Spirit is one and the same Spirit. It is both OT and NT concepts of anointing – being specifically set apart by God for his work as well as incurring an outpouring of the Spirit – that are picked up by contemporary, particularly Pentecostal, churches. The anointing on Hillsong Church referred to by Zschech in the quote above is based on the OT principle that God has set the church apart by giving them a distinct work, the composition and production of new congregational song for the Australian and worldwide church.

Aside from members of the church being 'chosen' by God to write new congregational song, the other use of the term 'anointing' within worship parlance refers to (a) certain moment(s) within a church service when the Holy Spirit 'comes in power' among the congregation. This is not exclusive to Hillsong but universally ubiquitous. Although strict definitions of this experience vary, many agree that it involves entering the presence of God and being ministered to by the Holy Spirit. Such a view is expressed in the following email posting to the internet Worship List:

> *I believe that anointing when referring to a corporate worship service can mean many things. But, the one thing that is common among all these is the manifest presence of Jesus in the service. The worship leader may be anointed, but that just means that Jesus has blessed him and 'anointed' his leading worship. The preacher may be 'anointed' simply meaning that the congregation senses Jesus' blessing on the words spoken, or a 'quickening' or 'confirmation' in their own heart the the [sic] preacher is speaking from God. The congregation may be 'anointed' to receive the word with all gladness, or to lift the high praises of God up, or to pray heartily. My per-*

sonal opinion is that this is simply Jesus' presence in the service operating severally [sic] *as He wills...blessing the WL* [worship leader], *the preacher, the congregation* (Jerald, Worship List posting, 16 October 2001).

This 'manifest presence' lies at the heart of much contemporary thinking about God's presence within the gathering of believers. While acknowledging that an omnipresent God must exist everywhere (Psalm 139:7-18), and hence outside of the worship gathering, the argument runs that there is something unique about the experience of God as part of corporate worship. It becomes a difference between the 'abiding' presence of God (which is a constant in the life of the believer) and the 'manifest' presence of God (which may be experienced within corporate worship). Such a manifestation may constitute a heightened awareness of the Holy Spirit, an enabling of spiritual gifts (1 Corinthians 12), or other deeper senses of God's presence. Due to the personal/emotional character of manifestation, many are intangible and unquantifiable. However, spiritual giftings within the gathering (the gift of tongues, healing, prophecy, etc.) are often thought of as tangible proof of God's manifest presence. Precedents of God's manifest presence are often taken from (and easily found in) the OT, most notably the *Shekineh* glory accompanying the consecration of the newly built temple by King Solomon (2 Chronicles 5:2ff.). In this account, after the appropriate religious observances had been conducted, 120 priests (replete with trumpets) and a huge chorus of singers, accompanied by cymbals, lyres and harps, began to sing praise and thanks to God:

> *Then the temple of the Lord was filled with a cloud, and the priests could not perform their service because of the cloud, for the glory of the Lord filled the temple* (2 Chronicles 5:13b-14).

One common perception is that the singing of congregational song releases the presence of God:[18] 'the view that praise singing brings God's presence to a meeting is one of the most solidly believed principles of praise' (Dickson, 1996: 7). As well as the dedication of the temple, the justification for this notion is often traced back to Psalm 22:3, 'Yet thou art holy, enthroned on the praises of Israel' (RSV), the belief being that as the people of God sing praises to him he manifests himself among them. However, Dickson (ibid.) notes that a contextual reading of Psalm 22:3 pictures:

> *Yahweh seated in his royal court being acknowledged by his loyal subjects as the universal king, as they publicly proclaim his mighty power and deeds.*

Such an interpretation removes the 'manifestation' of God, and rather places his people before him.[19] Of more consequence is the NT understanding that the people of God are actually the new temple of God: 'Do you not know that your body is a temple of the Holy Spirit, who is in you, whom you have received from God?' (1 Corinthians 6:19; cf. 2 Corinthians 6:16; 1 Corinthians 3:16). Given that God dwells in his temple, the NT shows that Christ, through his Spirit, dwells within the hearts of believers (John 14:15-26; 16:5-16). Given this understanding, it becomes clearer perhaps to view the manifest presence of God as his presence within the hearts of other believers present. It is this that separates the day-to-day abiding presence of God from the manifest presence experienced in the corporate worship gathering. One danger, of course, is that the 'anointing' of the Spirit can be facilitated or stoked by people (pastors, worship leaders, musicians, etc.) who are themselves seen to be 'anointed' by God.

Discerning this anointing remains a sticky problem – although a very real one – as the following Worship List post indicates:

> You can know when someone is anointed to do something when you feel the power of that anointing come upon you. For example: If someone has a worship leading anointing than [sic] you will feel in the Spirit that anointing. If someone does not have that anointing [then] the worship will be anointed because we are all anointed through the Anointed One, but the worship will be dry because that is not your anointing (Daniel, Worship List posting, 4 June 2002).

According to some pastors, the anointing these leaders and musicians have received from God is the 'unction of the Holy Spirit to empower and equip for the work of service' (ibid.). They believe that:

> ...these people have been anointed by God to do something and God responds. An anointed worship leader, it is believed, will lead people into the presence of God, because God will respond to this man/woman after God's own heart, and just like God filled the temple with a cloud of glory in Solomon's time he will fill our temple [church building] with his presence ... [the fundamental concept is that] God still anoints special people with special powers as an adjunct to the atonement. That anointing is a response to their spiritual purity and their moral purity and their giftedness (ibid.).

Some commentators are extremely zealous in their condemnation of anointing theology. In his corrective on the misuse of the term 'anointing', Fischer (1999b) considers the biblical use of the term in the NT. He exegetes 2 Corinthians 1:21-22 to contend that the anointing given to all believers is that they stand firm in their faith:

> And what is this anointing? It is when, having believed the gospel, God puts his Spirit in our hearts. Notice that this 'anointing' isn't something that can come and go; it isn't something that we can have more at one time and less at another; it isn't something that can be worked up; and it isn't something that some Christians have more than others! The notion of a Spirit that descends and departs according to human performance has always been pagan. Rather, this 'anointing' is something that God has done for everyone who is in Christ. It is something all Christians have... When we look at things that way, it becomes painfully apparent how so much 'anointing' talk is way off the track. The word is used in a way that is, in the end, experience-driven and not Scripture-driven (1–2).

Theology aside, one of the dangers of basing corporate worship around concepts of the anointing is the focus on subjective models of experience. That is, should the participant fail to experience God's anointing within the church service then they may feel failed. Likewise, the leadership team might consider the congregational meeting a 'failure' due to the lack of the Spirit's anointing over the meeting. Ever so subtly, the time of corporate worship becomes works-based. People are striving to attain, or provide, the anointing 'experience'. Bullock argues that a reliance on times of anointing is addictive, that in the end it becomes mandatory in the life of the believer, causing them to source it out more frequently and more intensely:[20]

> If your worship...is actually expressed through what you do until that 'anointing' comes in the service, then your confidence is in the wrong place. In the end you will need to worship more and go from service to service, anointing to anointing, movement to movement to maintain that, because it has to be worked up, and in the end it can't be maintained because it is based on what you do (interview with the author, 1999).

Due to human nature, various 'protocols' have emerged and are still emerging with respect to anointing theology. As it becomes an entrenched formula, a protocol effectually 'brings God down to man's level', so that people begin to strive after, and worship, worship itself. One clear example of this striving after experience can be found in the notion of 'glory worship', which has taken hold in the last five to six years. The concept of the 'glory' and the significance it holds within some quarters can be seen in the following posting:

> We had a glory conference at our church and moved into the glory dimension in our worship but after the conference found some trouble maintaining it. I personally think we should always aim to be there. It is something that is for everyone, not just a few super anointed people.

After experiencing that kind of worship, listening to old worship songs seems one-dimensional, like songs of the shadows. So you do need new types of songs to carry in the Glory. The old ones were just types and shadows pointing to this greater form of worship. In that sense, going back to regular worship after glory worship is a bit like going back into the old lesser covenant after experiencing...the new better covenant.

The gist of the conference was there are three realms : (1) faith; (2) anointing; (3) glory. You you [sic] need to go through the first two steps in your spiritual development to get to (3).

The way to worshipping in the glory was: (1) praise until the spirit of worship comes; (2) worship until the glory cloud comes...seed the glory cloud with your worship until it rains down on you and you enter into the eternal heavenly places where Jesus now lives. Healings are instantaneous and multiplied in this realm of worship. New songs abound and new rhythms are also a key to communicating the thoughts and intents of the heart of God (Carolyn, Worship List posting, 25 November 2001).

The works-based, or human effort, mentality of this paradigm is unmistakable. Interestingly a large part of the glory concept involves equipping those without an 'anointing' to enter into God's glory. Once again the reliance on music, as some kind of passage into God's presence, is highlighted, with the view being that certain songs in the contemporary vein are more suitable for ushering in the glory than older ones. Not that older songs are unbiblical, merely that they do not allow participants the time or atmosphere to reflect on God's presence. The sheer volume of lyrics present, numerous ideas covered, and archaic language are often cited as reasons for this unsuitability. The three steps outlined to attain the glory ignore NT teaching about worship (outlined in Chapter 3), which state repeatedly that no human effort or endeavour can afford greater privileges to any particular believers. Worship is a response to the initiative of God, a reaction rather than an action. Any fences or goalposts erected around corporate worship create, sometimes intentionally, an elitist mentality whereby some 'can' but others 'can't'. As another list member responded: 'If you don't find yourself in this glory cloud, you begin to wonder what you are doing wrong and it can be very discouraging' (Meka, Worship List, 27 November 2001).

What is common about movements such as the glory movement is the sheer hype and intensity of experience on offer, the superlative descriptions that surround it, and, ultimately, their fleetingness. There is no doubt that God may choose to manifest himself, or the Christian's relationship with him, in many forms. However, corporate worship that focuses on human abilities disregards scriptural worship and the theology of grace. These kinds of misconceptions are often caught up in generalised or jargonised notions like 'anointing' and 'glory'.

The Institution of Worship Leader

One of the most 'anointed' positions within many churches today is that of worship leader. In large churches the worship leader is usually a salaried member of the ministry staff.[21] The institution of worship leader is a human construct, with no biblical basis for the position.[22] It has its origin in the more traditional positions of 'song leader' and 'service leader' – in a sense combining the two. Part of the attraction many see in the position is the Christian celebrity that accompanies it – often more pronounced than that afforded to the pastors and teachers they are there to support. Yet many high profile Australian worship leaders are conscious of the dangers:

> I try to be as real as possible on stage and let my humanity show through. It is important that who you are on stage is who you are at home and around your friends (David Reidy quoted in Hallet, 1999: 59).

Essentially the worship leader guides the congregation through the service. They normally determine which songs will be sung, and guide the musicians through them (either by hand signals or pre-emptive vocal lines).[23] In this sense they often control the mood or emotional intensity of a gathering. More often than not worship leaders are singers or musicians (indeed many international worship leaders today were known first for their compositions rather than their leading), a fact which has contributed to errant thinking about the requirements of a worship leader, and overstated music's importance to worship. What can be said of worship leaders, in relation to congregational song construction at least, is that the 'band leader' role inherent within worship leading means that this person is often responsible for the live musicality of the songs. Most specifically they have a large role in determining the structure and timbre of pieces, through their control of repeated sections and band dynamics. Thus the worship leader, as positioned in most contemporary churches, is actively involved in the live musical production of congregational song.

Given the importance placed on the institution of worship leader, it is not surprising that many books are published each year on the 'how tos' of worship, as well as the personal reflections and experiences of famous contemporary worship leaders (e.g. Zschech, 2001; Redman, 2001). One of the first Australian worship leaders to gain a massive national and even international profile was Geoff Bullock. More a songwriter than a worship leader, Bullock was instrumental in the early success of Hillsong, and in shaping the culture of congregational song in Australia. He also propelled the notion that songwriters could double as worship leaders, and indeed gain prominence from such a position.

Part of Bullock's early encouragement came from Pastor Brian Houston, who convinced Bullock to latch on to the vision of the church, and 'praise and worship's' involvement in it. Houston recalled:

> ...there was this now infamous time when I spoke to Geoff...and said 'Geoff, I want you to start writing songs for the Lord, choruses – worship songs' – and Geoff said, 'I can't write worship songs, I can't write choruses' (taken from *Friends In High Places* video recording, 1995).

Bullock remained a somewhat reluctant ally, confident that music should be primarily composed and consumed as art, and equally convinced that his music represented a more avant garde approach to Christian music.

With the burgeoning success of the Hillsong congregational albums, and the growing influence of Hillsong Conference,[24] it was not surprising that overseas interest in Hillsong products began to develop. It was US publisher Integrity Music that secured the right to market and distribute Hillsong products via its Hosanna label. The relationship was launched with a live album, *Shout To The Lord*, recorded in November 1995. What is significant about the album is that it did not feature Geoff Bullock, the much-lauded Hillsong songwriter. For a variety of personal and ideological reasons Bullock decided to end his association with Hillsong Church.

Zschech Begins To Shout

> Before the Shout To The Lord *album...we had been practising for weeks, getting everything ready. And four days before recording, through various situations, he* [Bullock] *decided to move on. Brian Houston said, 'You have to lead this', and I said, 'I can't, I really can't.' But through Christ we can do all things. For the next 48 hours my friends got on the phone and said 'You can do this, you can do this.' I just thank God we had no video cameras there that night, because all of us cried our way through that project* (Zschech, panel discussion, 15 July 1999).

Unwillingly thrust into the limelight on Bullock's sudden departure, Darlene Zschech (composer of 'Shout To The Lord') would become the face and sound of HMA, and in some people's estimation, of Australian congregational music generally.

Zschech was a child pop-star in Brisbane. From the age of ten to fifteen she appeared on the Channel 9 program *Happy Go Round*. She joined a church at age fifteen, but it was several years before she found her niche role there. In the mid 1980s, she and husband Mark joined Hillsong Church, when the congregation numbered around 150:

> *I let go of my own thing, and from that moment I started to find what I was born to do... I wanted to be part of making church just the greatest place for people. My part in the puzzle was to help the church get free in their worship and praise to God* (Zschech quoted in Bagnall, 2001: n.p.).

Zschech initially joined the Hillsong music team as a backing vocalist. She was not restricted to background roles, however, recording her first album, *Make The Choice* (Shout Records), in 1987.[25] Given her abilities and passion for music it was not long before Zschech became Vocal Director, a role she 'absolutely loved' (Zschech, 1996: 81). There was a lot of pressure on Zschech to move 'up-front' and become a worship leader alongside Bullock, pressure she now attributes to God:

> *I loved to sing, especially in a back up role – but God had another plan. After about two years of trying to convince me, one day as Pastor Brian [Houston] was leading the meeting, he just walked off and left it to me. It was just as well I didn't have anymore time [sic] to think about it because I was now doing it!* (ibid.)

Zschech had been a prominent vocalist on both the *Power Of Your Love* and *Stone's Been Rolled Away* albums; however, it was the international success of *Shout To The Lord*,[26] her increasing profile within HMA, and Houston's goading that made her the suitable replacement for Bullock. Zschech recalled that while Bullock's leaving was difficult, because he had 'taught us so much' (interview with the author, 2002), the core values he instilled in the team were still the same, 'love God, serve Him with gladness...the [music] department is just a lot bigger, and is not so centred on one person' (ibid.). Other figures are important at HMA, particularly Reuben Morgan, (before leaving) Russell Fragar, Marty Sampson and Joel Houston, yet Zschech remains very definitely the lynchpin. In 2006 Zschech remains Worship Pastor at Hillsong Church, with an international profile matched only by four or five others worldwide,[27] a profile that sees her record and tour extensively each year. Zschech's influence has led to a proliferation of 'copycat' artists within the Christian Church. Walk into most evangelical churches in Australia that utilise contemporary music and it is not hard to find a female worship leader using techniques and nuances common to Zschech. This is easily read as exaggeration, but one must realise that Britney Spears or Gwen Stefani, or any pop diva of the moment, commands extraordinary influence in the life of their audience. The same is true of high profile Christian musicians. People, and not just younger people, are attracted to the talents and presence of the artist – more often than not a worship leader – and seek to emulate them in their own leading or ministry. This is the essence of the star-text itself, the reason people sing into hairbrushes in their bedrooms. Australia is somewhat unique in that our 'star to be revered' is a female singer/songwriter who has been at the forefront of the worship revolution in Australia and around the world. On the back cover of one of her latest volumes, Willow Creek pastor Bill Hybels rightly observed: 'When church historians reflect on the worship revolution that happened around the turn of the 21st century, Darlene Zschech will be credited for playing a major role' (Zschech, 2001).

6 Theomusicological Frameworks for Congregational Song Analysis

1. Engaging Theomusicology

In his largely pessimistic summary of the state of congregational music, Faulkner states that a portion of the current 'crisis' in church music is attributable to there being 'little, if any, theological investigation of the history or purpose of church music' (1996: 204) and that '[t]here is a lack of any widely held objective criteria that establish propriety or quality in church music' (ibid.). Dawn (1995) and especially Corbitt (1998) have developed tropes whereby theological affectivity and musical quality can be explored. These counter Faulkner's statement, as does the historical work of Wilson-Dickson (1992). This book takes the challenge further, aiming to totally disprove Faulkner's contention. The nature of the theological and musicological (i.e. theomusicological) investigation that follows, in conjunction with aspects discussed earlier, will result in an academic purview of the state of contemporary congregational song in the Western evangelical Church. In keeping with this ideal, songs have been drawn from many of the world's leading congregational song producers. There are many more examples of each category listed, yet the songs discussed provide valuable insights and criteria with which others can be tested.

Together with Chapter 7, this chapter offers analyses of each song category. The featured examples have not been chosen to represent the 'best' or 'worst' of each category, but rather as either typical songs and/or ones that point to additional elements that should be considered by any analysis of congregational song. And this is the nature of theomusicology. Congregational song is not produced in isolation; it is a consequence of numerous factors: denominational, national, economic and cultural – to name but a few. Theomusicological enquiry must necessarily deal with these external forces and secondary influences. Dealing only with the notes, or solely with lyrics, is a disservice to the discipline and the researcher alike. Many of the songs critiqued in the next two chapters offer springboards to further discussions and tensions, to further pressures and contexts, none of which are adequately dealt with through narrow investigation. To be fair, the analysis presented here cannot hope to cover all aspects inherent within the immanent, poietic or esthesic levels of operation (see below) of a text. Yet they do offer observations and methodologies that will serve future endeavours well. Such objective analysis is essential if congregational song is to expand creatively, and become increasingly relevant to both an increasingly insistent congregation, and an ever-secularising and culturally discerning world. As Keller states in advocating excellence in the use and performance of modern church music:

> *Without great music it is hard to capture transcendence and yet have simplicity. Nothing contributes to a hushed sense of awe better than music that is startlingly good... [Evangelistically] the better the aesthetics, the more it includes both insiders and outsiders, both newcomers and old-timers* (2002: 236).

Musicological Frameworks for Congregational Song Analysis

Any analytical investigation can be broadly understood as quantitative and/or qualitative. The former represents the size of the sampled body of work while the latter refers to meanings and signs embedded within the text itself. The ensuing deconstruction concerns itself with both approaches. As Shepherd (1991) has scrupulously detailed, all music is produced socially, thus qualitative analysis must necessarily consider the cultural, political, historical and economic circumstances that led to its creation. Indeed, McClary and Walser note that any formidable analysis of a contemporary (secular) music text must involve consideration of:

> *...the chords, melodic contours, and metric structures... The reconstruction of semiotic codes is crucial, both for grounding musical procedures (including rhythmic) in terms of various discursive practices and for explaining how the music produces socially based meaning. Verbal texts, performance styles, and video imagery need to be analysed carefully and in tandem with musical components. Modes of commercial production and distribution, the construction of band or star images, the history of a singer's career all have to be taken into account. And political issues (the positioning of the music with respect to class, race, gender) always must be dealt with seriously* (1990: 290).

To assist in this process, the analysis that follows will draw on the three levels of operation outlined by Nattiez (1990) and taken up by Hayward (1998). Nattiez's model involves separating the text into three diagnostic areas: immanent, poietic and esthesic. The immanent level represents 'the infra-textual elements of the music which can be adjudged to be "objectively" there when analysed by musicological methods' (ibid.: 8). Conventional musicology is inherently concerned with this level. In fact, it was the immanent, characterised as the geno-song – following Kristeva's notion of geno-text and pheno-text – that Barthes (1977) saw as monopolising contemporary musical study. For the present study, consideration of the immanent will rest on traditional musicological terms of inquiry suitably adapted[1] for contemporary music, and relevant to congregational song. These aspects include melody, rhythm, harmony, structure, dynamics, texture and timbre. Melodic inquiry will be primarily concerned with the 'singability' of congregational song (according to standard western parameters), since that remains a major function of the music. To this end, customary aspects of melodic contour and range are focused on. Faulkner states that twentieth-century congregational music is marked by:

> ...increasing public taste for stimulating, rousing, sensuously rhythmic music, paralleled by the growing influence of music of non-European cultures, especially music with African roots (e.g. jazz) that is propulsive, syncopated and rhythmically vivacious (1996: 193).

Rhythmic analysis will seek to verify Faulkner's claim. Particular attention will be given to rhythmic complexity produced through syncopation and accenting, as well as consideration of how the total rhythmic bed combines to produce the groove[2] of the song. The isolation of these grooves will prove particularly helpful in isolating generic similarities between congregational song and other forms of popular music. Harmonically, church music has enjoyed a long history of following musical and cultural trends (and often beginning them). In this respect harmony will be broadly viewed in terms of dominant (major/minor) tonalities. This will highlight whether contemporary western congregational song has followed the experimental harmonies of twentieth-century fine music, or the dominant three-chord model of the commercial popular industry. Also for consideration (as part of the immanent level) are changes in textural and timbral construction.

To return to Nattiez's three levels, the poietic refers to the perception of the musical work, its effects and relation to other works and sounds from the point of view of the personnel involved in its production (Hayward, 1998: 9); that is, the producers' discourse and perceptions. Although this can be awkward to adjudge in light of the many opinions and discourses that can emerge, primary focus will be given to the textural element of spatial preferencing[3] and the perception of the production process (and its discourses) by those involved.

Finally, the esthesic level of operation refers to the experience and perception of music by the listener/audience. Clearly this is the more challenging level to reify and analyse given that it is virtually impossible to survey all listeners in all listening situations. By incorporating evidence from the immanent and poietic levels, however, some degree of objectivity is also attainable.

Integrating album reviews, internet surveys and Christian Top 40-equivalent charts is a conveniently attainable method to glean insight into the esthesic level of textual operation.

As established earlier, the central text in contemporary congregational song, as in popular music more generally, is the recorded version, rather than the sheet music or score. Oftentimes songs are first heard on CD and then learnt without sheet music ever being consulted. These reproductions regularly aim to imitate the recorded version note for note and, where possible, instrument for instrument. As such, the ensuing analysis is heavily concerned with the recorded arrangement of the song, as well as its traditional musicological features. These latter features are largely discussed with the absence of quoted notation. While this primarily reflects difficulties in copyright licensing, it also mirrors the absence of notation in much contemporary congregational music.

Throughout the following sections, harmonic progressions are shown in figured bass. Although this system owes more to fine music than contemporary music (Kynaston and Ricci, 1978: 146), it is the most useful documentation for the predominantly simple harmonies found in congregational song. Where more complex jazz progressions are observed, they are written out in full.

Theology (Lyrics and Intent)
Theological investigation most obviously centres on the consideration of song lyrics. Using Nattiez's terminology, this involves study of the immanent level of the text in combination with an address to the esthesic, since while lyrics can be objectively apprehended and transcribed they are also subjectively internalised and ascribed contextual meanings. To a certain extent lyrics exemplify the crossover between all three levels, given the immanent and esthesic involvement already noted, as well as recognition that some lyrics come into existence at the poietic stage. Rock supergroup U2, for instance, are widely documented for originating lyrics because of, and at the time of, production (Flanagan, 1995). So too Geoff Bullock has repeatedly remarked that some of his songs have been improvised lyrically while in preparation for certain services, or prior to (and during) conferences or recordings (interview with the author, 1999). This is a common phenomenon within congregational songwriters.

As noted in Chapter 1, debates around the role of lyrical analysis within popular music studies are well documented. Excessive concentration on lyrics may lead to problematic interpretations regarding the presupposed meaning of the music. This is particularly true when the focus is on the lyrics as reproduced in CD packaging. Analysis of this kind, while literarily relevant, ignores the way the lyrics 'live' within the music. As Barthes (1977) notes, observation of the lyrical transcript ignores their pheno-textual power. Alternatively, lyrics cannot be overlooked and are an integral part of the text. Historically, lyrical analysis affords an important view of the cultural pertinence of lyrics. This is perhaps best demonstrated by the constant censorship lyrics attract, and in the case of congregational song, the blanket rejection or acceptance that can result from one lyrical reading.

In order to adjudge the theological intent of contemporary congregational song, classification of songs will be based on 'song-type'; that is, the theological function or purpose of the song will be the basis of classification.[4] The *intent* can then be critiqued in terms of meaning and, furthermore, the scriptural foundation for the song can be objectively considered in light of its intent. This methodology reduces traditional doctrinal and denominational influences that would otherwise bias the sample heavily in certain directions.[5] Throughout this study the acknowledged intents, or song-types, are:[6]

Anointing	– a song-type most prevalent in Pentecostal denominations which calls for the Holy Spirit's anointing to come upon a group (or individuals)
Body Unity	– songs that encompass the horizontal function within corporate worship to reflect the unity and purpose of believers
Call to Worship	– an invitation to the congregation to join in corporate worship (based on OT models, found particularly in the psalms)
Children's	– the only non-theological intent category. Refers to songs written for children which highlight various aspects of Christian life and belief
Communion	– songs specific to the celebration of the Lord's Supper
Confessional	– songs that acknowledge the singer's sinfulness and need of forgiveness
Credal	– statements of truth and faith
Eschatological	– songs focused on the end times, including heaven and the return of Christ
Evangelistic	– songs focused on sharing the Word of God with others for the purpose of conversion
Holiness	– praise songs about God the Father
Intimacy/Relational	– personal reflections on the relationship between participant and Godhead
Judgement	– songs declaring the judgement of God
Salvation (Christology)	– praise songs about Jesus Christ

Social Justice	– compassionate songs focused on community needs, and/or songs interrogating social injustice
Spirit	– praise songs about the Holy Spirit
Testimony	– songs emphasising strong testimonial accounts of believers
Thanksgiving	– songs of gratitude to the Godhead
Transformation/ Dedication	– personal commitments to life change and dedication based on God's will

Another consideration of the theological (lyrical) analysis of contemporary congregational song takes into account questions of immanence or transcendence; that is, is the repertoire focused more on our intimate relationship with God or his transcendent holiness? The common perception is that modern congregational song is reliant on the immanent: 'one cannot sing praise songs without noticing how first person pronouns tend to eclipse every other subject' (Hamilton, 1999: 32). To definitively ascertain the integrity of such statements each song will be classified according to point of view and terms of address or reference. The following model details the grammatical investigation in operation:

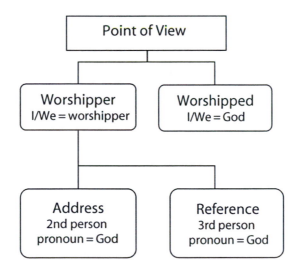

Figure 6.1: *Linguistic Analysis Model*

In considering the grammatical point of view, congregational song is either written from the point of view of God, or the point of view of the worshipper. The latter accounts for virtually all contemporary examples, with rare cases such as 'A New Commandment' (anon; arranged by B. Pulkingham, 1974), written as God speaking in the first person.[7] First person may not feature in congregational pieces, but is more prevalent in 'solo' songs used in the service to minister to the people. Still, this is a far cry from the hymns of Isaac Watts, who daringly wrote new words for Jesus and then quoted them in song (Marshall and Todd, 1982: 38). Due to the domination of songs written from the participant's point of view, the songs referred to subsequently fit solely with this group. Having determined this parameter it is possible to ascertain the terms of speaking, address or reference. Of course speaking (first person) has already been ruled out of the sample at the level of point of view, leaving only address (where God is addressed in the second person, e.g. 'You') or reference (where God is addressed in the third person, e.g. 'He'). A lack of personal pronoun is usually indicative of an implied term of reference (third person). Having gleaned this information it is possible to reflect back on whether the original point of view was individual or plural. The hypothesis underlying this investigation is that songs with a term of address (second person) are more individual than plural, and conversely, that third person terms of reference are necessarily plural rather than individual. Analysis of this grammatical information will substantiate the proportion of songs operating at the horizontal level in corporate worship, as opposed to those more vertically orientated.

In order to address other perceptions and generalisations pertinent to contemporary congregational music, the original word length (that is, irrespective of repetition) has been recorded along with the personal mention of the Godhead (see Appendix). Assessing the word length of songs is undoubtedly problematic at one level. That songs contain few words may not in fact dampen their affectivity. Martin Smith's 'Jesus' Blood' is one such song. Although the track actually contains three verses and a brief pre-chorus, the five-word chorus, 'Jesus' blood never failed me', is relentless, powerful and stirring. Indeed, many song-sets include only this chorus of the song as an intense climax to the time of corporate singing. Obviously the song recalls Gavin Bryars' acclaimed 'Jesus' Blood Never Failed Me Yet' (1971), a tape loop of a homeless man singing these evocative words that Bryars extended through increasing orchestration for about twenty-five minutes. Bryars' song was to have a profound impact on the minimalist movement, the general avant garde music scene, and clearly, even on congregational song some thirty years later. The brevity of the words was not a hindrance but part of the inspirational nature of the piece. This disclaimer provided, there is nonetheless a strong contention within worship practice that modern church music contains fewer words than traditional hymns, and that this deficiency certainly impacts on the usability and application of modern songs to the church service. A further decline in this general word length could be perceived as a lessening of modern song's theological purpose, and thus has been included in the analytical framework. A related area that begs investigation is the nature of repetition in contemporary congregational song. While various (strong) opinions can be heard on the subject, discussion needs to concentrate on whether we are singing fewer words but repeating them more often, or whether the brevity of modern songs allows for a greater number to be utilised within contemporary liturgical settings, thereby allowing for a greater coverage of themes, biblical ideas, experiences and testimonies to be sung.

Whether songs personally mention the Godhead is one way of scrutinising if modern songs have drifted more towards ambiguous love poetry than focused acts of worship. As music critic and historian Andrew Ford noted regarding songs that don't mention the Godhead:

> There is no clear message in songs like that, no hint of doctrine. As you listen, you might apply the words to God. But there's nothing to stop you thinking about the attractive girl sitting in front of you (Ford, *Music And Fashion: Heaven on Earth*, ABC Radio, 24 July 2005).

Clearly the contextual positioning of such songs within the church service, and the way they are led influence the personal address contained within them. Where possible such contexts must be addressed in analysis.

2. Rethinking 'Praise' Songs

As extensively detailed in Chapter 3, there is general misinformation present within the contemporary church about the theological nature of praise. While the term is often used to blanket large areas of congregational song, it actually occupies a far smaller proportion of the corpus. I have chosen to further delineate praise songs by ascribing them in terms of their address, i.e. as either being to God, Jesus or the Holy Spirit. The Bible states clearly that all three are worthy of praise, and indeed are to be praised (Ephesians 1)! Of course there are songs that mention multiple, or indeed all, members of the Trinity, often using different verses to refer to each. Obviously these songs have an important place in any song catalogue. They are not included as a separate category here in order to allow greater delineation between praise songs. Oftentimes the secondary theme distinction (as listed in the Appendix) allows for a clearer classification of the song, rather than grouping them together as, say, Trinity songs. Where the praise songs analysed below do change address or focus it has been duly noted.

Holiness

Holiness are praise songs about the character and deeds of God the Father. While it is apparent, based on statistical evidence from this current study, that Holiness songs are not as frequent as might be expected – and clearly do not feature as prominently as they did in more classic hymnology – there are a sizeable number of such compositions. It may be that the move away from songs exclusively focused on praising God reflects the growing intimate relationship sought between congregation members and Jesus. Nonetheless, the Bible is full of admonitions to praise God, and examples of those who do. Moving too far from this objective may not be positive for the general Church body.

One limitation on this song-type is that many songs may begin to focus on God the Father, but move quickly to discuss the work and attributes of Jesus. Such is 'Holy, Holy' (Fellingham), a song largely popularised by Tim Hughes. While verse one sings of the holiness of God and his eternal character, verse two echoes similar ideas but firmly declares Jesus as the focus of the worship. The chorus calls on the Christian body to 'Lift up His name, with the sound of singing', cleverly remaining non-specific in terms of address whilst simultaneously calling on the congregation to involve themselves in the (musical) adoration of the Godhead.

Similar problems of classification involve songs that could be deemed as belonging either to Holiness or Salvation song-types, given that they echo the third person praise of Revelation, without being overt about the direction of praise. Not quite fitting such a description, yet duplicating the language of Revelation, is Michael W. Smith's 'Agnus Dei'. A song that captures some of the joyous repetition of heavenly praise, as well as the awesome intensity of it, this relatively simple song increases its strength through a heavily centred, ascending melody line and subtle changes in syncopation. The force of the repetitive lyric is thus released yet given enough variation to maintain both interest and strength.

One clear example of a Holiness song-type is Vicky Beeching's 'Yesterday, Today And Forever'. The opening line provides the address, 'Everlasting God', while the song ultimately turns to addressing 'Yahweh' – the Hebraic name for God – in the bridge. The song is predicated on asserting the simple truth about God's character, 'Yesterday, today and forever/You are the same, You never change'. Propelled by dominant guitars and rock rhythms, the song is a triumphant declaration of this biblical truth.

'Lift Our Praise',[8] by Salvation Army songwriter Michelle Kay, is another strong Holiness song that exhibits a rhythmic groove and intensity often found in this category. The heavy funk groove of the song is initiated by the whole ensemble, with drums and bass locking together to form a highly syncopated backbone. A punchy brass riff provides additional energy, which is maintained via brass stabs throughout the piece. The full band sound is preserved with the onset of the group vocals. This full vocal sound accords well with the secondary Body/Unity function of the song, 'Come let's lift our praise'. The power of the chorus (which opens the song) is assisted by the verses. Although they ascend higher in pitch than the chorus, they are constantly building towards it, using the melodic ascent and ii-I$^{6/3}$-IV-V harmonic progression to create anticipation. The effect created is a triumphal, unifying one, indicative of the plural point of view. The song is also quite self-referential in parts, 'Let us raise our voice and sing', and extraordinarily positive, 'How good it is'.

One of the best-loved Holiness songs of the moment is Beth and Matt Redman's 'Blessed Be Your Name'.[9] Based around the classic I-V-vi-IV chord progression, the standout feature of the song is its lyrical construction. Although the song blesses the name of the Lord, without specifically delineating whether that be God or Jesus, the OT lyrical images used, and descriptions of characteristics ascribed to God throughout the Bible posit the song as a Holiness song-type. This 'investigatory' process is not required with a song like 'God He Reigns' (Sampson). Here the powerfully reverent lyrics clearly offer praise to God the Father: 'God He reigns, God He reigns/Holy is the Lord of heaven'. Emphasising the holy declarations is the song's slow (69 bpm) tempo. Melodically the song, like some of the great Christmas carols it resembles, calls on participants to extend themselves vocally; a minor 10th in the verse and minor 6th (though pitched higher) in the chorus. This expansive range allows the song to generate force and single out the declarative praise of the lyrics as the focus of the song.

'Blessed Be Your Name' features four verses (that alone is rather unusual within modern songs), but of more fascination is their construction. The verses are grouped in pairs, with the first of the duo calling on participants to bless the name of the Lord when things are positive in their life: 'In the land that is plentiful... When the world's "all as it should be"'. The second verse of each pair, however, reminds participants that God is to be praised even during tough times: 'Though I walk through the wilderness... On the road marked with suffering/Though there's pain in the offering'. Honesty like this, a move away from the triumphant praise of many other songs, is most scarce, and most refreshing. The pre-chorus summarises this position:

> *Every blessing you pour out I'll turn back to praise*
> *When the darkness closes in, Lord, still I will say:*

before going on to quite literally bless the name of the Lord in the harmonically and melodically simple, yet strong, chorus. Perhaps the most significant and challenging aspect of the song is the bridge: 'You give and take away... My heart will choose to say/"Lord, blessed be Your name"'. While many churches around the world focus on abundant living and the riches that may come through walking in step with the Spirit of God, 'Blessed Be Your Name' is a suitable reminder that all such gifts emanate from God, and find their end with him as well. We would do well in our modern songs to praise all aspects of God's character and deeds, without limiting ourselves to those most palatable portions.

Salvation (Christology)
The major, or dominant, Christian music producers today come mainly from strongly evangelical denominations; denominations devoted to the character and saving work of Jesus, the authority of the Bible, and personal life commitments to follow Jesus. This in part explains the dominance of Salvation song-types within contemporary congregational song. However, the Christian faith largely revolves around Jesus, the Christ, and as such he has long been a focal point for the creative adoration of Christians. The large proportion of contemporary songs about Jesus go some of the way to dispelling claims that all modern music is self-seeking, personal and centred around the one singing.

Not that Salvation song-types are particularly modern occurrences; they can be traced back to the beginnings of choruses. Indeed, popular songs in this category have the potential to dominate congregational song charts for many years. 'Lord I Lift Your Name On High' (Founds) is one such song. A simple binary song, it has proven extremely popular around the world.[10] Akin lyrically to 'Shout To The Lord' (see below), the verse involves a personal declaration about the joy of having Jesus in the participant's life and the desire to lift his name high, while the chorus switches to a more objective address, 'You came from heaven to Earth', and basic description of the gospel of Christ. The simplicity of the song has seen its widespread use in children's programmes, and the adoption of several physical routines that fit the song. The structure of the chorus also allows for a minor call and response to take place. The longevity of the song points to its universality amongst the Christian community, and among all age groups.

A similar, though slightly less pronounced, instance can be found in 'Ancient Of Days' (Harvill/Sadler). Structurally more involved than 'Lord I Lift', 'Ancient' utilises a main section A, which can be divided halfway throughout via a strong movement to the dominant chord, and a bridge section. The strong C major tonality is enforced via driving crochet beats in the bass and dominant I-IV-V harmonies utilised throughout.

Without doubt, the most famous Salvation song of the modern era is 'Shout To The Lord'. Now one of the most recorded and performed contemporary congregational songs of all time,[11] the album *People Just Like Us* (1993) was its commercial premiere. As Darlene Zschech's only contribution to the album, it marks the beginning of her career as an international, interdenominational celebrity within the Christian Church. Such is the success of the song that it is reportedly sung by thirty-five million Christians around the world every week (Brian Houston, *Australian Story*, ABC TV, 1 August 2005). The song draws from Psalm 98, 'Shout for joy to the Lord, all the earth' (98:4a), and represents a Salvation song with a strong Intimacy/Relational component. A rare quality of the song is that it uses both second person address and third person reference, as well as plural and individual point of view. These distinctions are fairly neatly separated into verse (second/individual) and chorus (third/plural) – although the second half of the chorus reverts back to second person individual. The balance of the song is also seen in the structure of the verse, where the first two lines speak of the character/title/attributes of Christ, while the next two personally respond to those. Likewise the first half of the chorus is praise, the remainder response.

Overall the song is biblically grounded as well as formally balanced and proportionate. 'Shout' begins with two synthesiser pads moving between the tonic and dominant chords. A woodblock taps over the top, simulating the spacious, quasi-indigenous Australian sound of clapsticks. Although this 'pre-intro' only lasts ten seconds, it need not have been there at all, considering that the now familiar piano introduction begins immediately after it. It may well be that – given 'Shout To The Lord's rapidly increasing popularity prior to recording – the producers sought to 'stamp' the song as Australian. Observing that many people now attribute 'Shout To The Lord' as the watershed moment in Hillsong Church's global aspirations, it would appear that this 'stamp' achieved the aim of bringing HMA onto the international Christian stage.

The verse of the song is based on a melodic line that ascends the third, fourth and fifth of the tonic chord, followed by the dominant. Rather than continuing upwards after the tonic, however, the second sequence drops to the G# below middle C. As such, it becomes one of the lowest notes in congregational song, well outside of the accepted vocal range of an average congregation. The highest note of the song, C# in the chorus, gives the piece a range of eleven notes. The chorus is pitched on the tonic (A) and is founded on the classic 'ice-cream change' chordal pattern (I-vi-IV-V). These factors, combined with an extremely conjunctive melody and small range (a fifth), make the chorus strong, powerful and catchy as a result.

Another powerful Salvation song from Hillsong illustrates the necessity of considering congregational song within its immediate performative context, whether that be on an album (as in this instance) or in a real-time liturgical setting. 'Jesus, What A Beautiful Name' (Riches) is track six from the album *God Is In The House* (1996), and it forms a musically and lyrically important pivot on that album. The strophic form of 'Jesus, What A Beautiful Name' is enhanced through key changes coinciding with each verse. The song begins in C major and moves through D major to E♭ major in the final verses. Track seven of the album then takes up in F major followed by track eight in G major. This build-up in tonal energy underpins the lyrics of track eight which call for a sincere and total dedication of one's life to God: 'Every breath that I take/Every moment I'm awake/Lord have your way in me'. Thematically the songs build on each other as well. As noted, 'Beautiful Name' is a Salvation song (with a Testimonial sub-theme) which utilises the third person term of reference and builds the foundation for the responsorial songs that follow – in keeping with the biblical principle outlined in Matthew 7:24-25. Tracks seven and eight are both Trans-formation/Dedication songs, augmenting their prayerful commitment through the use of second person individual address. In fact, 'Let The Peace Of God Reign' (seven) complements track six well by addressing God and the Holy Spirit directly in separate verses (while track six was about Christ). This too allows for a culmination of personal outpouring in the final track of the set.

Other notable musical nuances between the three tracks include the compound duple time signature of track six – one of only two variations from simple quadruple. Initially the song (six) is pitched quite low – in C major – which necessitates the melody dropping to G below middle C, yet this low tonality does allow for the two key changes to be comfortably accommodated. Overall the melody is quite conjunctive, with strong hymn-like movement. 'Jesus, What A Beautiful Name' is one of the best examples of an ascending tonal bass (C-D-E-F-E-F-G-A). It also features an additional 9/8 bar which, to some extent, increases the level of musicianship required to play the song.

One of the first songs to traverse denomination boundaries in Australia was Geoff Bullock's 'This Kingdom'. Now popular throughout the Western church, it was the Salvationist element of the song, combined with a strong Credal element – thereby meaning participants were singing exclusively *about* Christ – which allowed for its wholesale adoption within the Christian Church.[12]

As the title indicates, the dominant theological idea addressed is the kingdom of God (Mark 1, 4, 10, among others), and several structural devices are employed to reflect the power and promise of that doctrine. For example, five lines in the eight-line chorus begin with the conjunctive 'and', creating a growing list of 'kingdom' characteristics, and by inference, benefits of 'kingdom' membership. Both verses have the same structure, largely expressing the same ideas merely with different language. The last two lines of the verses, represented musically by the pre-hook, are the same, giving each verse uniform momentum into the chorus.

Considering other songs in this category, one finds the music of Robin Mark from Ireland and compositions like 'Be Unto Your Name' (DeShazo and Sadler) from the USA. The latter, along with Mark's 'Lion Of Judah', are fiercely Christo-centric in their approach. Both the aforementioned songs contain a simple triple metre, giving them a lilting yet emphatic feel. While 'Be Unto Your Name', like so many others, takes passages of praise (particularly from Revelation) and translates them into song, 'Lion Of Judah' seeks to map out more completely the gospel message and offer praise that all creation can take part in (Psalm 148). In many cases these triple metre songs feature simple crochet based melodies, especially those with greater tempi. The combination of triple metre and crochet, often syllabic melodic structures, not only provides a certain supremacy to the songs, it also allows those more attuned to the classic hymn tradition to engage with the music; given that many similarities exist between the tunes. Exposure to such songs allows congregants to become impartial in their attitudes towards modern song, which can then allow moves towards other compound metre Salvation songs that require a little more personal engagement, such as 'Hallelujah' (Myrin and Sampson). That so many popular Salvation songs exist around the world is testament to the Christology presence in today's church, and is definitely something to be capitalised on by music directors and worship leaders the world over. After all, it is the message of Christ that reconciles, heals and brings salvation (Romans 5:9-11).

Spirit/Anointing
Songs classified as Spirit songs are those that directly praise the Holy Spirit, while Anointing songs normally petition the Godhead to manifest his presence within the gathering or life of the believer in some way. They are grouped together here to reflect more their functionality within the corporate gathering. More often than not the songs occur together, often praise songs leading into a petition for the Holy Spirit's presence. The distinction between the abiding presence of God and his manifest presence has already been noted, and it is these categories of songs that most often align with seeking a greater manifest presence of God, for whatever purpose (understanding, spiritual gifts, forgiveness, etc.) the participant is in need of. This petitioning of the Spirit, more than anything else, is what troubles many traditionalists and Christians from mainstream denominations. Anointing songs, particularly, often call on the Holy Spirit to perform certain directives, 'come...fall...flow' etc. The petition to 'come', for example, raises theological questions for many, given that this event is normally associated with the conversion experience (Romans 8:14-16; 2 Corinthians 1:21-22). Others consider that such a request was fulfilled in the coming of the Spirit at Pentecost (Acts 2), and is inappropriately sought again. In either case, the appeal would *appear* to contradict those parts of the Bible that refer to the Spirit's constant presence within believers (e.g. John

7:39; 14:15-17; Romans 8:10-11; Galatians 3:2-5). If these appeals for the Holy Spirit's presence are based on errant understandings of his role within the believer's life, then certainly there are issues. However, what is more customary is that songwriters (and congregations) are seeking a greater recognition of the manifest presence of the Holy Spirit. Such requests of the Spirit are not peculiar to Pentecostals, or contemporary hymnody. In 1926, Reverend Daniel Iverson wrote the hymn 'Spirit Of The Living God', which begins: 'Spirit of the living God/Fall afresh on me'. Many other examples from hymnody exist, and continue to be sung in churches worldwide. Why is it we assume hymn-writers had a greater grasp of theology than contemporary songwriters?

There has been an assumption amongst the wider church that Pentecostal churches are dominated by these categories of songs, but present research has proven that a myth, with an average of only 19 per cent of songs surveyed referring to the Holy Spirit. There are, however, vast differences in the construction and quality of songs in these categories, as the following analysis highlights.

One of few songs to focus exclusively on praising the Holy Spirit, as opposed to other petitioning songs (see below), is 'Joy In The Holy Ghost' (Fragar). Fragar began his description of the track with: 'To write this song I decided to research the role of the Holy Spirit in the scriptures'. As a consequence the song is a biblical depiction of the attributes and roles of the Holy Spirit. It mixes practical and poetic language as it discusses the notion of the Holy Spirit dwelling in the hearts of believers (John 14:26-27). The song sets up a classic gospel blues groove. A compound quadruple feel is created by giving the quaver pairs a triplet feel throughout. The electric guitar plays blues licks in the bar breaks, while the brass section play a dotted minim, quaver-quaver *sforzando* punch on alternate bars. The groove is completed by a walking bass (which plays a chromatic blues turnaround at the conclusion of the verse) and a vamping piano. Contrastingly, the melody in the chorus is relatively stagnant (the first twelve notes all Cs), although still punchy and syncopated. There are no accidentals or blues notes in the melody; however, the choir perform long chordal harmonies, moving between the tonic and sub-dominant, which incorporate flattened thirds and sevenths. The song has been astutely arranged for maximum impact, with trademark genre traits and clichés. Unfortunately, such an arrangement is virtually impossible to replicate with average church resources, the most basic of which are people. The 1996 National Church Life Survey reported that the average Protestant congregation contained sixty-nine people. The average Assemblies of God congregation size was 115 (Kaldor *et al.*, 1999: 26). It is unlikely that either of these average congregations would be able to provide the musical skill and resources necessary to reproduce the rich sound of this song's possible arrangement.

More common Spirit focused songs are those dealing with various under-standings and manipulations of Anointing theology. Often harmonically simple and repetitive, these songs nonetheless display great variety in their presentation, even if their functional elements appear quite obvious from the outset. For example, 'Oh Holy Spirit' (Bullock) contains simple harmonic pat-terns (I-vi-IV-I in the verse and IV-I-IV-iii-vi in the chorus). The disjunctive melodic leaps contained in the song are easily executed in view of its slow tempo (84 bpm). Notably, the chorus is pitched lower than the verse, quite a rare phenomenon in congregational song. Lyrically the song is extremely similar to the other Anointing songs in calling for the Spirit to 'fall'. The verses are unique but uniform in structure:

> Address to HS
> 'Spirit of' …
> … 'fire'
> Role or attribute of HS
> Address to HS
> Request (reasonably vague in both verses)

'Holy Spirit Rain Down' (Fragar) is another that calls the Holy Spirit earthward. It addresses God in the second person and contains some degree of Intimacy/Relational categorisation. It deviates from the more dominant individual point of view, using the plural to further emphasise its Anointing function. 'Holy Spirit Rain Down' calls on the Holy Spirit directly to 'rain down' (i.e. be manifestly present amongst the congregation). While the sentiment behind the petition to the Spirit is biblically justifiable, it is the notion of asking the Spirit to 'come' which creates difficulties, given the NT understanding of his permanent indwelling within believers. As noted above, a dichotomy between abiding presence and manifest presence is perceivable. Significantly, it is not merely the lyrics that contribute to the song's basic supplication. Instrumen-tally the song builds throughout, with various instruments (especially flute, bass and piano) progressively becoming freer in their melodic improvisation. As such the song develops a slight jazz feel, particularly through the improvi-sation and harmonies provided by the piano. It is the lead vocal, however, that announces the 'arrival' of the manifest presence of the Holy Spirit. Leader Darlene Zschech improvises, 'Here it comes, here it comes',[13] a signal for other instrumentalists to increase the intensity of their own improvisation. Other vocalists begin a time of free worship, the many voices and melodies creating rich musical and emotional intensity. Zschech continues, 'Holy Spirit, you are welcome here…let your presence fill this place Jesus', in a sense confirming the successful appeal to the Holy Spirit.

One of the most innovative Holy Spirit songs of recent times is Tim Hughes' 'Consuming Fire'. It is innovative both musically and lyrically in moving away from any clichéd representations of the Holy Spirit or the desire for his manifest presence. Tonally centred in A major, the song opens with a vi^7-Vb-I-IV-vi^7-Vb-IV progression which clearly keeps the tonal centre at bay, causing the song to float and anticipate passionate heights to come. On most recordings or in performance this opening is played by high register keyboards playing only the minim chord changes, allowing the intensity of the vocal plea, 'There must be more than this/O breath of God come breathe within', to have pre-eminence over the sparse, non-centred accompaniment. The metaphor of 'breath' for the Holy Spirit's presence within the believer is well-established from biblical example (Job 32:8; John 20:21-22); traditional hymnody ('Breathe on us, LORD, in this our Day... The Holy Ghost receive' [Charles Wesley]); and also features prominently in the popular congregational song 'Breathe' (Barnett), 'This is the air I breathe/Your Holy presence living in me'. Less established in modern song is the metaphor of the Spirit as a 'consuming fire'.[14] It is this metaphor, though, that commences the chorus, with the A major tonal centre finally dominant through a simple I-Vb-vi^7-IV progression:

> *Consuming Fire, fan into flame*
> *A passion for Your name*
> *Spirit of God, fall in this place*
> *Lord, have Your way*
> *Lord have Your way, with us*

Furthering the imprint of the lyrics is a descending crochet triplet pattern used as a motif throughout. The triplet oscillates between a D-C$^\#$-A and D-C$^\#$-B descent, the latter obviously allowing for the dominant chord mid-phrase. This motif creates a falling motion throughout the chorus, which echoes the petition of the participant for the Holy Spirit to fall.

3. The Body of Christ

Corporate worship operates at both the horizontal and vertical levels of interaction. As noted previously, vertical songs represent those songs that speak directly from God to the congregation, and vice versa. Yet the horizontal operation does also take place within modern liturgical settings. Many of the songs discussed in the following song-types function at this horizontal level, and are often marked by a plural address ('we', 'us') that builds corporate longing and dedication from participants. These songs are more readily used at the beginning of services to engage and unite; however, their value as responsive mechanisms is also utilised.

While discussed together the following two song-types occupy different roles within the corporate gathering. Call to Worship songs are by nature far more specific than Body/Unity songs. They act to encourage people to join in the corporate worship that is beginning, or continuing. They are designed to ignite spiritual desire and build conducive environments for the exposition of Scripture, as well as stirring an atmosphere in which musical worship will be readily received by those in attendance. In contrast, Body/Unity songs can serve a variety of purposes. What does distinguish them, however, is their intention to unify a group of believers, to highlight that the group are 'all one in Christ Jesus' (Galatians 3:28). Could it be that the structure of modern churches, the physical constructs within which they take place are heightening this need for communal identification? On the one hand there are the mega churches, which often meet in non-traditional spaces, or purpose-built buildings.[15] On the other there are traditional churches which for the most part still adhere to a basic 'pews facing the front' type mentality. To a degree this is a movement away from previous physical environments, even within mainstream churches. For example, in the Holy Trinity church at York in England, the interior of the church is comprised of small booths which used to house the worshippers, often in family units.

Figure 6.2: *Holy Trinity Church, Goodramgate, York (UK)* (Author's collection)

There was undoubtedly a 'disciplinary' benefit to having family units in such a configuration, yet there is a deeper level to this construction. The notion that corporate worship is corporate – is something we enjoin in with others – is something unmissable in the booths at Holy Trinity. Irrespective of architectural design, there is no doubt that songs dealing with the body of Christ have a crucial unifying role to play in the modern church.

Call to Worship and Body/Unity

> *Do you feel the darkness tremble, when all the saints join in one song...?*
> ('Did You Feel The Mountains Tremble' [M. Smith]).

The opening three tracks of the Hillsong album *Touching Heaven, Changing Earth* provide a textbook opening to both a service and a live congregational recording; textbook in the sense of worship models, Pentecostal structure and song-type positioning. All three songs are up-tempo (around 160 bpm) and plural in address. That is, they operate at the horizontal level of corporate worship, motivating by including and propelling participants on their journey. Track one, 'That's What We Came Here For', is a Call to Worship song-type, which follows OT imagery of assembling at the gates of the temple and gradually moving deeper into the temple, and hence nearer to God's presence. Many, almost liturgical, accounts of this are found in the psalms,[16] although other practical accounts involving temple worship are scattered throughout the OT. The line 'Come into Your presence with praise' can be read as an OT idea (which would make it problematic in relation to NT theology), or as a metaphor of awareness. Other lines with dualistic meaning simultaneously reinforce the purpose of the gathering and various doctrinal ideas. For instance, 'There'll be singing and dancing' is at once a picture of heaven and a statement about the experience that awaits participants in the ensuing hour(s). Inherent to the motivational aspect is the use of Body Unity songs. Track three is such a song, yet it is perhaps more specifically related to Hillsong Church than the wider Christian Church. Lyrics such as, 'Anything can happen/And it probably will...something good is going on around here... This is a church on fire', require an experiential level of identification for listeners of the CD to engage with them easily. Though not overt, there is some degree of self-promotion in 'Church On Fire', with Hillsong Church clearly posited as the place where 'it' is happening. Such pronouncements about individual 'houses' of God are common throughout congregational song, and do offer participants a level of excitement and anticipation, knowing that they are privileged to be experiencing the corporate worship they have chosen to attend.

Musically the opening tracks are highly produced and tightly arranged with full band accompaniment. Track one takes its accents from the rhythm of the melody:

Figure 6.3: *Accent pattern, 'That's What We Came Here For'*

filling the musical bed with constant cymbals, and bongos that pan through the mix from Right to Left. Tracks one and three open with brass riffs which create style and energy in both instances. The opening brass riff is extremely rhythmic, and as it becomes buried in the mix, its unevenness is camouflaged:

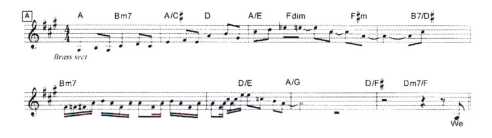

Figure 6.4: *Brass riff, 'That's What We Came Here For'*

The chromatically ascending off-beat melodic riff that announces track three is heavily based on a gospel funk sound. The clichéd sounding riff is similar to those made popular by the *Blues Brothers* movie. Such musical hermeneutics (as applied by Rosar, 2001) intensify the upbeat experience of the song, and indeed the opening of the album. There is a performative hazard underlying these associations with accepted cultural repertoire, however, which can give the album/service a distinctly 'theatrical' feel. Working against this, to some extent, is the consistency with which the style is maintained throughout the song, and its appropriateness to the lyrical content ('something very good, something good is going on around here'). Stylistic consistency is achieved through a gravelly male vocal, shuffle bass pattern and descending organ fills between phrases. The complexity of the brass part partially hampers performance of the song, with the vocalists missing the entry to the final chorus that follows the brass riff. Yet such orchestration, and by extension, difficulty, is to be applauded in our congregational song. Far too much modern music opts for the lowest common denominator, rather than extending musicianship, and thus compositional outcomes. Another Body Unity song that incorporates similar riffs and rhythmic variety is 'Your People Sing Praises' (Fragar).

Once again an uptempo song, 'Your People Sing Praises', runs at 171 bpm. It is worth pausing to note that these categories of songs often operate at faster tempi, a fact consistent with the motivational elements often inherent to Call to Worship and Body Unity songs. What is of consequence within the general corpus of congregational song is the lack of moderate tempo (90-120 bpm) songs being written and performed.[17] The polemic between fast songs and slow (often most reductionistically referred to as 'praise' songs and 'worship' songs, respectively) signifies a lack of ingenuity and creativity. It may also, in part, reflect a general tendency among pastors/worship leaders etc. to plan congregational songs based on whether they are fast or slow. For example:

> I divide my master song list into two categories – fast songs and slow songs. I find this to be the easiest distinction because the mood of most services can blend into one of these two categories (Sorge, 1987: 275).

'Your People Sing Praises' features a combination of second and third person address, with plural point of view. Overall, this blend of address incorporates individual congregants into the larger body of believers, heightening the Body Unity theme. However, the song switches address mid-verse and is subsequently less clear in its identificatory process. One lyric of particular significance within the song is the line, 'Your people sing praises/Let laughter fill the world'. This seemingly innocuous line takes on greater significance in light of recent Pentecostal history. Fragar's song was written in 1995 and, as he explains in the music's header, was conceived to allow people to praise God in their individual manner, yet with a pure and contrite heart:

> Everyone had their own way of praising God, which probably makes life very interesting for God! I'm quite sure that the most important thing to Him is not the language, the style, the volume or the tempo; He looks at the hearts of those who are worshipping (GIITH Music Book).

What is significant is that 1995 was the year of the Toronto[18] Blessing, a phenomenon where Pentecostal churches in Toronto, Canada were reported to have received an outpouring of the Holy Spirit which resulted in congregational members laughing uncontrollably in services.[19] Deemed an anointing, people reported being so overcome with the Spirit's 'presence' that they appeared drunk or hysterically happy. Thus Fragar's song would appear to be a reference to, and endorsement of, the Toronto Blessing, one of the most significant and reported happenings in recent Pentecostal history.

As pre-empted above, 'Your People Sing Praises' calls on the full resources of orchestration and features a heavily arranged sound. Indicative of this is the reliance on brass section riffs to begin the piece. These riffs are used to set the feel or groove of the piece, and are often the only – or at least primary – vehicles that achieve this end. A good example is the syncopated, calypso melodic riff that announces 'Your People Sing Praises':

Figure 6.5: *Melodic riff, 'Your People Sing Praises'*

The riff, played by the brass section over the top of the full band, presents a carefree, animated and rather stimulating beginning to the Body Unity song. The calypso feel is enhanced through the use of auxiliary percussion executing a variety of sixteenth patterns, marimba keyboard sounds, and syncopated bass lines emphasising the third beat (or anticipation of it). Contrastingly, the melody itself is quite straight, with little accenting, and certainly no calypso-style accents. Much of the melody does, however, draw on the basic crochet-quaver-quaver rhythm of the opening melodic riff, giving it a certain lilting quality. Where this is abandoned in order to accommodate lyrics (e.g. 'and everything else that we've got') the result is a jarring stylistic break which could well have been avoided through more careful lyrical editing. Harmonic structures throughout are very simple, IV-V-I in the verse and V-I in the chorus, again stressing the reliance on arrangement to create mood.

One song that cleverly manipulates its melodic construction in order to maximise its Call to Worship functionality is 'Come, Now Is The Time To Worship' (Doerksen). The opening crochet on the word 'Come' is followed by three rest beats, effectively filling out the bar. As such, 'Come' sounds prominently and

forcefully; seemingly inviting and instructing simultaneously. Even more dominant is the protracted extension of the word 'worship' in the third bar; held over
the bar's length with slight melisma on the final eighth note of the bar to land
strongly on the one in the next beat. Aside from the length of the note, it rises
above the rest of the melody, both in pitch and texture. The note effectively does
call out, to all and sundry, to come and share the worship experience on offer.
Resembling a heartfelt cry, the note seeks out those mingling outside, at the back
of the building, or even contemplating participation. This most effective musical
technique generates a song that sits comfortably at the beginning of corporate
worship (see *I Could Sing Of Your Love Forever 2*, 2001 as an example) and creates a
functional Call to Worship song through musicality as well as lyric. Fittingly, the
song is directed firmly at other believers, 'Come, just as you are before your God',
and uses an individual, second person address to further its request.

One identifiable danger for Body Unity songs is that they call the people
together, seek to unify them, but are misleading or ill-directed in the focus of
this collective energy. One song that illustrates this problem, albeit an older
tune but still one widely sung in churches today, is 'Latter Rain' (Bullock).
'Latter Rain' uses plural address to build a Body Unity song that explores the
ambiguous notion of the 'latter rain'. The chorus reads:

> *These are the days of the latter rain*
> *Days of power, days of grace*
> *This is the time the fire will fall*
> *To make this land holy*
> *To make this land, holy to the Lord.*

Nowhere in modern translations of the Bible is the phrase 'latter rain' mentioned, although the King James Version (KJV) of the Bible does use the phrase
'latter rain' in Jeremiah 5:24 and Joel 2:23, where it speaks of a 'former and latter rain'.[20] The context of the passages suggests a seasonal reference, rendered
as 'autumn and spring rains' in the NIV. However, many view these passages as
referring metaphorically to God's promise to pour down blessings, in the tor-
rents of the 'latter rain', just prior to the climax of history. During that time:

> *There would be a worldwide resurgence of faith, and the healings and*
> *miracles that had been so evident in the first years of Christianity would*
> *happen again as a prelude to the second coming of Jesus Christ, this time to*
> *establish his visible church* (Cox, 1996: 47).

On a more surface level, the lyrics are inconsistent metaphorically, e.g. 'the
fire will fall' and 'the rain will fall', further confusing the thematic concerns. In
retrospect, Bullock considered the song more conceptually:

[The song] *was based on the whole Pentecostal idea that there is a double portion, and there are greater anointings – more of God for those who seek Him. And in the end times there is going to be this heightening of anointings* (interview with the author, 2002).

Social Justice

One category vastly under-represented in modern church music is songs dealing with Social Justice. Remembering that many define worship as adoration and action together, this lack of action-focused songs is troubling. Congregational song has tremendous power to call the Church body together in order to achieve socially responsible goals. Failure to sing (and act) on these responsibilities, yet to regale ourselves with personal dedications of belief and transformation, is to stand somewhat hypocritically among the wider community.

To be fair, one of the larger contributors to this category, the Salvation Army, has not been widely surveyed for this analysis. Indeed, their internationally recognised songs 'I'll Fight' (Rowe), 'Let Justice Roll' (Rowe), 'Break Me' (Strickland) and 'The World For God' (Grinnel) go some way to redressing the lack in this area. However, and it is a big however, they do not represent a major international music producer, and as such their songs, while perhaps widely sung within the Army, are not generic across a large body of churches. Furthermore, it is problematic if the larger denominations and producers leave all Social Justice songs to the creative forces of the Salvation Army, based on the assumption that is 'what they do', and by inference *not* what we do. A feature of the Army songs mentioned here are heartfelt concerns for the 'lost' and 'broken hearted', promises to 'deny [my]self', and active verbs 'searching', 'reaching out', 'fight' and 'calling' that speak of the participant's desire to seek out a functional faith response to those less fortunate.

One rare song that does tackle issues of social justice directly in relation to a worship practice setting is 'Let Us Rise To Worship' by Geoff Bullock. At a mammoth 208 words, it is easily the lyrically longest of all songs in the survey sample for this volume. Despite this, it only mentions the name of Christ twice in the coda. The track's title may have distinct connotations for many Christians, particularly those actively engaged in congregational song, given the prevalence of such wordings.[21] As Bullock noted:

[the song] *talks about if we lift our hands to worship let us reach out hands that care. In other words, if we are going to sing then we better know what we are singing about* (interview with the author, 2000).

The lyrics draw much of their content from Luke 4:17-21, where Christ teaches on the social responsibilities of the Church (see also James 1:27). It was Bullock's own social concerns that created conflicts, both internal and external, during public seminars to promote his *Hands of Grace* book and CD. Long an ambassador for aid organisation World Vision, Bullock found the tension between what he was doing and why became too strong:

> *I got to a point where I was doing Hands of Grace seminars, and I'd be talk-ing about the World Vision children and trying to get people to realise that if we are going to sing, let's sponsor a child first and then sing. How could we possibly sing about the love of God being in us, and then walk past the* [World Vision] *table to buy a CD? I suddenly had these crises... I'd walk out and there would be the World Vision table, which to me was a fitting response, and my table of CDs and all these 'Mel Gibson'* [style] *photos, airbrushed with blue eyes... I found it a contradiction, a contradiction that was in me* (interview with the author, 2000).

Such sentiments are clearly heard in lyrics such as:

> *Let our songs be brought to silence*
> *If our voices are not heard*
> *Beyond the music and the singing*
> *When our hearts remain unstirred.*

The track begins with piano and acoustic guitar, while gentle female vocals provide the lead. The sound continues in much the same vein, and is similar to the entire album from which it is taken, *Deeper and Deeper*. The melodic rhythm is simple yet predominantly off the beat, propelling the piece forward and giving further impetus to the lyrics. While there is a blend of conjunc-tive and disjunctive movement, the basic direction of the verse and chorus is descending. Given the number (and length) of verses this tends to result in a lack of variety over the course of the entire song. The use of some chromatic diminished chord progressions does provide some additional colour.

Communion
Another category minimally evident in this survey were those songs con-cerned exclusively with Communion, or coming to the Lord's table. Early 1980s examples such as 'Broken For Me' and 'Around The Table' appear to have few contemporaries. Indeed, no specific song was found that deals in sufficient depth with the subject matter as to be considered a Communion song-type. Of interest, however, is news that Hillsong is planning to release a 'communion' album in 2006. This will ostensibly contain songs which are uti-lised during communion services but have never been recorded. Frequently, it is felt that these songs fall outside the rubric of standard congregational

song releases. It is worth pondering why songs used within communion (or deemed appropriate to that setting) do not qualify for categorisation as Communion song-types. Perhaps we have become too hung up about the sound of these songs, their emotional impact and musical ingenuity, and have forgotten the basics about the situation they are serving. To this end, Christian City Church's *Sante* (née *Prayerworks*) series also falls into this group, with their songs often incorporated into the communion service, without acting in a traditional congregational song manner. Nonetheless, this is a category that needs urgent attention within the modern church, and will help to ensure the continued centrality of the Lord's Supper to contemporary liturgy.

7 Corporate Worship Gets Personal

While one aim of theomusicology is to objectively observe the nuances of various religious music, there comes a point where a degree of subjective analysis is almost unavoidable, particularly when the researcher is involved in the scene. 'Corporate worship gets personal' definitely hints at the types of congregational song to be scrutinised below, but it also acknowledges a more subjective, personal tone that necessarily runs through the chapter. Theomusicology cannot only report the successful and creatively stimulating, it must also present the awkward and uncomfortable aspects of the music. There are some tough questions and arguments within the world of congregational song, and Chapter 7 seeks to consider some of these.

1. 'As For Me...'

So begins one of Darlene Zschech's more famous songs ('All Things Are Possible'), and so encapsulates, many would argue, the basic tenor of congregational song today. More often than not critics point to the dominance of personal intimacy present in the lyrics of modern songs; the focus on the individual, on the participant singing rather than the subject of their worship – God. It is important to remember that this intimacy is not in itself a new thing. Much of the classic hymn canon deals with personal, experiential stories and testimonies. Isaac Watts (among many choices) will more than suffice as an example. As Marshall and Todd (1982) have noted, Watts's 'favored metaphor for the love between Jesus and the individual Christian is that of erotic passion' (53). They go on to note that to Watts:

> Jesus has a 'charming Name'; he is 'the dear Object of our Love', who 'lights our Passions to a Flame' (XVI). The 'Infinite Lover' (XXI) makes my dying bed
>
> > Feel soft as downy Pillows are,
> > While on his Breast I lean my Head
> > And breathe my Life out sweetly there (ibid.).

Here, then, the use of human love, and even sexuality, is almost too realistic (ibid.: 54). One can but ponder the magnitude of similar terms being sung in songs today. And while we may not possess the sensibility of seventeenth-century love poetry, even in their day such songs were designed to shock. This example is provided to temper, somewhat, current critical musings on the intimate and overtly affectionate songs of today.

The concept and practice of detailing an intimate, personal relationship with God through congregational song is not new. Concerns about such language are not new. What does appear valid in today's argument is the sheer quantity of songs in this ilk, not their existence.

In a 2002 survey of over 150 contemporary songs,[1] I found that the use of individual point of view in contemporary congregational song is customary. It appeared in 71 per cent of songs surveyed. This lack of plural point of view was indicative of a deficiency in Body Unity songs, and songs involved in the horizontal level of corporate worship. Despite one of the most popular contemporary congregational songs ever ('Shout To The Lord') employing both individual and plural points of view, only 5 per cent of other songs in the survey did so. Coupled with individual point of view was the fact that we are singing in second person address over 60 per cent of the time, a combination which adds to the intimacy of the songs.

Song-type classifications across the survey material proved to be rather limited. Only three song-types were found in more than 10 per cent of songs, while merely six song-types account for 85.5 per cent of all songs. The Intimacy/Relational song-type was unquestionably the dominant category. 34.8 per cent of songs fell into this classification. The second highest average classification was Transformation/Dedication – the category closest to Intimacy/Relational. It was dominant in 13.1 per cent of songs. Salvation songs, the first designated praise category to feature, come in third with 12.3 per cent.

The personal, experiential character of contemporary congregational song manifests itself through these figures. Over half the songs analysed were primarily concerned with the relationship between the participant and the Godhead. Of these, over 70 per cent were written from an individualistic point of view, and over 60 per cent addressed the Godhead in the more informal second person address. Some see this as indicative of Pentecostal expectations: 'The feeling dimension of worship is important to [Pentecostals as] they expect to "sense the presence of God"' (Hughes, 1996: 16). Yet Piggin (1996) argues that this relational, experiential desire is not exclusively Pentecostal, but essentially evangelical:

> *Evangelicalism is concerned to foster an intimate, even intense personal relationship with Jesus Christ. The creation and development of this rela-*

tionship is understood as the work of the Holy Spirit... Evangelicalism, then, is experiential, Biblicist, and activist. It is concerned with the Spirit, the Word, and the world (vii).

This present study identifies several song-types that, when banded together, amount to a more intimate, personal and individual type of modern song; namely Intimacy/Relational, Transformation/Dedication, Confessional, Testimony and Thanksgiving songs. To assume that any, or all, of these songs are negative is narrow-minded. Confessional songs, for instance, have a huge role to play in contemporary liturgy, and indeed, all of these song-types have their place in the modern church. Yet inferior songs from these categories can seriously impact on the life of the church and the believer. Care needs to be taken in seeking out the best quality songs from all of these categories, and ensuring that the context in which they are performed is carefully thought through and monitored. Most often these songs are used as responsive tools within the service. Thus they require something before them, a sermon, presentation, Bible reading, etc., in order that participants find themselves responding to God (the vertical dimension of worship in Woodhouse's schema – see p. 18). Used without appropriate contextualisation these songs can all too easily become meaningless. For instance, it is hard to sing a song dedicating one's life to Jesus if he has not been mentioned.

These songs have the power to call upon sentimentality and emotionalism without directing the participant's gaze towards God. They also have the power to manipulate the emotions of participants within the gathering, making them *feel* as though they are experiencing something they are not. That said, music remains a powerful tool in allowing believers to express the inexpressible.

Intimacy/Relational

Intimacy/Relational songs involve personal reflections on the relationship between participant and Godhead. In one sense these are the most personal, individual and idiosyncratic songs in the congregational realm. There are literally hundreds (thousands?) of these songs in popular circulation. They range from the purely subjective to identifications with biblical characters or situations (most commonly from the Psalms). What marks this category is the focus on the relationship, in whatever state that may be, between the participant and God.

'Jesus, Lover Of My Soul' is one example of an extremely intimate song, echoing ideas found in Psalm 40 (especially verses 2, 12 and 17).[2] This is reinforced in the original CD recording of the song through the male vocalist echoing lines and adding further personalised improvisations, 'I love you Jesus, you know I need you Jesus'. There are some complex rhythmic ideas in the melody line (e.g. bars 7-8 and 11-12), although the simple harmonic progression (I-V$^{6/3}$-vi-IV-V) employed throughout does compensate for this. The song contains disjunctive melodic leaps that are easily executed in view of its slow tempo (76 bpm).

In reality the vast number of modern songs falling into this category makes close scrutiny of them rather redundant. General characteristics are that Intimacy/Relational songs tend to be slower in tempo. Formerly songs in this category have tended to be mistakenly identified as 'worship' songs – in the previous 'praise and worship' genre branding. Certainly they are responsive and need to be treated as such. Often these songs place an emphasis on melodic contour rather than harmonic or timbral creativity. That said, songs of this nature do often build in intensity, thus creating more impetus for the emotionalism of the song to take effect.

Popular songs of this persuasion include 'Jesus You're All I Need' (Zschech), 'Glory To The King' (Zschech), 'And That My Soul Knows Very Well' (Fragar and Zschech), 'You Rescued Me' (Bullock), 'Just Let Me Say' (Bullock), 'Unfailing Love' (Bullock), 'Lord, I Thirst For You' (Sadler), 'My Heart Yearns For Thee' (Baroni), 'When The Tears Fall' (Hughes), 'You Are God In Heaven' (Redman and Redman), 'Intimacy' (Redman), and quite literally, many many more.

Transformation/Dedication

Reuben Morgan's popular composition, 'I Give You My Heart', is an excellent example of a Transformation/Dedication song, and a good example of how important contextual positioning is in the use of congregational song. On the album in which it premiered (*God Is In The House*), the song operates as the climactic point of the song set. It follows two other songs, the first an excellent Salvation song that clearly describes the person of Jesus, while the second is another Transformation song that calls on the Holy Spirit's help in the sanctification process. Thus, 'I Give You My Heart' operates as the summary, the decision point. Its lyrical declaration of life dedication is all the more powerful in this context. Being a live congregational album, it highlights the function of the song within a liturgical setting.

The song benefits from carefully detailed arranging which extends the 26-bar song (in simple binary form) to a mammoth 7:50 minutes. The well-known opening melodic riff is doubled on a resonant keyboard sound and electric guitar. It is more syncopated than much of the main melody and temporarily withholds the tonality of the song. The riff returns between repeats of the verse:

Figure 7.1: *Melodic riff, 'I Give You My Heart'*

The lyrics are introduced by a solo male voice over the top of rim-shot drums and a triangle riff which provides most of the rhythmic propulsion in the opening verse. Sparkling keyboard pads also underlay the melody. The sound produced is reminiscent of the 'boy-band' pop sound of the late 1990s. The song features a break-down section after the chorus, where the melodic riff is reintroduced. The singers improvise as a period of 'free worship' or 'singing in the Spirit' is established. This section typifies free worship times that are common to many churches worldwide. In this case, the same lyrics are sung to new melodies. Drums and other instruments cease at this point, leaving keyboards and bass to provide the harmonic foundation for vocal improvisations. The free worship ends with leader Zschech signalling a return to the chorus, through which instruments reinsert themselves, and build once again to a full, powerful and emotionally strong sound. This extension of the basic song is a typical example of practices commonly experienced with this song-type. Such manipulations allow participants time to reflect and (re)dedicate their lives to God.

'The Power Of Your Love' (Bullock), is one of the most popular contemporary songs of the last decade.[3] Significantly, on close examination, the song addresses a number of theological issues. While the song is about seeking renewal and forgiveness, the petition 'Hold me close/Let your love surround me' is awkward in that it is asking God to do something that he has already done. As Bullock himself notes:

> ...it should be 'you hold me close and you let your love surround me, you've brought me near etc'. We are pleading with God to do something he has already done, which means we don't know he has done it (interview with the author, 2000).

Furthermore, the song contains corporeal requests such as, 'Draw me to your side' and 'Let me see you face to face',[4] which – admittedly – could be interpreted as figurative requests for closer intimacy with God. Robin Ryan observes that it has become customary for the God/man relationship to be lyrically couched in corporeal metaphors. To go back on such terminology now would be 'dehumanising and distancing, that is, less conducive to evangelism' (personal communication with the author, 6 June 2002). Overall the lyrical content of the song is a blend of confessional and dedicatory statements, mixed with some theologically problematic ideas. Musically, 'The Power Of Your Love' is a blend of the predictable and the innovative. It utilises standard pop-bass accents (1, 2+, 3, 4+) with accompanying snare accents on two and four. The sensory word painting, 'I'll rise up like the eagle' sees the melody rise to the highest note (E^b), as does 'By the power of your love', where a leap of a minor seventh from 'the' to 'power' adds melodic intensity to the words. The range of the verse (11) is quite large and incorporates both conjunctive and disjunctive movement. Bullock employs a descending tonal bass line, which at times moves in contrary motion with the melody giving the piece further textural colour. Indeed, the piece ends with a seven note descending bass line that moves down an octave from the tonic. These compositional techniques combine to give the song a musical symmetry and strength.

The song 'The Potter's Hand' (Zschech) is based on imagery of God as a potter; moulding, shaping, creating with clay – symbolising his people. This idea is borne out numerous times in the OT:

> 'O house of Israel, can I not do with you as this potter does?' declares the LORD. 'Like clay in the hand of the potter, so are you in my hand, O house of Israel' (Jeremiah 18:6).

> You turn things upside down, as if the potter were thought to be like the clay! Shall what is formed say to him who formed it, 'He did not make me'? Can the pot say of the potter, 'He knows nothing'? (Isaiah 29:16)

Yet Zschech borrows more than the imagery. In perhaps the most famous 'potter' passage, Isaiah (64:8-9) writes: 'Yet, O LORD, you are our Father. We are the clay, you are the potter; we are all the work of your hand... Oh, look upon us, we pray, for we are all your people.' The petitional aspect of this passage lies at the heart of Zschech's song. It posits itself as a prayer, requesting God to 'take...mould...use...fill...call...guide' the participant in accordance with God's will. The strength (and popularity) of the song is reflected by the high production value accorded to it on the album *Touching Heaven Changing Earth*. Careful spatial preferencing of the flute, acoustic guitar, piano and muted trumpet allows a light band beginning to occupy a relatively large spatial domain. An off-beat triangle pattern can be heard in the background-mid of the Left channel. Further highlighting the significance placed on the song is the free worship segment which begins about 5:00 minutes into the song.

Once again instrumentalists improvise freely while Zschech exhibits both vocal facility and spiritual fervour. In a rather rare occurrence for such a recording, Zschech initiates a second such time near the conclusion of the song. The song contains some colourful harmonic progressions throughout, and adheres to relatively simple quaver-based rhythm patterns. The simple dotted-crochet, quaver pattern of the chorus is enhanced through its ascending character, adding power to the list of requests presented. A leap (a fourth) in the final bar, combined with syncopated accents, provides a necessary climax to the chorus. The chorus does run the risk of becoming cyclical by remaining unresolved on the dominant chord. All in all the song represents an archetypal Transformation/ Dedication song, combining strong biblical images with astute compositional devices to draw the participant towards an increased life commitment and purpose in following Christ.

Confessional

Confessional songs, which acknowledge the singer's sinfulness and need for forgiveness, have been part of Christian experience since OT times. Indeed, King David's ruminations on his own sinfulness in Psalm 51 have been the basis of most confessional songs in the modern era. Perhaps the best known, 'Create In Me A Clean Heart' (Green), released back in 1984, is virtually a direct transcription of parts of the Psalm:

> *Create in me a pure heart, O God,*
> *And renew a steadfast spirit within me.*
> *Do not cast me from your presence*
> *Or take your Holy Spirit from me*
> *Restore to me the joy of your salvation*
> *And grant me a willing spirit, to sustain me* (Psalm 51:10-12).

Becomes:

> *Create in me a clean heart, O God*
> *And renew a right spirit within me...*
> *Cast me not away from your presence O God*
> *Take not your Holy Spirit from me*
> *Restore unto to me, the joy of my salvation*
> *And renew a right spirit within me.*

Clearly this literal translation could easily posit the song as Credal in the current framework, yet it is, like so many other modern songs, its functionality that distinguishes it. This direct appeal to God's forgiving and cleansing kindness, based on the participant's self-awareness, is the feature of confessional songs. Many traditional churches incorporate formal times of confession during their liturgy, making the continued production of Confessional songs extremely important to the modern church culture. One of the most recent, and specifically tailored, examples of the Psalm 51-based confession song is 'Hiding Place' (Crabtree and Smith). The verse takes a simple list-like structure, each line detailing places the participant 'finds' God, i.e. draws near to God and experiences a relationship with him. Although the Godhead is not directly mentioned, statements like 'Your word' and 'talking to You when I pray' clearly posit God as the subject of the second person address. What is curious is that the songwriters' ruminations on situations where they draw closer to God move them to a confessional state in the chorus:

> *Create in me a clean heart*
> *As I come away with You*
> *Wash away all of my stains*
> *And restore to me the joy I have in You*
>
> *You are my hiding*
> *You are my hiding place*

Again the connection to Psalm 51 is obvious, adapted here in the second line to reflect the focus of the song. This less literal interpretation is useful both in introducing congregants to the original text, and also incorporating confessional elements within more 'standard' intimately relational songs. Obviously musical arrangement is a vital ingredient to the success of a Confessional song. In the case of 'Hiding Place', the arrangement involves acoustic and electric guitars (panned Left and Right giving an openness and 'vulnerability' to the mix) propelling the song through integrated rhythmic patterns over a synth pad. While the song builds steadily into a medium paced rock song, with the ensuing arrangement to accompany that, there is a breakdown on the chorus late in the song (4:05 mins) that allows more reflection and less victoriousness in the mood. One element that does tend to contrast with the song's message are the loud, grainy interjections of the male leader, the tone of which are often at odds with the congregation's place within the song.

One song that combines thoughtful writing and unmistakeable Confessional elements is the Parachute band's 'Salvation Song' (Collins, Huirua and de Jong). Lyrically the song contains images of repentance, 'in my heart I bow my knee', before making fundamental gospel statements: 'I believe, Jesus you are God and You died for me'. The melody at this point contains a strong rise to the dominant note on 'believe', setting up an easy scalic descent with straight quavers on the rest of the phrase. In fact, the simple quaver movement of the melody, combined with the three two-bar motifs on which the verse is built, allow an easy, gentle performance from the participant, creating a thoughtful contemplativeness to the song. The chorus takes the previously stated characteristics of, and attitudes towards, Jesus, and responds to them:

> *I turn away from my sin Lord and turn to You, to You*
> *I know that You're saving me Lord*
> *I turn away from my sin Lord and turn to You, to You*
> *I thank you for saving me Lord*

Here the melody features the only semi-quaver of the song, on 'turn away', the sensory word-painting of the rhythm giving a sense of both the action itself and the emphatic nature in which it is felt. Strongly repeating the dominant note of the scale for the opening declaration – with more syncopation than anywhere else in the song – the melody then returns to easy quaver movement up and down the scale. This musical declaration followed by dedication echoes such things as the Anglican confirmation service, where confirmees declare their faith through renouncing the Devil and 'turning' to Christ. Similar themes are present in baptism services and services of dedication the world over. Capturing the vitality and magnitude of these events, and of forgiveness itself, is the achievement of 'Salvation Song's writers.

One complicating factor with Confessional songs is that they often develop into areas of commitment. Once the confession has been made, an acknowledgement of forgiveness in the songwriter moves them naturally towards statements of (re)dedication. For example, the opening of 'Refresh My Heart' (Bullock) may indicate a confessional aspect to the song by invoking the Holy Spirit's presence, not as an initial conversion experience but rather as a re-establishment of commitment and relationship – an idea possibly adapted from Paul's request in Philemon 1:20. The second person, individual address adds to the personal plea of the opening lines. Yet, subsequent to this refreshing, the songwriter vows, 'And I will worship you/With all of my heart', moving the song in the direction of Transformation/Dedication. This is further evidence of why songs of this personal, experiential nature need to be carefully considered before being planned within corporate worship, to ensure the messages conveyed through the music are those desired or warranted at that particular moment of the service.

Thanksgiving and Testimony
These two categories have been amalgamated here to indicate the connection between them. Songs of Testimony, which recount the work of God in the life

of the believer, often lead into Thanksgiving – songs of thanks to the Godhead. Similarly, giving thanks to the Lord – a clear instruction for all believers from the Bible (1 Thessalonians 5:18) – can develop into consideration of God's previous intervention in one's life. The following discussion begins with songs of Thanksgiving.

The Dennis Jernigan song, 'Thank You, Lord', is popular across denominations for its earnest yet simple declaration of thanks. The song, in simple triple metre, is a fulfilment of several verses in the Bible which call on believers to thank God for his provision, salvation, grace, etc. (see 1 Thessalonians 5:18; Colossians 4:2; Hebrews 12:28). As such, it delivers a simple message through simple delivery, with a strong gospel sound created through the syllabic crochet melody. Here the arrangement and original composition fit quite closely, creating a piece that holds pronounced resemblance to the late nineteenth-century gospel songs of Sankey and Crosby. The dotted minim rhythm of the chorus melody allows for meditative reflection on the simple 'thank you' lyric. Despite its simplicity, the song still manages to build to climax through largely stationary crochets (with some scalic movement).

Another older song in this category, routinely sung around the world, is 'Give Thanks' (H. Smith). Dating back to 1978, Smith's song is in simple binary form, the first section almost instructing believers: 'Give thanks with a grateful heart', but also providing justification for such instruction, 'because he's given Jesus Christ, his Son'. This justification is a key to Thanksgiving songs. The trap for some writers attempting to express thanksgiving is that they neglect to provide the reason for the response. A call to give thanks devoid of any mention of God's character, deeds or saving work holds little value.

Most atypical in 'Give Thanks' is the song's reliance on minor tonalities throughout. One might expect songs of thanks to be predominantly written in more uplifting major tonalities, and even though 'Give Thanks' is indeed major, it lacks a strong tonal centre allowing a greater freedom of harmonic ideas to develop. Section two actually begins on chord iii, and rarely lands on the tonic (iii-vi^7-V-vi-ii^7-V-IVb-Vb-Imaj^5). Lyrically this section moves towards accepting the grace of Jesus:

> *And now let the weak say, 'I am strong'*
> *Let the poor say, 'I am rich'*
> *Because of what the Lord has done in me*

To highlight the connection between Thanksgiving and Testimony songs, it is revealing at this point to consider Reuben Morgan's 'What The Lord Has Done In Me'. Technically a Testimony song-type, the song draws from the same passage, beginning:

Let the weak say 'I am strong'
Let the poor say 'I am rich'
Let the blind say 'I can see'
It's what the Lord has done in me

As with 'Give Thanks', the first verse of the song is drawn heavily from NT passages that reflect a testimonial deliverance (2 Corinthians 12:10; James 2:5; John 9:39), while the chorus responds in praise of Christ (drawn from Revelation 5). A balance is thus established between the personal testimony of the participant and recognition of the one responsible for their journey. Verses two and three centre around images of baptism and symbolic cleansing, to such an extent that the song could even be used in conjunction with a baptismal liturgy.

The song is in simple triple metre which, combined with its three verse/chorus structure, creates a strong hymn-like feel. Although possessing a degree of syncopation, the melodic elements also resemble strong hymn-like flavourings.

Returning to Thanksgiving songs, two more contemporary instances are 'Thank You, Thank You For The Blood' (Redman) and 'Thank You' (Pringle). The latter song begins with an evocatively sparse rendition of the song's chorus, with acoustic guitar and synth pad underneath strong yet considered male vocals. The evocative mood is assisted through the falling melody over the IV-V-vi progression:

Figure 7.2: 'Thank You' chorus (excerpt only)

The song goes on to combine appropriate heartfelt thanks with their foundations:

Thank You
For the promises You made
For the gift of life You gave...
For the chance to live again
For Your grace that never ends
Always I will sing Your praise

Unlike the resonate praise of the chorus, the verses are strongly tonally centred, allowing a lightness and ease to the lyrics. This also assists in building to the worshipful chorus. In keeping with the nature of the song, and modern compositional trends, the song contains a bridge that is more a reflection on the relationship between participant and God. There is no need to view such contemplation as being outside the bounds of a Thanksgiving song.

Another Reuben Morgan Testimony song worth discussing is 'My Redeemer Lives'. Given that the song opened the live corporate worship album *By Your Side* it is instructive to note especially the recorded arrangement, as it brings certain nuances to bear and once again showcases the primacy of the recorded text in contemporary congregational song. 'My Redeemer Lives' represents not only an upbeat, feel-good beginning to the album – represented sonically through the cheering and clapping of the congregation – but it also demonstrates the participants' willingness to identify with a testimonial account as the beginning of their corporate worship. A highly syncopated acoustic guitar riff (combined with improvised electric guitar licks) and remaining rhythm section establish a solid rock/funk groove. In the verse and chorus this groove is maintained via a busy syncopated bass riff. The verse's simple I-IV harmonic pattern creates a gospel-inflected sound (furthered through the flattened seventh note), while the chorus utilises a standard I-IV-vi-V progression. The gospel-feel is enhanced by the lyrics, which provide personal testimony of the believer, employing gospel-inflected terms, 'I know He's rescued my soul/His blood has covered my sin', in the process. The chorus is simply 'My redeemer lives' repeated four times, again capturing a gospel flavour through the separated statements and melodic shape.

A feature of this recorded version of the song is a cappella breakdown of the chorus. The vocals (lead, backing and choir) split, with some continuing the chorus melody while others sing another vocal line. While resembling an echo, or call-and-response style, this section is more accurately an unusual example of polyphony within congregational song. Both melodies are rhythmically and melodically independent and do overlap. Accompanying the vocals are tom tom fills, mixed to pan from Left to Right as each bar progresses (simultaneously moving from small to larger toms). There are also syncopated clapping patterns well forward in the mix. Notably these clapping patterns can be heard the world over when this song is performed, another example of the primacy of the recorded text. The overall effect of this section creates an Afro-American (Christian) feel, with the heavy production and arrangement underscoring the worth of the song, and simultaneously the value of participants being where they are, and declaring their collective faith.

2. Looking Ahead and Looking Back

Eschatological

This category of songs, most pointedly those concerned with heaven and/or the return of Christ, appears to have waned somewhat in common collections. While songs with these descriptions do exist, 'Hallelujah Song' (Redman), 'Midnight Cry' (Day and Day) and 'I Can Only Imagine' (Millard) – see analysis below – it remains that there are far less such themed songs. Going back many years, the hymnbook *Golden Bells* (1925) contained numerous songs concerned with heavenly issues. In personal communications some Christian musicians have proposed that modern life in the Western world is far more affluent and enjoyable than previous decades. If so, then Christians' desire to see the return of Christ, or to take their place in heaven immediately, might have diminished. Combine this with modern teaching on the abundant life that can be experienced by the believer, or the general positivism present in many contemporary churches, and it's easy to see why thoughts of the 'end times' have been pushed further back in the collective psyche.

As mentioned, Bart Millard's 'I Can Only Imagine' is a notable exception to the general deficiency in this category. Perhaps the worldwide popularity of this song will see more writers turn their attention to heavenly considerations. Millard, as literally implied in the title, dares to imagine what existing in heaven will be like. The chorus is occupied by genuine questions: 'Will I dance... [or] be still? ...stand... [or] will I fall? Will I sing... [or even] be able to speak at all?' Accentuating these question binaries is an inventive musical technique. For the most part the melody of each question rises the interval of a second on the last word (except one which remains static). This shape mirrors that commonly involved in normal speech, where a rise in pitch is often the marker of inquisition. The chorus concludes with the honest assessment of these ponderings, 'I can only imagine'. The triumph of the song is that it never claims more than it knows, with the only factual occupations of heaven sung about – seeing the face of God and worshipping him forever – being those easily gleaned from Scripture. In conclusion, the song is easy to identify with due to the universality of its lyrical enquiry. It takes little 'imagination' to envisage a variety of possible uses for the song in contemporary corporate worship.

Evangelistic

As songs focused on sharing the Word of God with others for the purpose of conversion, Evangelism songs have a large role to play in many contemporary services. They can be particularly significant in the context of a seeker service. Broadly speaking, songs in this category divide into two easily distinguishable types. The first are songs that encourage Christians to witness to non-Christians, to share the gospel, and basically fulfil the great commission (Matthew 28:18-20). The second branch are those songs directly aimed at non-believers, in order to explain the work of Christ and (ideally) bring them to salvation. This direct approach, with singer(s) addressing non-believers, has a strong heritage in country and western music. Indeed, these versions tend to be far more aggressive in their appeal than modern congregational songs. A great example is the Hank Williams tune, 'Calling You':

> *When you've strayed from the fold*
> *And there's trouble in your soul*
> *Can't you hear the blessed Saviour calling you?*
> *When your soul is lost in sin*
> *And you're at your journey's end*
> *Can't you hear the blessed Saviour calling you?...*
>
> *He will take you by the hand, lead you to that promised land,*
> *Can't you hear the blessed Saviour calling you?*

Williams goes on, verse after verse, to further burden anyone who might have remotely wandered from the path of the Lord. In Williams' teaching the only way to escape the miry bog you might have found yourself in is to hear (perhaps once again) the call of the Lord and follow him. However, Williams' religious compositions merely reflected the 'fire and brimstone' of Southern preaching traditions. Modern Evangelistic songs tend to be a little more delicate in their approach, and often map out the work and person of Jesus, rather than threatening congregants! 'So You Would Come' (Fragar) is an example of such a song.

The classification printed on some copies of the 'So You Would Come' sheet music lists the song as 'an altar call song'. That is, a song written for people who 'don't know God' inviting them to become Christians. Such an event within the modern church service is not uncommon, with 'altar calls' – so named because the congregants literally move forward to the front of the church, the altar[6] – a feature of most gatherings. Commonly they occur towards the conclusion of the service, after the sermon. Quite often instrumental music accompanies the movement of the people to the front of the church. Actually using a song to facilitate this conversion opportunity is rarer nowadays,[7] probably due to a sparsity of these forms of evangelistic songs in the contemporary congregational repertoire.

'So You Would Come' is exceptional because God is not the object of the song, in fact nor are other Christians. The song speaks directly to non-Christians in second person address. It contains a simple gospel presentation which is nonetheless intimate and quite poetic: 'And every tear you cry/Is precious in His eyes'. The dominant lyrical strength, however, lies in the realisation that the impetus for (and success of) salvation is attributable only to God. The summary, 'Everything was done, so you would come', is heightened by the contextual consideration that congregants have been invited to 'come' forward, to represent their spiritual movement physically. The song (as it appears on *All Things Are Possible*) begins with a detailed introduction from leader Darlene Zschech that explores the lyrics of the song and calls people to become Christians, to 'come to God'. The 33-second introduction, which occurs over light electric piano chordal movement, is a solid, impassioned statement of gospel truth. After the introduction the piano takes over, with a noticeable rise in volume and rhythmic consistency. More marked is the audible jump from the live recording, during Zschech's speech, to the studio overdub which begins with the piano introduction, free from the hiss and noise of the live piano sound, combined with remarkably clean, clear vocals from Zschech. Well crafted in terms of the song's intent, the production keeps the vocals well clear of the band, even foregrounded well above any band swells. Melodically the verse contains leaps of fifths and sixths, combined with complex rhythmic movement. The inclusion of these elements points to the 'performance' nature of the song that, while intended for the corporate worship setting, is designed to be performed *for* the congregation rather than *by* them. 'So You Would Come' represents perhaps the most competent, comprehensive example of the Evangelistic song within the genre of contemporary congregational music.

The other type of Evangelistic song is that which seeks to motivate the congregation into evangelising and witnessing to the world around them. The aptly named 'Tell The World' (Douglass, Houston and Sampson) does just that. While the verse contains testimonial ideas, largely reflecting on the participant's dedication to live a life worthy of the calling they have received, the chorus, however, switches to the third person when it states:

> Tell the world that Jesus lives
> Tell the world that
> Tell the world that
> Tell the world that He died for them
> Tell the world that He lives again

The bridge returns to a second person address, enjoining Jesus himself in the mission: 'Come on, come on, we'll tell the world about You'. What is striking about the recorded version of the song is the powerful rhythm (created through punchy drum rhythms and driving – heavily distorted – electric guitars). Combine this with deep male vocals and the song generates a momentum that serves well the purpose of the song. Furthermore, the personally contemplative verse and bridge are almost entirely (but for one bar) constructed over chord vi, thus the arrival of the chorus with its tonally strong I-V-vi-IV progression only enhances the message being proclaimed. Breakdown sections, mainly the bridge, with prominent audience clapping and repeated sloganistic phrases, further the unified commitment being sung about.

A slight modification to standard Evangelistic song modes is to sing enthusiastically about receiving Christ, and then 'question' the audience about where they stand. 'Can't Stop Talking', another Russell Fragar composition, uses exactly this technique. A fast-paced song (152 bpm) with an elaborate melodic riff as an introduction, 'Can't Stop Talking' is actually climaxed by a bridge section, featuring a particularly grainy male vocal which addresses the audience with simple crotchet-based questions. These questions, 'Do you know Him?', are answered by the female backing vocalists, 'Yes, I do'. As such, the bridge provides a strong evangelistic and motivational element. This is underscored by electric guitar accompaniment, a sliding bass on the first beat, and the gradual introduction of the full band with brass lines and an increasingly improvisatory bass line. This builds into a return of the chorus, pre-empted by a rock and roll styled 'Hey, hey, hey' from the choir. The chorus is underscored by a funk-blues harmony (I^7-^{b}VII-$IV^{6/3}$) and introduces flattened thirds and sevenths into the melody. A strong double crotchet at the start of the phrase gives power to the words 'Can't stop' and 'best thing'. Overall the extreme groove of the song, and clever lyrical construction, make for a convincing celebration of being in relationship with Jesus.

Credal
As has been noted elsewhere, Credal songs can easily fall into other categories based on their functionality. Given that these songs involve statements of biblical truth, and more often than not, direct transcriptions of Bible passages, they can actually fall into a variety of themed areas. Holiness and Salvation songs can often have secondary Credal themes. What is important in any catalogue is making sure that Credal songs are represented. The modern church will soon suffer if it neglects to sing the Scriptures. One Australian publisher almost solely devoted to this song-type is EMU Music. EMU's mission statement is to: 'Provide churches with songs of the Word – being biblical, Christ focused and contemporary' (http://emu.mu/about/, accessed 24 January 2006). Although some of their music has been criticised for being too literal, and consequently less poetic and musical than is desired, at least there is one organisation dedicated to constantly delivering this area of con-

gregational song. EMU Music's executive director's own composition, 'We Are His People' (Percival), supplies enough example of the lyrical concerns of the organisation. The chorus reads:

> *By grace we are saved*
> *Through faith, not from us but*
> *God – not our words or boasting*

which is almost a direct quotation of Ephesians 2:8-9 and indicative of the Scriptural accuracy of EMU Music songs.

'Holy One Of God' (Bullock) is in essence a series of biblical truths about Christ, written in third person reference, without any formal point of view. In this way it reflects the heavenly worship described in Revelation 4–5. Its Credal nature is confirmed by its biblical quotations (John 1:29; Mark 1:24; 1 Corinthians 15:54; Isaiah 9:9; Revelation 5:12). The song is divided into two sections, marked by a written key change from E major to A minor. Two female vocalists take the lead in section one with a male singing in the background. Yet in section two the male vocal takes over, adding brawn to the powerful lyrics, 'Suffered hell and death... Death is swallowed up in victory'. Throughout the song the grain of the voice is unusually prominent, with respiration, vocal cavity and physical mouth noises adding bodily accentuation. Such techniques increase the space of the enunciation and therefore the power of the vocality (Evans, 2000; 2001). Further enhancing this earthy organic sound is the lead guitar which plays high-pitched squealing, sliding notes deep in the mix, replicating a groaning, painful physicality underneath lyrics such as, 'Rejected and despised/Suffered crucified'. Rather than destabilising the piece, a loose tonal centre, particularly in the second section, contributes to the exultant, revelatory intent of the song.

Judgement

It is concerning that no songs declaring the judgement of God could be found in this survey. While some songs do make passing reference to the wrath of God, there was no song with a detailed focus on Judgement. Now to be sure this is not the most uplifting topic to sing about – but it is a major theme of the Bible. To ignore it is to pick and choose our theology. As with Eschatology songs, hymns dealing with the judgement of God were a common feature of older hymnbooks. The 'fear of the Lord' was often the source of musical deliberation, with a strong rhythm and urging organ the perfect accompaniment. The performing media may have changed in many churches but the ability to deal with challenging topics has not. Again it might be the positivism emanating from largely Pentecostal churches (but filtering into traditional mainstream denominations) that has contributed to this poverty of Judgement songs. Either way our theology is lacking if we ignore any of the characteristics of God.

'Feminising' Congregational Song

The following section moves out of song-type analysis, into a broader critique of a perceivable trend in contemporary congregational song. It is not an area popularly dealt with, and not one broached lightly. To be fair, the subject is far too dense to be adequately dealt with here. But to ignore it would be to limit the future opportunities for dialogue and analysis. And whether we are comfortable with discourse on the subject is irrelevant. The fact remains, that in researching this volume, a common complaint/observation/concern from practitioners and participants alike was that much modern song was somehow 'feminine' in construction. Such a notion raises considerable debates that continue to unfold within popular music studies. The following ruminations do not masquerade as the definitive answer – or even an answer at all – but rather bring the issue into public debate for further scrutiny. The more we dissect modern song to ensure it is serving the best purposes for the majority of believers the better.

Sophie Drinker (1995) argues that: '[Women] have been spiritually starved... by the long tradition of the Church, and by the requirement that, in matters of the spirit, they accept men's formulations and men's music' (262). In contrast, one of the most dominant discourses within contemporary churches is that the 'new' music used in corporate worship has become, in some way, feminised. This feminisation, it is argued, occurs not only through songwriting and performance but is also somehow inherent within the music itself. To this end, many male Christian organisations (especially prison ministries, for example) have complained that contemporary congregational music is unusable in their context. In preliminary interviews for this book, many males confirmed a sense of isolation or inadequacy being created in their worship due to this 'gendering' of the music. Colloquially within the Church, songs of this ilk are known as 'Jesus is my girlfriend' songs. In one sense this colloquial understanding might be viewed as a continuation of nineteenth-century trends (noted in Chapter 2) that saw feminine 'overtones of sexuality and sentimentality' (Balmer, 1999: 35) emerge in evangelical music.

The possibility that music, particularly instrumental music, can somehow be gendered is both a contentious and vibrant area of discussion. Still the most seminal work remains Marcia Citron's (2000) investigation of gendered sonata form – notably that pertaining to Cecile Chaminade. As she usefully notes, however, 'This analysis is an exploration of possibility... It is not intended as an explanation of everything that goes on musically... To a great extent, of course, these are matters of judgement' (145). Yet, as the oft-cited McClary and Walser (1990) note, if we are to analyse the fullness of popular music experience we must 'bring one's own experience as a human being to bear in unpacking musical gestures, to try and parallel in words something of how the music feels' (288–89). As one who has both studied and *felt* this music, and spoken with many more also involved in its production and reception, I would encourage future researchers to engage with such a sentiment.

The historical exclusion of women from the creative power in the Church has been well documented (Citron 2000: 143). Yet as Drinker (1995) notes, without the feminine, 'Christian art would have lacked much of its beauty. Without the alleluia, triumphant cry of women's ancient rites, Christian music would have been deprived of its most gracious song' (153):

> *Early Christian annals are filled with references to the participation of women in music. The leaders clearly wish to utilize this musical talent to further Christian ideals* (ibid.: 159).

Both the Roman historian Pliny and first-century Jewish scholar Philo report the involvement of women in songs of the church (ibid.: 158–59). This continued throughout the fourth and fifth centuries, testified to by the likes of St Ambrose of Milan (ibid.: 160). Such freedom, though, was steadily outlawed from the middle of the fourth century onwards. Due to the association of prostitutes with musical instruments, female performance on them was forbidden (ibid.: 178). Ultimately, the involvement of women in congregational singing was also forbidden, 'even when they were in church with their families' (ibid.: 179).

This brief history is presented to show that female involvement in congregational song has swung wildly throughout the ages. From huge involvement in the early church; to prohibition; to the current state where women increasingly occupy key positions in the production and propagation of liturgical-based musics, the female creative input has in no way been a steady involvement, and has exhibited pendulum type association – due mainly to the edicts of male Church governorship. Complicating even this aspect of the argument is whether or not the level of female involvement in performance and/or production of congregational song influences the 'feel' of the music anyway.

But how different are modern songs in expressing a sentimentality and relational focus from those that have come before? 'Just Let Me Say', a classic Geoff Bullock composition, features constant dedications of love, which form the lyrical motif for the song and are perceived by some as being 'feminine'. Indeed, the opening line is an example: 'Just let me say how much I love You'. It is fair to say that similar sentiments exist in many well-loved hymns, 'I Need Thee O I Need Thee' (Hawks and Lowry) and 'I've Found A Friend, O Such A Friend' (Small and Stebbins), for example. Perhaps timbre and performance of modern songs places greater sentimentality on them than previous hymns. Certainly the context in which they are utilised is all important.

In thinking about lyrics one must remember that 'language [is] inseparable from its emotive context, in the social exchange between performer and listener. A song's metaphorical connotations lie not in its words alone' (Nehring, 1997: 141). Citing Greil Marcus, Nehring notes: 'More often it is the music, or a phrase, or two words heard, jumping out as the rest are lost, that seem to fit one's emotional perception of a situation, event, or idea. A pattern of notes or the way in which a few words happen to fit together hit a chord... "Message", in music, isn't meaning alone' (Marcus, cited in Nehring, 1997: 142). While Marcus was referring more specifically in this instance to rock and punk songs where the distinct delineation of words being sung is not always attainable, the notion of emotional affectivity, as a force the listener is required to process, is important in the current discussion. Clear pronunciation and heightened production of lyrics are markers of congregational song, thus rather than snatching at words here and there, consumers are free to experience the full emotional impact portrayed in the musical construction. As Nehring (1997) points out, such emotional impact is crucial to our experience of music, and should be part of our analysis of it. While I am not equating emotive aspects of music with femininity, I am suggesting that certain emotional qualities of contemporary congregational song are produced, and are perhaps being consumed, as feminine.

One popular aberration to the soft textures often associated with feminised congregational song is Tim Hughes' song 'Beautiful One'.[8] Sung throughout the Western Church, Hughes' song features extremely poignant and tender lyrics:

> *Beautiful one I love you*
> *Beautiful one I adore*
> *Beautiful one my soul must sing*

yet offsets these with strong textural elements. The strong guitar introduction strips back to arpeggiated accompaniment with the onset of lead male vocals that contain a rather masculine grain, along with strong rock accents in the drums.

Despite the timbral strength contained within elements of the arrangement, the piece repeatedly strips back to a sparse density, only to be propelled in the chorus through heavy drums, bar chord electric guitars and piano over the higher registers. Despite the strength in the chorus and the stronger rhythmic presence through this section, and heavy rock accents in earlier verses, the lyrics draw the song back more intrinsically to love song forms and sentiments. 'Beautiful One' is a good example of using textural elements to counterbalance the sentimentality of the lyrics. More importantly, perhaps, it represents a song with strong feminine traits that is composed and performed by one of the world's leading (male) congregational song practitioners.

Harmonically speaking, so-called 'female movements' of works, according to Citron (2000), are more tonally disruptive, longing for a return to the masculine harmonic strength (139). It is common in contemporary congregational song to have a bridge or middle section that possibly equates to the development section of the sonata form. Often a repeated section, this bridge is regularly removed from the tonal centre of the song; is extremely 'personal' in lyrical nature; and more often than not is repeated extensively. There may well be a correlation between these reflective, emotionally concentrated sections and particular feminine ideologies.

One of the strongest arguments against a perceived feminisation of congregational song revolves around the songwriters, the vast majority of whom are male. That said:

> Composition itself is basically a technical discipline whose language is available to men and women alike; an interval or a chord is not inherently gendered... There is no style that issues from inherent traits in female biology. It cannot be claimed that every female composer writes in a style that all women composers utilize, that is unmistakeably their own, and that cannot be found in works by men (Citron, 2000: 159).

There is, then, much in this area that warrants future investigation. A qualitative study on the male composers of Intimacy/Relational songs (especially those perceived to be feminine in nature) might be a useful starting point.

What does it matter if congregational song is in some way gendered feminine in current manifestations? Is it even a problem worth addressing? Well, perhaps for the majority of the Christian population presumably the answer is 'no, not really'. Yet we return here to notions of vernacular music. For if congregational song is to represent the immediate lived experience of its participants, it must be able to speak for all members of the constituency, which in this case involves not only males, but males from all spheres of life. One danger is that the current proliferation of 'gendered' worship music is merely an outgrowth of certain cultural factors (Citron, 2000: 160). If so, these cultural factors – which one would have to inevitably tie to the Pentecostal Church – are not indicative of the entire Christian body of believers and may well inhibit future works of the Church. Sara Cohen has examined how rock as a genre is 'produced as male through the everyday activities that comprise the scene; through the sensual, emotional aspects of the scene; and through the systems of ideas that inform the scene, including the contested concept of "scene" itself' (Cohen, 1997: 17–18). Likewise the sensual, emotional aspects of the Pentecostal corporate worship experience may be driving a necessary feminisation of the music mandatory in such an environment.

8 Conclusion: 'When the Music Fades'

In the introduction to *Open Up the Doors* I noted that the book was concerned with placing contemporary congregational song firmly within the realm of vernacular music studies, and popular music studies more generally. The goal was to expose the modern music of the Church to academic enquiry and observe its evolution, in style and message, and the practical contexts in which it is being produced. That is, to examine both the message and the medium of transmission; its function and form. Some of the more general trends of modern church music are identified later in this conclusion. But it would seem to me there are several key areas to be considered by those working in, caring about, learning about, or simply enjoying, congregational music.

1. Imagination and Variation

The early years of the twenty-first century would appear to mark the end of a progressive but comfortable cycle of congregational music. And I say this rather prophetically, or at least optimistically. For this has not quite happened yet, but it certainly needs to. If congregational music is going to impact the world outside the doors of the church, and greater impact the lives of those inside, then the time has come to break through tried and true – and tired – musical forms. As was noted in Chapter 2, the greatest danger an artform faces is an attitude that says, 'More of the same, as much as you can' (Routley, 1977: 66). To that end, continuing to produce the current glut of what I'll label, 'not-quite-middle-of-the-road soft pop, with reverb', is neither wise nor acceptable.

Frost and Hirsch note that 'imagination takes courage, as it involves risk' (2003: 189). The time has come for this risk-taking, to step out in faith and move congregational song beyond the doors we have placed around it. For some producers this will involve enormous financial risk. Yet the consequence of non-action could be the steady demise and depleted influence of modern church music. The risk might be losing congregation members – those who don't want to stray from what they have always known. It's very conceivable to imagine a church in ten years that doesn't want to cease singing the standard binary form 'choruses' they have always known. Such an insulated attitude will ultimately insulate the Church from the world. If I'm correct in assuming that heaven isn't full yet then such an elitist, resistant attitude seems pointless.

There are so many musical genres available today, an almost exponentially expanding world of musical opportunities. We must be willing to experiment with new musical forms and new timbres. I am aware that pockets of the Church are already utilising dance rhythms, or sampled loops, or digital effects, or punk rock, or hip hop beats and rhymes, but these remain exceptional cases. These courageous risks need to occur in mainstream denominations and churches. Not all of them will be successful, which is why objective analysis and understanding will become ever more crucial to those working with arts in the Church. There are debates, arguments and impassioned opinions now – and the music being produced is hardly that offensive.

'The contemporary traditional church is increasingly seen as the least likely option for those seeking an artistic, politically subversive, activist community of mystical faith' (Frost and Hirsch, 2003: 6). Imagine if this were not the case. Re-imagine a Church that is at the forefront of music culture, pushing musical boundaries, giving expression to the joys, fears, trials and salvation of its members. A Church that survived the transition from the traditional to the contemporary, and moved bravely into the avant garde. Perhaps this, at the very least, needs to be the dream.

Missional Focus
Part of what is being discussed here, in terms of music cultures anyway, is a 'missional' church (Frost and Hirsch, 2003). Part of the objective of the missional church is to exist within the world, to, in a way, become part of the world. The missional church is at once *in* the church but not *of* the church. Clearly the evangelistic opportunities of such a church, in moving away from a model where you simply seek to attract people to your services – and to your music – to one where the music is created in the midst of the world, perhaps with the help of the non-churched, are enormous. Similar ideas have entered the imaginations of musicians through the centuries. Much of the great Renaissance and Baroque art music was designed solely to bring glory to God, despite its secular settings. Perhaps hymn-writer John Wesley best expressed it:

> *When it is reasonable to sing praise to GOD they do it with the spirit and with the understanding also; not in the miserable, scandalous doggerel of Hopkins and Sternhold, but in psalms and hymns which are both sense and poetry, such as would sooner dispose a critic to turn a Christian than a Christian to turn critic* (quoted in Marshall and Todd, 1982: 60).

This is, in part, the striving of the church songwriter; to produce sense and poetry, truth and art, that so compels the soul as to turn them towards the things of God. What is most insightful here is that Wesley derides another tradition – an accepted musical practice – in favour of that which excites and convicts. Rather than being bound to sameness for sameness' sake, he longs for innovative song that turns the hearts of critics. We face a constant battle to ensure that contemporary congregational song does not turn hearts the other way; as Wesley put it, turn Christians into critics of the faith:

> We believe that the missional church will be adventurous, playful and surprising... It will gather for sensual-experiential-participatory worship and be deeply concerned for matters of justice-seeking and mercy-bringing (Frost and Hirsch, 2003: 22).

Herein lies one of the great challenges to modern churches, let alone those seeking to be missional in approach. Carson (1992), Volf (1992) and others have long touted the importance of 'action' within our corporate worship; of the need to practise those truths and concepts so often revealed during both private and corporate worship. It is imperative that as a body of believers we remain 'deeply concerned' for justice and social action. Around the world we have unfortunately come to realise that, politically, being 'deeply concerned' about something doesn't really amount to anything. The Church must be different. Church arts must be different. We must reflect a social action both in theme and in practice. In the music surveyed for this volume, the greatest absence occurred in Social Justice songs and Judgement songs. While the latter (song-type) title may sound a little sinister, it is only really connected to songs concerned with justice at their core. Why is the modern Church not writing songs that concern these practical outworkings of faith? Many churches are heavily involved in social welfare, healthcare, legal rights and other pastoral issues, but our art, in particular our congregational song, should reflect this also. If not only to remind congregants, then also to make bold declarations to the world about the Church's love for the lost and disenfranchised.

Increased Understanding of Functionality and Context
Throughout all the analysis presented in *Open Up the Doors* I have tried to stress the importance of dealing with contextual forces that have led to the text in question. These forces are many and varied. They may include the denominational history of the church involved; equipment and financial resources – particularly where production discourses are concerned; personnel; the social climate at the time of writing/recording; the body of work preceding the song in question; commercial imperatives; or audience expec-

tations. Congregational song is produced in the midst of these, and many more, forces that influence the text. Perhaps the greatest artery feeding congregational song is the scriptural element. Some have argued that, due to the primacy of the Word within congregational song, only those trained in theology should compose congregational works. I disagree with such a contention. Undoubtedly biblical knowledge is crucial, but so is experience of faith, grace, forgiveness, salvation, sin, etc., and fortunately it is not only the biblical scholar who has experience in these. Furthermore, songwriting remains an artform; one to be practised by those gifted (and perhaps trained) in it. Consequently there is substantial pressure on writers of modern church music to ensure they are biblically equipped. Moreover, they must be aware of the theological climate in which they compose. Andrew Ford notes:

> *Music in the medieval church was a way of presenting scripture and liturgy as clearly and memorably as possible. In the beginning was the word. A lot of modern Christian music is far more concerned with establishing mood. But in terms of music fashions, the question remains the same as ever. Is music responding to theology, or is it the other way round?* (Ford, 'Music and Fashion: Heaven on Earth', ABC Radio, 24 July 2005).

In answering Ford's question songwriters must remain objective in their analysis of what personal factors are contributing to the song's evolution. They must put their lyrical convictions through Scriptural tests. As theomusicological scholars we must try to remain objective in our assessment of various songs and liturgies used to support them, and not just view words on the page in isolation. Congregational song finds itself in transition, on the cusp of greater relevance and impact. It needs to look objectively at itself, as a genre within the broad gamut of popular music today, and re-evaluate the ways in which it seeks to serve those within, and those outside, the doors.

More Localisation
Another area that needs to be on the agenda of theomusicologists is the disappearance of the 'local' within congregational song. Like a giant, global sausage machine, modern congregational song producers are running their material through the funnel of global acceptance. Obviously there are huge economic benefits to producing a music that is acceptable and popular the world over. But there are opportunity costs to this 'transglobal' mentality. The 'McDonaldisation' of congregational song is not going to be the best thing for local congregations battling with specific issues, or celebrating a particular, Spirit-inspired revival.

John Newton wrote of his own 'hope [that] most of these Hymns, being the fruit and expression of my own experience, will coincide with the views of real Christians of all denominations' (quoted in Marshall and Todd, 1982: 91). This was not a marketing ploy for world domination, simply a hope that his theology was in line with that of reformed Britain. There is in modern church music a need to differentiate between the universal and the idiosyncratic. The former is well and truly represented in the current repertoire of the Church. Indeed it is a significant contributor to a global Christian unity, even a partially ecumenical unity, among Christian churches in the Western world. It is the latter, the individual nuances of denominations, churches, revivals, missions or other strategies, that are being lost. We have become consumed with the idea of producing a music that will be acceptable, and perhaps profitable, on the world stage. As a result the individual needs and desires of local churches are not being met by their artists. There are few things more powerful than songs written out of the teaching *of* a local church, *for* that local church. There is a difference between Newton's hope and a lowest common denominator mentality.

This transglobal acceptance is perhaps best realised in Canada and Australia, which both seek to establish vibrant congregation music in the face of North American precedents and imports. John Foote notes that:

> From a societal perspective, an underlying consideration in Canadian audience research is the question of delivery and consumption of massive quantities of foreign (particularly American) content, and the implications of this for Canadian society and values (2002: n.p.).

But this is only one side of the equation. Not only is there a massive foreign music consumption level for those countries whose music industries (across all genres) operate in the shadow of the North American, there is also the more concerning realisation that texts being produced in these countries seek only to replicate their American counterparts. By seeking to produce music that is acceptable to an American market, the local inflections and peculiarities are lost. No single group of songs, no matter how popular globally, can reach all the needs of individual churches. This is why local songs, specific to congregations perhaps, are necessary. This is not always an option for smaller congregations or churches, but in those instances one would hope someone at a denomination level is being assisted to provide music that serves its members.

While Hillsong senior pastor Brian Houston may state: 'I clearly want our church to stay [Australian], not to be too impacted by American culture' (Brian Houston, 'Australian Story', ABC TV, 1 August 2005), the music being produced by his church no longer speaks exclusively to an Australian sensibility. Gone are all 'Great Southland' style songs, and calls for national revival, replaced instead with the opening cry of the title song of the album *People Just Like Us*, 'All over the world people just like us/Are following Jesus'. Indeed the promotional material for that album spelled out even more clearly its objective: 'This album is an expression of the worldwide ministry of His dynamic church'. Given the sheer number of Australian churches and songwriters aping those from Hillsong, it quickly becomes apparent how individual nationalistic idiosyncrasies can disappear. Yet once again we must remember that the local context produces the song-text. For instance, Darlene Zschech alluded to Hillsong's local and national influence in an interview in 2001:

> *In the last 12 months the Church is becoming stronger, we are really starting to take our place as a Church in our community. And that is reflected in the songs we are writing.*[1]

Given this kind of awareness, it would be unfortunate if those songs produced did not speak openly and transparently to the contexts in which they were birthed.

A similar phenomenon has occurred in Canada where '[m]any Pentecostal churches now view [Toronto's] Airport Vineyard-style worship as the only legitimate worship... Their focus of energy is to replicate it in their churches' (Careless, 1999: n.p.). This would be fine were Airport constructing corporate worship tools designed to specifically reach the Canadian psyche. However, although they are the largest producer of congregational music in Canada, much of their music is simply Vineyard music from below the border recorded in Toronto or given an international gloss to serve the Vineyard church the world over. As with mainstream Australian congregational song, Canadian congregational music examined for this volume revealed very little sense of a nationalistic focus. Only one Vineyard song even mentioned Canada, and then only as part of a longer list of countries and continents. More troubling perhaps for the Canadian church is the wholesale adoption of Australian and US music. As Posterski and Grenville note:

> *Canadians often look to America [and I would add Australia] for models of effective ministry. We think they have the answers. We forget the questions may be different. Given the clear differences between the faith experiences of the two countries, it is clear the challenge of encouraging Canadians to integrate Church and faith demands a 'made in Canada' solution. The challenges are here. So are the solutions* (quoted in Bibby, 2004: 5).

This insightful observation should resonate throughout many countries. The challenges facing churches are not always those facing the Church. Thus a globalised song culture is not always going to be that which is required by local churches. In the Canadian example, as a minimum there is the need to combine the use of non-Canadian resources with a thorough and clear reading of Canadian culture and Canadian religious developments (Bibby, 2004: 5).

Returning to one of the key theses of this book, if people are involved in a corporate gathering, and share music as part of that, then the vernacular experience of that music can only be achieved with like communities of people taking part in the music production. Johnson's (1998) notions of vernacular music (discussed in Chapter 1) outline the necessary relationship music must have with the conditions of production and consumption, and 'their relationship to the community that produces them' (8). The music must close the gap between producer and consumer, enabling the audience to participate in the production of the music.

2. General Congregational Song Trends

Scrutinising the analytical statistics, revealed via the analysis of material for this book (see Appendix for a complete breakdown of elements), highlights some important trends and developments in congregational song composition.

Looking initially at the average word length, it could be argued that congregational song has become progressively wordier. While this varies from album to album, and songwriter to songwriter, there is nonetheless a discernible rise in word lengths. The negative perhaps is that these rises are quite minimal. The average word length across all songs surveyed was ninety-eight words per song. This figure at least provides a benchmark by which future songs and trends can be measured.

The dominant Godhead reference employed throughout the survey was 'Lord' (occurring in 49.6 per cent of all songs). God was the next most prevalent title, averaging 41.7 per cent, while Christ was named in 37.6 per cent of songs. When references to 'Lord' and God fell, references to Christ tended to increase. There is no direct reference made to the Godhead in approximately 14 per cent of songs.

There are two ways of viewing this lack of direct reference in the repertoire of congregational song. The first, outlined in Chapter 4, is representative of a creeping secularisation. This might be perceived as a danger for the contemporary church. For when the songs of the Church cease to sing about God they will become mere social and personal commentary. Clearly this is not the

case at this point in history, and what is important in corporate worship programmes is a balance between praise of God and personal response to that
praise. Frost extols the second possible paradigm, noting that:

> Hebrew people don't make the distinction between secular and sacred,
> they talk about the holy and the not-yet-holy. So anything can be holy
> to the degree to which we [Christians] take it over and see the degree to
> which it reflects God's design or God's grace. If you take a song, for exam-
> ple, that doesn't mention God or faith but affirms justice, then we can
> make that holy by the degree to which we see it as faith enlarging. There is
> a distinction between that – what the Hebrews do – and what Christians
> do, which is often to make the arrow more pointy, to preach Jesus in some
> way (interview with the author, 2002).

This process involves far more risk and negotiation on behalf of the Church
and its members; a process of being in the world but not of the world. Yet
this is exactly the process major congregational song producers and the huge
Contemporary Christian Music (CCM) industry are involved in. They take the
music of the secular culture and 'redeem' it, by bringing it into the Church and
giving it holy meanings and functions.

Fischer (1994) identifies a precarious balance at work in this secularisation:

> God has always preferred to put his messages at odds with the world. More
> often than not, he slants his messages counter-culturally. He works against
> the grain... Jesus stood both inside and outside of culture. This ability of
> the gospel to transform as well as transcend – to stand outside of culture
> as well as inside – is the aspect of the gospel that our present contemporary
> efforts lack (52–53).

Fischer contends that the CCM industry, as well as congregational song more
generally, is too entrenched 'in' the world to be successful in leading anyone
'out' of it. This may be too extreme a position, yet the importance of the negotiation between resistance and accommodation cannot be overstated. How
successful this process of negotiation will be, for both the CCM and congregational music, remains to be seen. Worthy of further investigation, it certainly
marks a bold attempt to secularise the sacred for the purpose of redeeming
(or re-sacralising) vast quarters of secular culture and the people who inhabit
them.

Diversity
Alarm at the lack of diversity in congregational song is growing. Hamilton, for
instance, notes that:

It is fruitless to search for a single musical style, or even a blend of musical styles, that can assist all Christians with true worship. The followers of Jesus are a far too diverse group of people – which is exactly how it should be. We need, rather, to welcome any worship music that helps churches produce disciples of Jesus Christ. We need to welcome the experimental creativity that is always searching out new ways of singing the gospel, and banish the fear that grips us when familiar music passes away. For this kind of change is the mark of a living church – the church of a living God, who restlessly ranges back and forth across the face of the Earth seeking out any who respond to his voice (Hamilton, 1999: 33).

Two important points are presented here. Firstly, it is important that any music considered helpful to the people of God in their collective worship of him be welcomed into the contemporary church. Churches that cordon off their music programmes to that which is tried and tested risk encasing themselves in an irrelevant, inwardly focused, alienated culture. This is not supported by Christ's call to his people to go *into* the world. The second point raised by Hamilton is that the modern Church needs to embrace experimental creativity that seeks to tell the gospel story.

The danger looming for congregational song songwriters and producers is that if they continue to conform to similar, safe compositional techniques, and allow their music to be typecast into fairly narrow stylistic bands, then they will be historically stereotyped as representing a single musical idiom. A diet that consists of only one food type will ultimately become destructive. Likewise, as historical contexts have shown (Chapter 2), any Christian group that seeks to subsist on a limited diet of congregational song will ultimately be deprived of many new and fresh aspects integral to the Christian journey.

Musical Trends

We have definitely seen the parameters of what has always been acceptable church music be stretched and enlarged to accommodate the generations coming through (Zschech, interview with the author, 2002).

A number of musical trends have become evident in relation to the material studied in this volume. Firstly, music has generally increased in tempo over the past decade, songs becoming more rhythmically complex, incorporating greater syncopation and funk elements. Most songs conform neatly to pop, rock, funk, or funk-rock stylings, yet the prevalence of off-beat rhythms has undoubtedly already pushed some music beyond the capacity of average church musicians. Faulkner's assertions about the rhythmic qualities of congregational song becoming increasingly 'propulsive, syncopated and rhythmically vivacious' (1996: 193) would appear valid. This trend towards rhythmic complexity has also been attributed more specifically to Pentecostal tendencies: 'While the words [of Pentecostal music] may be simple and frequently repeated, the rhythms may be very complex compared with those in the hymns used in other denominations' (Hughes, 1996: 16).

What has not become more rhythmically adventurous is the diversity in metre. More than 90 per cent of congregational song is written in simple quadruple time, echoing the common rhythmic groupings of popular music. A greater reliance on other time signatures, particularly those drawn from non-Western music, would only enhance the power of congregational song to reach differing groups of people.

Vocal ranges vary according to the songwriter, with vocalist/songwriters more disposed towards wider ranges in their work. Where ranges are small, the chorus is often pitched higher than the verse to compensate. Most melodies remain conjunctive, necessitating in many a greater range to enable musical variety and sustainability.

3. The Heart of Contemporary Congregational Song

In 1997, Matt Redman wrote a song entitled 'The Heart Of Worship', a song that could, potentially, refocus the corporate worship culture of the Western Church. Due to the time lag involved in the adoption of congregational song, the song has only begun to be heavily utilised and recognised since 2000. By late 2002, 'Heart Of Worship' had registered on the CCLI Top-25 congregational charts in Canada, USA and the UK. These countries represent a more developed – or at least historically extended – worship culture. Those countries (including Australia) with a more recent acceptance of, and involvement with, contemporary worship styles, are yet to be drawn in by the lyrical sentiment expressed in the song. Redman's pastor at Soul Survivor, Watford (UK), Mike Pilavachi, explained that 'Heart Of Worship' was written after a period of immense challenge and self-examination. The church, which had grown in a similar fashion to Hillsong Church, was (arguably) at the forefront of corporate worship in the UK. They had a brand new building, state-of-the-art sound and lighting, renowned musicians and songwriters, and links with huge summer worship festivals held around the UK (which later spread internationally). Yet the church had made the act of corporate worship itself the object of their worship: 'We seemed to be going through the motions but I noticed that although we were singing the songs, our hearts were far from him [God]' (Pilavachi, 2000).[2] Fischer has also noted this development in North American churches as a social by-product of the individualistic baby-boomers:

The 'me' decade of the '80s has rolled over into the church. Instead of coming before God in humility and fear, grateful for the breath to honor and serve him, we are more likely to come before him now to be blessed – to have our current desires bestowed upon us and to praise him on the basis of what we will receive in return (1994: 9).

In a remarkable step for a church of its size and reputation, Pilavachi dispensed with the band. He challenged the congregation to think about what they were *bringing* to corporate worship every time they walked through the door. For a while, the church meetings were stifled and uncomfortable – and largely silent. But a change began to exert itself in the understanding of the congregation, and in their heart for worship: 'The truth came to us: worship is not a spectator sport, it is not a product moulded by the taste of the consumers. It is not about what we can get out of it; it is all about God' (ibid.).

Out of this refinement and fresh understanding of corporate worship – and the state it had deteriorated to – Redman penned the song 'The Heart Of Worship'. For him it was evidence that the 'songs of our hearts had caught up with the songs of our lips' (Redman, 2001: 78). While the confessional element of the song is quite apparent, it is the implied commentary on tangential corporate worship that has most deeply affected other churches:

> *When the music fades*
> *All is stripped away,*
> *And I simply come.*
> *Longing just to bring,*
> *Something that's of worth,*
> *That will bless your heart...*
>
> *I'm coming back to the heart of worship*
> *And it's all about You,*
> *All about You, Jesus.*
> *I'm sorry Lord for the thing I've made it,*
> *When it's all about You,*
> *All about You, Jesus.*[3]

Churches that connect with Redman's song are those who feel they too have strayed from the true purpose of worship. Perhaps one day churches like Hillsong will feel the need to pen their own 'Heart Of Worship', but for now such an acknowledgement does not fit the vision. Instead Zschech feels:

a great responsibility to make sure our worship team and all it represents...
[is] *operating in truth, and with great passion and commitment. Once you*
are not feeling the pressure to 'perform' for others or when you become secure
enough in who you are in Christ, your inner desire becomes much more
about making His church glorious (interview with the author, 2002).

Congregational song and the corporate worship culture it is part of has become many things. In some circles it has become an industry, which can be 'extremely unhealthy, because industry and market and business and pride and ego and money all fly in the face of what worship really is' (Michelle Kay, interview with the author, 2002). In other places it is a performance practice akin to any other amateur cultural group, and in still others it has become a purely experiential, feel-good focal point for the soul. These shortcomings aside, there is much in the contemporary church culture to be lauded. As people the world over mourn the tragedy of increasingly frequent and senseless terrorist attacks it becomes more pointed than ever that vernacular music, particularly congregational song, and the corporate structures that house it, possesses a power to unify, heal, express emotion and provide hope.

A degree of scrutiny with regards to congregational song will always be valid given its ability to subtly transform both the theology of the Church and its relationship to the world around it. Yet all the intellectualising, analysis and philosophical tropes in the world cannot replace the fact that, while humans may consider only the outward appearance, God looks at the heart (1 Samuel 16:7). If the Church is to remain authentic in their worship, Christians will need to remember this, and be constantly seeking to shape their own hearts into a heart of worship.

Appendix:
Song Classification and Analysis

Song	Songwriter	Type (primary)	Type (2nd)	Address	POV	Words	Lord	Jesus	HS	God	Tempo	Time	Verse range	Ch range
Above All	Leblanc	Salvation		2nd	Individual	88	No	No	No	No	67	Quadruple	m7	8ve
All For Love	Fieldes	Intim/Relational	Salvation	2nd	Individual	115	Yes	No	No	No	67	Quadruple	m7th	M6th
All I Do	'Galanti, Bedingfield'	Testimony		2nd	Individual	113	Yes	No	No	No	142	Quadruple	m7	5th
All of My Days	Stevens	Trans/Dedication	Holiness	2nd	Both	91	No	No	No	No	82	Quadruple	m6	5th
All The Heavens	Morgan	Holiness		2nd	Plural	57	Yes	No	No	Yes	67	Quadruple	m7	m7
All Things Are Possible	Zschech	Salvation	Intim/Relational	2nd	Individual	129	Yes	Yes	No	Yes	120	Quadruple	7th	6th
And That My Soul Knows Very Well	Fragar/Zschech	Intim/Relational		2nd	Individual	80	No	No	No	No	81	Quadruple	6th	6th
Angels	Sampson	Salvation		3rd	None	77	Yes	Yes	Yes	Yes	110	Triple	m7	M6
Awesome In This Place	Davies	Body Unity	Intim/Relational	3rd	Plural (Ind)	85	Yes	No	No	Yes	151	Quadruple	m7	M6
Beautiful One	Hughes	Intim/Relational	Salvation	2nd	Individual	108	No	No	No	No	120	Quadruple	8ve	5th
Beautiful Saviour	Bullock	Salvation		3rd	Individual	67	Yes	Yes	No	No	96	Triple	7th	6th
Because Of Your Love	Fragar	Testimony		2nd	Individual	91	No	No	No	Yes	165	Quadruple	6th	6th
Before The Throne	Fragar	(Instrumental)					No	No	No	No		Quadruple	N/A	N/A
Believe	Lasit	Testimony	Trans/Dedication	2nd	Both	196	Yes	No	No	No	78	Quadruple	11th	Tritone
Better Than Life	Sampson		Testimony	2nd	Individual	130	Yes	No	No	No	99	Quadruple	Tritone	m7
Blessed	Zschech, Morgan		Body/Unity	2nd	Plural	72	Yes	No	No	No	86	Quadruple	5th	4th

Key:

Type (primary) = the primary song-type evident in the song; Type (2nd) = the secondary thematic song-type, if present, evident in a song; (Salvation) = an implied, though not stated, song-type classification; Address = terms of address used for Godhead; POV = point of view of participant; Words = total number of words in published version of song (no repeats); Lord = actual reference to 'Lord' in printed lyrics; Jesus = actual reference to 'Jesus' in printed lyrics; HS = actual reference to the 'Holy Spirit' in printed lyrics; Tempo = beats per minute of primary recorded version; Time = time signature; Verse range = vocal range of the verse; Ch range = vocal range of the chorus (where separate melody to verse)

Song	Songwriter	Type (primary)	Type (2nd)	Address	POV	Words	Lord	Jesus	HS	God	Tempo	Time	Verse range	Ch range
Blessed Be	Bullock	Salvation		3rd	Individual	56	Yes	Yes	No	No	164	Quadruple	5th	N/A
Blessed Be Your Name	Redman/Redman	Holiness		2nd	Individual	151	Yes	Yes	No	No	115	Quadruple	M9th	4th
Breathe	Barnett	Intim/Relational		2nd	Individual	49	No	No	No	No	65	Quadruple	m7	m7
By Your Side	Sampson	Trans/Dedication		2nd/3rd	Both	111	Yes	No	No	Yes	124	Quadruple	7th	5th
Can't Stop Praising	Faletolu, Sampson	Testimony		2nd	Individual	164	Yes	No	No	No	112	Quadruple	10th	11th
Can't Stop Talking	Fragar	Testimony	Evangelistic	3rd	Individual	106	No	Yes	No	No	152	Quadruple	7th	6th
Carry Me	Sampson	Intim/Relational		2nd	Individual	78	No	No	No	No	78	Quadruple	M6	8ve
Church On Fire	Fragar	Body Unity		3rd	Plural	108	No	Yes	Yes	No	165	Quadruple	5th	7th
Come Now Is The Time To Worship	Doerksen	Call To Worship	Salvation	God/Man	None	59	No	No	No	Yes	98	Quadruple	4th	5th
Consuming Fire	Hughes	Spirit		2nd	Plural	63	Yes	No	Yes	Yes	77	Quadruple	m7	5th
Creation Stands In Awe	Bullock	Salvation		2nd	Plural	167	No	No	No	Yes	71	Quadruple	9th	9th
Deeper and Deeper	Bullock	Intim/Relational		2nd	Individual	74	No	No	No	No	95	Triple	7th	6th
Dwell In Your House	Ewing	Trans/Dedication		2nd	Individual	121	Yes	No	Yes	No	100	Quadruple	9th	5th
Dwelling Places	Webster	Intim/Relational	(Salvation)	2nd	Individual	86	No	Yes	No	No	77	Quadruple	m7th	5th
Eagles Wings	Morgan	Trans/Dedication	(Evangelistic)	2nd	Individual	52	No	Yes	No	No	75	Quadruple	4th	7th
Emmanuel	Badham	Salvation	Body/Unity	2nd	Plural	94	Yes	No	No	Yes	80	Quadruple	9th	M6
Emmanuel	Morgan	Salvation		2nd	Individual	79	Yes	Yes	No	Yes	71	Quadruple	5th	8ve
Ever Living God	Badham	Salvation	Holiness	2nd	Plural	62	No	No	No	Yes	75	Quadruple	M6	m7
Evermore	Houston	Trans/Dedication	Testimony	2nd	Individual	74	Yes	No	No	No	137	Quadruple	5th	4th
Everyday	Houston	Trans/Dedication		2nd	Individual	123	Yes	No	No	No	111	Quadruple	m7	m3rd
Everything That Has Breath	Morgan	Holiness	Credal	3rd	Individual	76	Yes	No	No	No	149	Quadruple	m6	5th

Song	Songwriter	Type (primary)	Type (2nd)	Address	POV	Words	Lord	Jesus	HS	God	Tempo	Time	Verse range	Ch range
Exceeding Joy	Webster	Testimony		3rd	Individual	101	Yes	Yes	No	Yes	72	Quadruple	m9th	5th
Faith	Bullock	None		None	Individual	68	No	No	No	No	120	Quadruple	6th	N/A
Faith	Morgan	Trans/Dedication	Intim/Relational	Both	Individual	83	Yes	No	No	No	127	Quadruple	8ve	m6
Father Of Lights	Fragar	Holiness	Testimony	3rd	Individual	82	No	No	No	No	182	Quadruple	5th	7th
For All You've Done	Morgan	Salvation	(Testimony)	2nd	Individual	61	No	Yes	No	No	133	Quadruple	m7th	m6th
For This Cause	Houston	Intim/Relational		2nd	Individual	120	No	No	No	No	79	Quadruple	m6	5th
Forever	Sampson	Intim/Relational		2nd	Individual	117	No	No	No	Yes	78	Quadruple	m9	8ve
Forever And A Day	Badham	Testimony	Trans/Dedication	2nd	Individual	99	No	No	No	No	114	Quadruple	m6th	M7th
Forever And Always	Bullock	Intim/Relational		2nd	Individual	114	Yes	No	No	No	90	Quadruple	8va	8va
Free	Sampson	Testimony		God/Man	Individual	179	No	Yes	No	Yes	99	Quadruple	8ve	m3rd
Free To Dance	Zschech	Testimony	Intim/Relational	2nd	Individual	116	Yes	Yes	Yes	No	132	Quadruple	4th	5th
Friends In High Places	Fragar	Intim/Relational	Testimony	3rd	Individual	128	No	No	No	Yes	154	Quadruple	8va	6th
Glorified	McPherson	Holiness	Intim/Relational	2nd	Both	78	Yes	No	No	No	113	Quadruple	8va	m7th
Glorify Your Name	Holmes/Zschech	Salvation		2nd	Individual	75	Yes	Yes	No	Yes	72	Quadruple	8ve	5th
Glory	Bullock	Salvation		2nd	Plural	52	Yes	Yes	No	Yes	88	Quadruple	5th	8va
Glory	Morgan	Salvation		3rd	Plural	81	Yes	No	No	Yes	112	Quadruple	m10	m7
Glory To The King	Zschech	Intim/Relational	Holiness	2nd	Individual	107	Yes	Yes	No	No	75	Quadruple	6th	6th
God He Reigns/All I Need Is You	Sampson	Holiness	Salvation	Both	Individual	58	Yes	No	No	Yes	69	Quadruple	m10th	m6th
God Is Great	Sampson	Salvation	Holiness	2nd	Plural	125	Yes	Yes	No	Yes	153	Quadruple	11th	Tritone
God Is In The House	Fragar/Zschech	Intim/Relational	Testimony	3rd	Individual	109	Yes	Yes	No	Yes	158	Quadruple	7th	8va
God So Loved	Morgan	Salvation	Credal	3rd	None	50	No	No	No	Yes	84	Quadruple	8ve	M6
Grace Abounds To All	Bullock	Salvation		Both	Plural	73	No	No	No	No	82	Quadruple	8va	8va

Song	Songwriter	Type (primary)	Type (2nd)	Address	POV	Words	Lord	Jesus	HS	God	Tempo	Time	Verse range	Ch range
Grace And Mercy For All	Bullock	Intim/Relational	(Salvation)	3rd	Plural	180	No	No	No	No	104	Quadruple	8va	8va
Great In Power	Fragar		Holiness	3rd	None	70	No	No	No	No	120	Quadruple	5th	6th
Hallelujah	Myrin/Sampson	Intim/Relational	Salvation	2nd	Individual	97	No	No	No	No	144	Triple	5th	5th
Have Faith In God	Bullock	Intim/Relational		2nd/3rd	Individual	89	Yes	No	No	Yes	85	Triple	6th	4th
He Shall Be Called	Fragar	Salvation	Call To Worship	3rd	Note	86	Yes	Yes	No	Yes	132	Quadruple	5th	8va
Hear Me Calling	Bullock	Intim/Relational		2nd	Individual	52	Yes	No	No	Yes	83	Quadruple	9th	5th
Heart Of Love	Bullock	Intim/Relational	Salvation	3rd	(Individual)	94	No	No	No	No	77	Quadruple	6th	4th
Here I Am To Worship	Hughes	Salvation	Intim/Relational	2nd	Individual	98	No	No	No	Yes	72	Quadruple	4th	5th
Here to Eternity	Zschech, Moyse	Body Unity	(Salvation)	2nd	Both	76	No	No	No	No	142	Quadruple	9th	m6
Hiding Place	Crabtree/Smith	Intim/Relational	Confession	2nd	Individual	85	No	No	No	No	115	Quadruple	8ve	8ve
Highest	Morgan	Holiness	Salvation	2nd	Plural	46	Yes	No	No	Yes	78	Quadruple	M6	8ve
His Love	Badham	Testimony	Holiness	2nd	Both	94	Yes	No	No	No	153	Quadruple	5th	5th
Holding On	Bullock	Intim/Relational		2nd	Individual	56	Yes	Yes	No	Yes	138	Quadruple	8va	8va
Holy Holy	Fellingham	Holiness	Salvation	3rd	None	86	Yes	Yes	No	Yes	85	Quadruple	8ve	4th
Holy One Of God	Bullock	Credal	Salvation	3rd	None	56	No	Yes	No	Yes	76	Quadruple	8va	8va
Holy Spirit Come	Bullock	Anointing	Trans/Dedication	2nd	Plural	67	No	No	Yes	No	80	Quadruple	8va	N/A
Holy Spirit Rain Down	Fragar	Anointing		2nd	Plural	75	No	Yes	Yes	Yes	72	Quadruple	7th	8va
Holy Spirit Rise	Bullock	Intim/Relational	Anointing	2nd	Individual	84	Yes	Yes	Yes	Yes	80	Quadruple	6th	6th
Home	Sampson	Intim/Relational		2nd	Individual	123	Yes	Yes	No	Yes	146	Quadruple	m6th	8ve
I Adore	Morgan	Salvation	Holiness	Both	Both	110	Yes	Yes	No	Yes	78	Quadruple	8ve	M6
I Am Carried	Bullock	Intim/Relational	Testimony	2nd	Individual	167	No	No	No	No	80	Quadruple	9th	8va
I Am Overwhelmed	Bullock	Intim/Relational	Testimony	2nd	Individual	169	No	No	No	No	75	Quadruple	8va	9th
I Believe	Bullock	Intim/Relational	Eschatology	2nd	Individual	86	No	No	No	Yes	125	Quadruple	min6th	5th
I Believe The Promise	Fragar	Spirit	Call To Worship	3rd	Both	155	No	No	Yes	Yes	156	Quadruple	9th	10th

Song	Songwriter	Type (primary)	Type (2nd)	Address	POV	Words	Lord	Jesus	HS	God	Tempo	Time	Verse range	Ch range
I Can't Wait	Fragar	None	(Testimony)	2nd	Individual	82	Yes	No	No	No	165	Quadruple	6th	N/A
I Could Sing Of Your Love	Smith, M	Intim/Relational	Trans/Dedication	2nd	Individual	107	No	No	No	No	90	Quadruple	M6	5th
I Feel Like I'm Falling	Badham	Intim/Relational		2nd	Individual	114	No	No	No	Yes	131	Quadruple	6th	5th
I Give You My Heart	Morgan	Trans/Dedication		2nd	Individual	62	Yes	No	No	No	77	Quadruple	4th	7th
I Just Want To Praise The Lord	Bullock	Holiness		2nd/3rd	Individual	48	Yes	No	No	Yes	98	Quadruple	6th	5th
I Know It	Zschech	Testimony	Salvation	3rd	Individual	125	No	Yes	No	No	88	Quadruple	7th	9th
I Live To Know You	Zschech	Intim/Relational	Trans/Dedication	2nd	Individual	110	Yes	Yes	Yes	Yes	77	Quadruple	6th	9th
I Simply Live For You	Fragar	Intim/Relational	Trans/Dedication	2nd	Both	120	No	No	No	No	70	Quadruple	8ve	8ve
I Surrender	Bullock	Intim/Relational	Trans/Dedication	2nd	Individual	102	Yes	No	No	No	82	Quadruple	5th	5th
I Will Bless You Lord	Zschech	Intim/Relational	Holiness	2nd	Individual	72	Yes	No	No	Yes	105	Triple	6th	5th
I Will Love	Webster	Salvation	Trans/Dedication	2nd	Individual	82	Yes	Yes	No	No	64	Quadruple	Tritone	4th
I Will Rest In Christ	Bullock	Trans/Dedication	Intim/Relational	3rd	Individual	177	No	Yes	No	Yes	65	Quadruple	8va	5th
I Will Run To You	Zschech	Holiness	Trans/Dedication	2nd	Individual	98	No	No	No	Yes	82	Quadruple	10th	9th
I Will Worship	Bullock	Trans/Dedication		Both	Individual	98	Yes	Yes	No	No	85	Quadruple	6th	6th
I Will Worship You	Bullock	Salvation	Trans/Dedication	2nd	Individual	50	Yes	No	No	No	88	Quadruple	5th	5th
I'll Love You More	Eastwood	Trans/Dedication	Confession	2nd	Individual	67	Yes	No	No	No	80	Quadruple	min5th	7th
I'll Worship You	Bullock	Trans/Dedication	Intim/Relational	2nd	Individual	82	Yes	No	No	Yes	83	Quadruple	8va	9th
In Freedom	Puddle	Body Unity		3rd	None	73	No	No	No	No	134	Quadruple	8va	2nd
In Jesus' Crown	Bullock	Testimony	Salvation	3rd	Plural	95	No	Yes	No	No	95	Quadruple	6th	5th
In The Name Of The Lord	Bullock	Body Unity		3rd	Plural	83	Yes	No	No	Yes	110	Quadruple	6th	6th
In The Silence	Iannuzzelli	Intim/Relational		2nd	Individual	100	No	No	No	Yes	60	Quadruple	8va	7th
In Your Hands	Morgan	Intim/Relational		2nd	Individual	97	No	No	No	No	74	Quadruple	5th	4th
Irresistible	Zschech	Intim/Relational		2nd	Individual	71	Yes	No	No	No	76	Quadruple	8ve	m6

Song	Songwriter	Type (primary)	Type (2nd)	Address	POV	Words	Lord	Jesus	HS	God	Tempo	Time	Verse range	Ch range
It Is You	Zschech	Intim/Relational	(Testimony)	2nd	Individual	80	Yes	Yes	No	No	75	Quadruple	4th	8ve
Jesus Lover Of My Soul	Grul/Ezzy/McPherson	Intim/Relational		2nd	Individual	58	No	Yes	No	No	76	Quadruple	6th	8va
Jesus The Same	Badham	Salvation		3rd	Plural	105	No	Yes	No	Yes	72	Quadruple	5th	5th
Jesus You Gave It All	Gower	Trans/Dedication		2nd	Individual	90	Yes	Yes	No	No	87	Quadruple	7th	8va
Jesus You're All I Need	Zschech	Intim/Relational	Salvation	2nd	Individual	84	Yes	Yes	No	No	75	Quadruple	6th	5th
Jesus, What A Beautiful Name	Riches	Salvation	Testimony	3rd	Individual	92	No	Yes	No	Yes	53	Comp Duple	9th	N/A
Joy In The Holy Ghost	Fragar	Spirit	Testimony	3rd	Both	151	No	No	Yes	Yes	173	Quadruple	7th	5th
Just Let Me Say	Bullock	Intim/Relational	Salvation	2nd	Individual	199	Yes	No	Yes	Yes	76	Quadruple	8va	N/A
King Of Kings	Bullock	Salvation		3rd	None	85	Yes	Yes	No	Yes	93	Quadruple	5th	5th
King Of Love	Riches	Salvation		2nd	None	42	Yes	Yes	No	No	137	Triple	5th	M6th
King Of Majesty	Sampson	Intim/Relational		2nd	Individual	83	Yes	Yes	No	No	115	Quadruple	m10	M3rd
Know You More	Zschech	Trans/Dedication		2nd	Individual	129	No	No	No	No	67	Quadruple	m6th	4th
Latter Rain	Bullock	Body Unity		3rd	Plural	124	Yes	No	Yes	No	88	Quadruple	8th	9th
Let Creation Sing	Morgan	Salvation	(Holiness)	2nd	Plural (Ind)	105	No	No	No	Yes	151	Quadruple	m6	4th
Let The Peace Of God Reign	Zschech	Trans/Dedication	Spirit	2nd	Individual	117	Yes	No	Yes	Yes	65	Quadruple	8va	9th
Let Us Adore	Morgan	Salvation		3rd	Plural	92	Yes	Yes	No	Yes	80	Triple	m7	4th
Let Us Rise To Worship	Bullock	Social Justice	Trans/Dedication	2nd (3rd)	Plural (Ind)	208	No	(Yes)	No	No	82	Quadruple	8va	8va
Let Your Presence Fall	Willesdorf	Anointing		2nd	Plural	39	Yes	No	No	No	74	Duple	min7th	8va
Lift Our Praise	Kay	Holiness	Body/Unity	Both	Plural	96	Yes	No	Yes	Yes	97	Quadruple	7th	6th

Song	Songwriter	Type (primary)	Type (2nd)	Address	POV	Words	Lord	Jesus	HS	God	Tempo	Time	Verse range	Ch range
Light To the Blinded Eyes	Bullock	Testimony		2nd	Individual	153	No	No	No	No	73	Quadruple	9th	7th
Longin' For Your Touch	Iannuzzelli/Uluirewa	Intim/Relational		2nd	Individual	68	Yes	Yes	No	No	87	Quadruple	5th	6th
Lord I Give Myself	Zschech	Trans/Dedication	Intim/Relational	2nd	Individual	80	Yes	No	No	Yes	67	Quadruple	8va	N/A
Lord Of All	McPherson	Salvation	Trans/Dedication	2nd	Individual	76	Yes	Yes	Yes	No	74	Quadruple	m5th	5th
Lord Of All Mercy	Bullock	Holiness	Trans/Dedication	2nd	Individual	167	Yes	Yes	No	Yes	90	Quadruple	4th	7th
Lord Of The Heavens	Fisher	Salvation		3rd	Individual	65	Yes	Yes	No	Yes	69	Quadruple	8va	5th
Lord We Come	Bullock	None	(Body)	2nd	Plural	62	Yes	No	No	No	136	Quadruple	6th	5th
Lord Your Goodness	Morgan	Intim/Relational	Holiness	2nd	Individual	66	Yes	No	No	No	132	Quadruple	6th	9th
Lost Without Your Love	Bullock	Intim/Relational	Trans/Dedication	2nd	Individual	101	Yes	No	No	No	110	Quadruple	m7th	5th
Love Divine	Bullock	Holiness	Intim/Relational	3rd	Individual	69	No	No	No	Yes	91	Triple	6th	8va
Love You So Much	Fragar	Intim/Relational		2nd	Individual	93	Yes	Yes	No	No	78	Quadruple	8va	8va
Made Me Glad	Webster		Holiness	2nd	Individual	84	Yes	No	No	No	81	Quadruple	m9	5th
Magnificent	Badham	Salvation		2nd	Plural	80	No	Yes	No	No	80	Quadruple	m7	m7
Make Me Your Servant	Fragar	Trans/Dedication	Evangelistic	2nd	Individual	59	Yes	No	No	No	120	Quadruple	min7th	8va
Mercy	Bullock	Intim/Relational	Holiness	2nd	(Individual)	101	Yes	No	No	No	106	Quadruple	9th	5th
More Than Life	Morgan	Intim/Relational	(Salvation)	2nd	Individual	103	No	No	No	No	68	Quadruple	M6th	4th
Most High	Morgan	Trans/Dedication	Holiness	Both	Individual	75	Yes	No	No	No	162	Quadruple	m6	M6
My Best Friend	Houston, Sampson	Testimony	Intim/Relational	God/Man	Individual	121	No	Yes	No	No	108	Quadruple	10th	4th
My Greatest Love Is You	Fragar	Intim/Relational	Holiness	2nd	Individual	50	No	No	No	No	70	Quadruple	8va	8va
My Heart Sings Praises	Fragar	Intim/Relational	Holiness	2nd	Individual	107	No	No	No	No	94	Quadruple	9th	m6th
My Hope	Zschech	Holiness		2nd	Individual	71	Yes	No	No	No	73	Quadruple	8ve	m7
My Redeemer Lives	Morgan	Testimony	Salvation	2nd/3rd	Individual	74	Yes	No	No	No	132	Quadruple	7th	5th

Song	Songwriter	Type (primary)	Type (2nd)	Address	POV	Words	Lord	Jesus	HS	God	Tempo	Time	Verse range	Ch range
Need You Here	Morgan	Intim/Relational	(Salvation)	2nd	Individual	89	Yes	No	No	No	73	Quadruple	M9	Tritone
No Higher Place	Bullock	Intim/Relational		2nd	Individual	130	No	No	No	No	88	Quadruple	6th	m7th
No Longer I	Bullock	Intim/Relational	Confessional	3rd	Individual	105	No	Yes	No	Yes	80	Quadruple	7th	4th
Now Is The Time	Bullock	Call To Worship	Testimony	3rd/2nd	Individual	95	No	No	No	Yes	84	Quadruple	8va	9th
Now That You're Near	Sampson	Intim/Relational		2nd	Individual	128	Yes	Yes	No	Yes	119	Quadruple	5th	M6
Oh God Of All Comfort	Bullock	Intim/Relational	Holiness	3rd	Individual	148	Yes	No	No	Yes	58	Comp Duple	6th	6th
Oh Holy Spirit	Bullock	Anointing	Spirit	2nd	Individual	48	Yes	No	Yes	Yes	84	Quadruple	6th	6th
Oh The Mercy Of God	Bullock	Holiness	Salvation	Both	Plural	136	No	Yes	No	Yes	90	Triple	7th	9th
One Day	Morgan	Intim/Relational		2nd	Individual	73	Yes	No	No	Yes	133	Quadruple	M6	M6
One Desire	Houston	Intim/Relational	Trans/Dedication	2nd	Individual	119	Yes	Yes	Yes	No	77	Quadruple	8ve	M6
One Way	Douglass/Houston	Salvation	(Int/Relational)	2nd	Individual	125	No	Yes	No	No	134	Quadruple	10th	4th
Open The Eyes Of My Heart	Baloche	Intim/Relational	Holiness	Both	Individual	49	Yes	No	No	No	118	Quadruple	M6th	5th
People Get Free	Fragar	Body Unity	Testimony	3rd	Individual	9	No	Yes	Yes	No	165	Quadruple	m6th	6th
People Just Like Us	Fragar	Body Unity	Eschatology	2nd	Plural	138	No	Yes	No	No	152	Quadruple	7th	5th
Praise His Holy Name	Zschech	Holiness	Thanks	3rd/2nd	Both	64	Yes	No	No	Yes	116	Quadruple	5th	8va
Pressing On	Bullock	Trans/Dedication	Eschatology	Both	Individual	79	No	No	No	No	110	Quadruple	5th	m3rd
Reaching For You	Badham	Intim/Relational	Testimony	2nd	Individual	88	No	No	No	No	61	Quadruple	m9	M6
Refresh My Heart Lord	Bullock	Trans/Dedication	Confession	2nd	Individual	55	Yes	No	Yes	No	84	Quadruple	8va	8va
Rock Of The Ages	Bullock/Zschech	Salvation	Credal	3rd	Individual	77	Yes	No	No	Yes	97	Quadruple	8va	min7th
Salvation	Bullock	Testimony		2nd	Individual	94	Yes	Yes	Yes	No	117	Quadruple	6th	8va
Salvation Is Here	Houston	Testimony		3rd	Individual	127	No	No	No	Yes	115	Quadruple	8ve	m6
Saviour	Zschech	Salvation	Holiness	2nd	Both	120	Yes	No	No	No	70	Quadruple	m7th	M9th

Song	Songwriter	Type (primary)	Type (2nd)	Address	POV	Words	Lord	Jesus	HS	God	Tempo	Time	Verse range	Ch range
Shelter House	McPherson	Spirit	Intim/Relational	2nd/3rd	Individual	125	Yes	No	Yes	Yes	105	Quadruple	m7th	8va
Shout To The King	Davies		(Holiness)	Both	Both	111	No	No	No	Yes	128	Quadruple	M6	5th
Shout To The Lord	Zschech	Salvation	Intim/Relational	2nd/3rd	Both	102	Yes	Yes	No	No	76	Quadruple	10th	5th
Shout To The North	Smith, M	Body Unity	Salvation	God/Man	(Plural)	128	Yes	Yes	No	Yes	184	Triple	M6	5th
Shout Your Fame	Myrin, Bedingfield, Galanti; Nevison	Salvation	Trans/Dedication	2nd	Individual	185	No	Yes	No	Yes	114	Quadruple	8ve	8ve
Sing (Your Love)	Morgan	Trans/Dedication	Testimony	2nd	Individual	62	Yes	No	No	No	69	Quadruple	8ve	m7th
Sing Of Your Great Love	Zschech	Trans/Dedication	(Eschatology)	2nd	Individual	127	Yes	Yes	No	No	71	Quadruple	6th	5th
So You Would Come	Fragar	Evangelistic		Not God	None	109	No	No	No	No	62	Quadruple	7th	6th
Song Of Freedom	Sampson	Intim/Relational		2nd	Individual	49	No	No	No	Yes	109	Quadruple	8ve	m7
Song Of God	Sampson	Salvation	Intim/Relational	Both	Individual	93	Yes	No	No	No	164	Triple	5th	8ve
Stay	Munns	Trans/Dedication	Intim/Relational	2nd	Individual	78	No	Yes	No	No	52	Quadruple	6th	5th
Steppin' Out	McPherson	Body Unity	Evangelistic	3rd	Plural	121	No	Yes	No	Yes	107	Quadruple	3rd	6th
Still	Morgan	Intim/Relational		2nd	Individual	57	No	Yes	No	Yes	70	Quadruple	5th	8ve
Surrender	Bullock	Trans/Dedication	Intim/Relational	2nd	Individual	181	Yes	No	No	No	75	Quadruple	8va	m7th
Take All Of Me	Sampson	Intim/Relational		2nd	Individual	104	No	Yes	No	No	70	Quadruple	m7th	m7th
Tell The World	Douglass/Houston/Sampson	Evangelistic	Testimony	Both	Individual	126	No	Yes	No	No	145	Quadruple	4th	m6th
Thank You	Pringle	Thanks	Salvation	2nd	Individual	74	No	No	No	No	68	Quadruple	8ve	8ve
Thank You, Lord	Jernigan	Thanks		2nd	Individual	79	No	Yes	No	No	110	Triple	9th	7th
That's What We Came Here For	Fragar/Zschech	Call To Worship	Holiness	2nd	Plural	128	Yes	No	No	No	162	Quadruple	9th	6th
The Great Southland	Bullock	Body Unity	(Revival)	3rd	Plural	126	No	No	No	No	77	Quadruple	8th	9th
The Love Of God Can Do	Fragar (C&R)	Holiness		3rd	None	118	No	No	Yes	Yes	150	Quadruple	6th	8va

Song	Songwriter	Type (primary)	Type (2nd)	Address	POV	Words	Lord	Jesus	HS	God	Tempo	Time	Verse range	Ch range
The Potter's Hand	Zschech	Trans/Dedication		2nd	Individual	102	Yes	No	Yes	No	77	Quadruple	7th	4th
The Power And The Glory	Bullock	Intim/Relational	Testimony	2nd	Individual	131	Yes	No	Yes	Yes	80	Quadruple	6th	6th
The Power Of Your Love	Bullock	Trans/Dedication	Intim/Relational	2nd	Individual	127	Yes	No	Yes	No	84	Quadruple	11th	min7th
The Stone's Been Rolled Away	Bullock	Testimony	Intim/Relational	3rd	Individual	79	No	Yes	No	Yes	120	Quadruple	5th	5th
The Time Has Come	Bullock	Body Unity		3rd	Plural	131	No	No	No	No	154	Quadruple	7th	4th
There Is Nothing Like	Myrin/Sampson	Sal/Hol/Spirit		2nd	Individual	84	Yes	Yes	Yes	Yes	74	Quadruple	m10th	5th
This Is How We Overcome	Morgan	Testimony		2nd	Both	60	No	No	No	No	136	Quadruple	6th	5th
This Kingdom	Bullock	Salvation	Credal	3rd	Plural	96	No	Yes	No	Yes	85	Quadruple	6th	8va
This Kingdom Of Love	Bullock	Salvation	Intim/Relational	Both	Both	127	No	Yes	No	Yes	97	Quadruple	8va	6th
This Love In Me	Bullock	Intim/Relational		2nd	Individual	41	No	No	No	No	88	Quadruple	9th	N/A
Through It All	Morgan	Intim/Relational		2nd	Individual	62	Yes	No	No	No	76	Quadruple	M6	8ve
To The Ends Of The Earth	Houston, Sampson	Trans/Dedication	(Salvation)	2nd	Individual	102	No	Yes	No	Yes	73	Quadruple	8ve	M3rd
To You	Zschech	Intim/Relational		2nd	Individual	90	No	No	Yes	No	80	Quadruple	M6	m7
To You Alone	Morgan	Salvation		2nd	None	70	Yes	Yes	No	No	66	Quadruple	M6th	m7th
Touching Heaven, Changing Earth	Morgan	Body Unity		2nd	Plural	111	Yes	No	No	Yes	160	Quadruple	8va	6th
Trading My Sorrows	Evans	Testimony		3rd	Individual	108	Yes	No	No	No	120	Quadruple	M6	M6th
Unfailing Love	Bullock	Intim/Relational	Salvation	3rd	Individual	115	No	Yes	No	Yes	87	Quadruple	9th	7th
Walking In The Light	Zschech	Intim/Relational	Salvation	2nd/3rd	Individual	112	No	Yes	No	No	163	Quadruple	7th	5th
We Proclaim Your Kingdom	Bullock	Salvation		2nd	Plural	86	Yes	Yes	No	Yes	80	Quadruple	8va	6th

Song	Songwriter	Type (primary)	Type (2nd)	Address	POV	Words	Lord	Jesus	HS	God	Tempo	Time	Verse range	Ch range
We Will Rise	Bullock	Body Unity		3rd	Plural	112	No	No	No	No	162	Quadruple	4th	6th
Welcome In This Place	Webster	Spirit		2nd	Individual	82	No	No	Yes	Yes	70	Quadruple	4th	4th
What The Lord Has Done In Me	Morgan	Testimony	Salvation	3rd	Individual	90	Yes	Yes	No	Yes	72	Triple	9th	8va
What The World Will Never Take	Crocker/Ligertwood/Sampson	Testimony	Trans/Dedication	2nd	Individual	105	No	No	No	Yes	125	Quadruple	m6th	M6th
Whenever I See	Bullock	Intim/Relational		2nd	Individual	134	No	No	No	No	82	Quadruple	9th	7th
With All I Am	Morgan	Trans/Dedication	Intim/Relational	2nd	Individual	93	No	Yes	No	No	69	Quadruple	8ve	M6th
With You	Morgan	Intim/Relational		2nd	Individual	68	No	No	No	No	127	Quadruple	8ve	m7
Within Your Love	Bullock	Intim/Relational	Confession	2nd	Individual	92	Yes	No	No	No	90	Quadruple	5th	6th
Wonderful God	Davies	Holiness		2nd	Plural	87	No	No	No	Yes	71	Quadruple	8ve	5th
Worthy Is The Lamb	Zschech	Salvation	Thanks	2nd	Individual	92	Yes	Yes	No	No	76	Quadruple	9th	M6
Yes And Amen	Fragar	Intim/Relational		3rd	Individual	99	No	Yes	No	Yes	183	Quadruple	10th	7th
You Are Holy	Morgan	Holiness	Intim/Relational	2nd	Individual	43	Yes	No	No	Yes	67	Quadruple	m6th	8va
You Are My God	Bullock/Dunshea	Intim/Relational	(Holiness)	2nd	Individual	67	Yes	No	No	Yes	88	Quadruple	11th	8va
You Are My Rock	Bullock	Salvation		2nd	Individual	56	Yes	No	No	No	168	Quadruple	12th	4th
You Are My Song	Bullock	Intim/Relational		2nd	Individual	119	No	No	No	No	65	Quadruple	8va	5th
You Are My World	Sampson	Intim/Relational	Testimony	2nd	Individual	109	Yes	Yes	No	Yes	80	Quadruple	5th	4th
You Are Near	Morgan	Body Unity	Holiness	2nd	Plural	61	No	No	No	Yes	73	Quadruple	M6	Tritone
You Are The One	Bullock	Intim/Relational	Salvation	2nd	Individual	147	No	Yes	No	No	72	Duple	4th	5th
You Are Worthy	Zschech	Holiness	Trans/Dedication	2nd	Individual	127	Yes	No	No	No	67	Quadruple	M6th	m6th
You Are/You Are Lord	Va'a, Zschech	Trans/Dedication		2nd	Individual	116	Yes	Yes	No	Yes	71	Quadruple	m7	5th
You Call Us Near	Bullock	Intim/Relational		Both	Plural	139	No	No	No	Yes	93	Comp Duple	5th	5th
You Gave Me Love	Morgan	Testimony		2nd	Individual	121	No	No	No	No	195	Quadruple	6th	5th

Song	Songwriter	Type (primary)	Type (2nd)	Address	POV	Words	Lord	Jesus	HS	God	Tempo	Time	Verse range	Ch range
You Give Me Shelter	Bullock	Holiness	Intim/Relational	2nd	Individual	100	Yes	No	No	Yes	125	Quadruple	8va	5th
You Placed Your Love	Bullock	Trans/Dedication		2nd	Individual	65	Yes	No	No	No	168	Quadruple	4th	6th
You Rescued Me	Bullock	Intim/Relational	Salvation	2nd	Individual	83	Yes	No	No	No	80	Quadruple	8va	9th
You Said	Morgan		Evangelistic	2nd	Individual	81	Yes	No	No	No	78	Quadruple	6th	7th
You Stand Alone	Stevens, McPherson	Intim/Relational		2nd	Individual	77	Yes	Yes	No	Yes	78	Quadruple	8ve	8ve
Your Grace & Your Mercy	Bullock	Intim/Relational		2nd	Individual	114	No	No	No	No	88	Comp Duple	8va	8va
Your Love	Bullock	Intim/Relational		2nd	Plural	67	No	No	No	No	148	Quadruple	4th	6th
Your Love	Morgan	Testimony		2nd	Individual	72	No	No	No	No	82	Quadruple	5th	5th
Your Love Is Beautiful	Morgan, Badham, McPherson, Hednroff	Testimony	Intim/Relational	2nd	Individual	89	No	No	No	No	121	Quadruple	8ve	9th
Your Love Keeps Following Me	Fragar	None	Intim/Relational	2nd	Individual	82	No	No	No	No	167	Quadruple	min6th	8va
Your Name	Zschech	Salvation	Trans/Dedication	2nd	Individual	125	Yes	Yes	No	Yes	132	Comp Duple	min7th	5th
Your People Sing Praises	Fragar	Body Unity		2nd/3rd	Plural	138	Yes	Yes	No	No	171	Quadruple	8va	6th
Your Unfailing Love	Morgan	Intim/Relational	Testimony	2nd	Individual	66	No	Yes	No	No	76	Quadruple	7th	4th
You're All I Need	Bullock	Intim/Relational	Salvation	2nd	Individual	112	No	Yes	Yes	Yes	76	Quadruple	8va	6th
Yours Is The Kingdom	Houston	Salvation		2nd	None	96	Yes	No	No	Yes	141	Quadruple	m7th	5th

Notes

Introduction

1. In 1968, David and Dale Garratt produced a 45 rpm in New Zealand, called *Scripture In Song*. This pioneered a concept that spread throughout the world over the next decade. In 1971 they published their first words book by the same title, and in this and all subsequent publications, they gathered together a wide variety of songs and choruses from all over the world.
2. A fuller exploration of the difference between, and worth of, contemporary choruses and hymns will be introduced in Chapter 4.
3. 'Did You Feel The Mountains Tremble?' (M. Smith).
4. See, for example, Reed (2003).
5. This list was initially developed for subscribers to *Perfect Beat: The Pacific Journal of Research Into Contemporary Music and Popular Culture* to facilitate ongoing discussion around popular music studies in the Asia-Pacific region. As such it also included members of the Australia/New Zealand branch of the International Association for the Study of Popular Music (IASPM).
6. My version of the debate that ensued can be found in Evans (1999a).

Chapter 1

1. See Hayward (1998: 7–16), Whiteley (1997: xiii–xxxvi), Shuker (1994) and Middleton (1990) for exegesis of the academic evolution of contemporary music studies.
2. See Dawn (1995) on gender positioning within worship.
3. Johnson's paper can be found at http://www.arts.unsw.edu.au/jazz/Arch/BJAR/. This version is a conglomeration of three separate conference/seminar papers on the topic. The page numbers cited refer to those from the website printout.
4. See, for example, Evans (2000).
5. Johnson later notes that Australia's 'celebration of military tradition', Anzac Day, is probably the biggest employer of musicians for the biggest audience in one day (1998: 4). Yet this assertion, and his earlier arts attendance figures, under-represent the substance and proliferation of vernacular music, particularly the ubiquitousness of congregational song. Kaldor *et al.* report attendance estimates for the major denominations in Australia to be 1,759,100 (1999: 15). Even if we exclude the Catholic denomination, which, despite a recent move towards contemporary music styles, still exhibits a penchant towards fine music traditions, the average weekly attendance comes out at 884,100 – roughly five times the weekly attendance at formal musical events. Given that, theoretically at least, all parishioners are involved in the production and consumption of

congregational music, such numbers highlight the chasm that exists between what is studied in contemporary music, and what is experienced.

6. Curiously, as will be detailed in later chapters, one of the aims of current congregational song producers is to reflect audience *participation* on all their audio and audio-visual recordings.

7. See the albums *You Outlast* (2001) and *Now And Forever* (2003) as examples.

8. To compare jazz to congregational song has more than musical implications, as Johnson points out: 'Jazz is [also] an instructive case study for other vernacular "arts" in debates on cultural value' (2000: 26). For other connections between jazz and congregational song, see Begbie (2000), Clarke (2002) and Moore (2002).

9. The descendents of Levi, son of Jacob, were chosen by God to be priests and serve in the ritual practices (Tent/Temple, etc.) of the Old Testament (see Numbers 3–4).

10. Chris Thompson, Vice-President of Integrity Creative Group, contends that this vertical level of operation is the key to defining the (commercial) success of congregational song, 'God to man – man to God, a vertical relationship musically and spiritually' (cited in Price, 1998: 6).

11. Many thanks to Tim Chavura for this observation.

12. Chavura, T. (2005) 'Expressions of Protestant Congregational Music Practices in Contemporary Australian Worship Conferences' (unpublished Honours dissertation, Macquarie University, 51).

13. Liesch compares this to the role of prompter in a theatrical or musical production, that is, someone who is totally familiar with the text, aware of individual needs, and mindful of any possible stumbling blocks to the performance. 'When his job is well done, it normally goes completely unnoticed by the audience' (1996: 125). In Christian terms, '[w]orship leaders perform "up" to God and "down" to the people, simultaneously' (ibid.).

14. Dawn (1995) finds the practice of applauding during worship subtly destructive of genuine community, and argues strongly that it unnecessarily elevates those applauded while simultaneously downgrading the importance of those who applaud (156–57).

Chapter 2

1. See Sadie (1980), Grout (1960), Hanning (2002) and Ferris (1999) for worthwhile accounts.

2. For more complete expositions of early Christian worship and liturgy see Peterson (1992), Cullman (1953), Martin (1964), Rowley (1967) and White (1993). For complete histories of congregational music see Faulkner (1996), Hustad (1981), Wilson-Dickson (1992), Long (1972), Etherington (1962) and Routley (1967, 1977).

3. Faulkner (1996: 52–58) cites many examples of this revulsion.

4. Ambrose himself wrote a number of hymns in the contemporary style of the day and was more than aware of their emotional and spiritual impact:

> They also say that the people are led astray by the charms of my hymns. Certainly; I do not deny it. This is a mighty charm, more powerful than any other (quoted in Wilson-Dickson, 1992: 36).

5. Note that this term, common in popular music parlance, has a religious reference point.

6. See the example provided in Ferris (1999: 61).

7. Two of the best sources of English music from the Middle Ages are the *Eton Choir Book* and the *Old Hall Manuscript*. These volumes highlight the fact that church music was clearly distinguished from any other type of music, simultaneously ahead in ingenuity and imagination (Routley, 1977: 12).

8. Many still argue with this, however, and seek to situate the start of the Reformation more contextually within the sixteenth century. See Scribner (1986) for further discussion.

9. It has never been definitively proven that Luther wrote the melody, though the music is generally ascribed to him.

10. Organs had begun to be installed in churches around the fifteenth century, though they were used to double the voice parts for security, not to play against the melody. Singing was mostly in unison though the choirs would have known part-singing. The organ was used as a substitute for the voices, and hence rejected by some reformers (especially Calvin and Zwingli). Interestingly, given the contemporary disputes that rage over congregational instrumentation – and the current reverence for the organ in mainstream churches – history shows that the use of the organ in churches was a continual source of controversy until the late seventeenth century.

11. A common legend regarding this adaptation is that Luther, and others, used German beer songs as the basis for reworded hymns. While he may well have been influenced by songs of the day – from all quarters – there is no historical evidence for a reliance on 'bar tunes'.

12. Valuable investigations on the effects of the Enlightenment on church music can be found in Routley (1967) and Blume (1974).

13. A seeker-service is the fashionable term for a church service designed around the needs of non-Christians. It is largely stripped of all Christian jargon and ritual practice for the purpose of making newcomers feel comfortable and allowing them to 'seek' God without the usual cultural baggage that many associate with the Church. Basden (1999: 88–95) discusses the origins and evolution of the seeker-service.

14. Queen Victoria also ruled at the height of the Oxford Movement, which re-introduced elements of Catholic theology and liturgical practice into the Church of England. One result of this movement was the development of the High Church or Anglo-Catholic Church, which largely imitated the traditional Catholic Mass and incorporated translations of Latin and Greek hymns.

15. Patrick Appleford and the Quaker Sydney Carter were two other famous dissenting hymn-writers at this time. Carter wrote *9 Carols Or Ballads* between 1960 and 1964. His 'Lord Of The Dance' (1963) became a landmark of international significance in its signal for musical change across the church. In Melbourne, Anglican Reverend James Minchin wrote *Jazz In The Church* in 1964, a collection of old hymn texts that he set to jazz rhythms – some of which were published internationally.

16. The final Psalter, the current collection of 150 psalms, is not thought to have been officially collated until the third century BC, though earlier collections can be traced

back to the period of Solomon's temple, or even to the time of David (Stek, 1985: 781). The textual notations regarding the occasion of composition of the Psalms are also somewhat ambiguous, 'since the Hebrew phraseology used, meaning in general "belonging to", can also be taken in the sense of "concerning" or "for the use of" or "dedicated to" ' (ibid.: 782). Given this, Davidic involvement in the Psalms was fundamental to their composition, development and function.

17. For a complete exploration of the Psalms' place within ancient liturgy see Mowinckel (1967).

18. A useful history and summary of this scholarship occurs in Guthrie and Motyer (1970: 446–51).

19. Many believe, however, that several of Paul's unidentified quotations focusing on Christ are actually excerpts from early hymns (e.g. Philippians 2:6-11; Romans 11:36; Colossians 1:15-20) (see Kauflin, 2002: www.crosswalk.com).

Chapter 3

1. For useful discussions on the inappropriateness of this term see Hayward (1998: 3–7), Feld (1994), and Taylor (1997).

2. For example, see Basden (1999: 17); Carson (2002: 18); Dawn (1995: 76–77), and Corbitt (1998: 53).

3. Peterson usefully notes that nowhere in the Bible is worship actually defined. Considerations of the terminology of worship, in its various contexts, do, however, provide a useful mosaic by which we can relate appropriately to God (1996: 10; 1992: 56). For a thorough academic investigation into the terminology and experience of worship throughout the Bible see Peterson (1992).

4. While there are other Greek words associated with worship activities and attitudes within the Bible (e.g. *leitourgia*), the three outlined here give sufficient insight into the meaning 'systems of worship', especially considering the close relationship between the words.

5. Peterson (1992: 70–72, 79) elaborates further on the *seb-* stem used to reflect notions of awe and reverence.

6. Bullock (1998) observes that the statement of Christ in John 4:24 has produced an encyclopaedia of worship theology and practice. He prefers to view the story as a whole, noting that it is 'a chance meeting between God, revealed in the flesh as Jesus, and a social misfit, an outcast by religion, birth and gender [which] shows us *who* we should worship and *why*' (82).

7. Carson (2002) makes the valuable observation that worship, as it exists as a phenomenon within God's creation, cannot 'be defined as *necessarily* arising out of the gospel' (27). His point being that the angels who orchestrate the praise of heaven do not worship out of an experience of redemption. For our part here, however, we will restrict our discussion to the worship responses of humans.

8. Psalm 96:1-6 is a helpful example of this, where the call to praise God is followed by proclamation of his character and deeds.

9. The orality of praise is important, both in understanding the role of the believer and the possible place of music within praise:

> *As verbal acknowledgement, praise is response to what we see or experience. Praise does not express a yearning or wish but responds to something given to us... When praise acknowledges, it proclaims truth; otherwise it is flattery and deceit, deceiving both the one praised and the one doing the praising* (Keck, 1992: 1167).

10. The *Ring of Praise* (1985) songbook does this by specifying in its subject index separate listings for 'Exultant Praise', 'Meditative Praise', 'Rejoicing Praise' and 'Personal Praise'. These categories appear to have been delineated according to the singer's place within the song, clearly disregarding strict biblical notions of praise.

11. For example, Hillsong have released *The Secret Place: Hillsong Instrumental Series Volume 1* (2000) and are planning an album of 'communion' songs for 2006. The possibilities of instrumental music and 'journey' music are beginning to be explored by numerous parties around the world. In Australia Dave Gleeson from Melbourne and Prayerworks from CCC lead the way. Undoubtedly this is a music that will become increasingly important to future corporate worship and theomusicological studies.

12. A similar, though more abstract, idea is presented by Corbitt (1998), who states that 'worship music' should be Christ-centred, God-directed, Spirit-empowered and expressive of, and edifying to, the church (as community) (72).

13. Carson also chooses to adopt the term corporate worship, while simultaneously recognising the 'ambiguities inherent within it' (2002: 49). Timothy Keller is more disparaging, labelling it a 'somewhat inelegant term' but nonetheless employing it throughout his useful study of alternate corporate worship forms (2002: 207).

14. Corbitt (1998) notes that the element of unity is of fundamental importance to the community of believers:

> *The members of the community live in constant yearning to attain unity, unity with God and unity with each other.* [Corporate worship] *offers an event when the community can come together and hope to find unity... The community comes face to face with God, and in his presence seeks affirmation and healing. As the community builds physical unity with one another through praise, it comes to a point of realizing the sins and powers that prohibit unity... The event is not totally complete; it is a process... From this event, the individual responds in continued life service* (55).

15. Note too John Frame's excellent analogy of a worker in the King's palace, where service, respect and homage are occurring all the time, yet when the King enters the room 'something special happens' (1996: 33).

16. This sense of nostalgia is an underlying feature of all debates centred on the use of traditional liturgy and corporate worship. Feld (2001) notes that the same sense of nostalgia is largely inherent to the Bosavi people of Papua New Guinea who, ironically, are involved in the production of a contemporary guitar-based music (unpublished Trajectories conference paper, Macquarie University, 2001).

17. Unfortunately they often invoke misleading statistics and generalisations to assist their argument. One example of this, cited in Dawn (1995: 180), quotes a letter questioning why the church (in the USA) continues to utilise music that is foreign to 98 per cent of the population. The basis for this contention is that only 2 per cent of the

US population listen to classical music. Clearly this fact alone does not make hymns foreign to the other 98 per cent of the population. Furthermore, the protagonist allies classical music with traditional hymnody. Given the discussion on the popular (and sometimes secular) beginnings of hymnody outlined in Chapter 2, this is clearly a misnomer, yet one that is regularly manifested throughout the modern church.

18. The term 'blended' is used to refer to services that contain elements of both contemporary and traditional worship, frequently music. Many see the blended service as the obvious way to appease different preferences within the church. In opposition, others argue that the blended service ultimately appeases no one and only serves to further disenfranchise all parties. They contend that blended services should only be used as a transitional bridge from traditional to contemporary styles, and (though highly unlikely) vice versa. For further discussion on blended services see Basden (1999: 104; 110–12) and Webber (1998).

19. For example, 'seeker-driven churches, purpose-driven churches, permissive churches, resurrected churches, twenty-first-century churches, metro metamorphosis-size churches and new apostolic churches, just to mention a few' (Boschman, 1999: 27).

20. Boschman (1999: 75) provides a list of predominantly Protestant and Pentecostal worship metamorphoses throughout history, arguing that each created an entirely new culture of worship. For instance, he cites the death and resurrection of Christ, the coming of the Holy Spirit at Pentecost, the Reformation, the translation of the Bible into vernacular languages, the Great Awakenings of the eighteenth century, the rise of the Charismatic Movement in the 1960s and 1970s, and the Toronto Blessing of 1995.

21. LeFever (1997) agrees and raises the notion that people worship differently due to the fact that we all learn differently, i.e. some respond to verbal stimulation, some visual, and others tactile.

22. Indeed, several seeker services that I have been involved in have drawn heavily on the use of well-known hymns, in an effort to appeal to the more mature audience attracted to the event.

Chapter 4

1. Corbitt himself distinguishes between 'sanctuary' music (that used within a church context) and 'street' music (that used outside the church) (1998: 37). Such delineation works effectively in his broader cultural and intercultural investigation.

2. See Goodall (1995) for detailed exposition of these terms.

3. Even more pointed is Corbitt's notion of critical contextualisation, developed in order to import secular music, particularly in non-Western environments, directly into corporate worship situations. Considering the magnitude of this idea, his rather brief rationalisation argues that one can reject, accept or 'deal with' secular music (1998: 280). This latter option he marks out as contextualisation of the music within biblical principles. However, inside the rubric of intercultural music studies, such a process is more readily viewed as syncretism (which he attributes to blind acceptance of secular musics). The frequent result of syncretism is a new music, a by-product of the intersection of two distinct cultures (see Kartomi, 1981).

4. A similar phenomenon occurred, and continues to take place, in the USA, much to the chagrin of some commentators: '[t]he vast majority of Christians in America are unwilling or unprepared to engage the secular, except to regularly make it the object of their protest' (Eberly quoted in Boschman, 1999: 37).

5. An interesting parallel can be drawn with the assertion by C. S. Lewis (1970) that music of the church was merely fifth-rate poems set to sixth-rate music. Clearly those living at the turn of the new millennium are not the only ones to have ever struggled over style and quality issues in congregational music.

6. This latter outcome confirms Gilbert's assertion that: 'A vital difference between the secularization of the "Church" and the secularization of the wider culture is that the involvement of the Churches in the former process is to a significant extent *active* as well as simply *reactive*' (1980: 106, original emphasis).

7. Dawn also includes evangelistic songs that call on people to 'believe and be saved' (1995: 171). Although these songs are clearly not meant for the edification of believers, they can, and do, have a place within specifically focused types of corporate worship.

8. These are songs largely composed for Christian camps and conferences, usually aimed at adolescents. The songs are often characterised by simple, contagious melodies and are frequently accompanied by preset body movements and clapping patterns. How Dawn distinguishes these from a plethora of 'standard' congregational songs that could fall into this category remains problematic.

9. See particularly Liesch (1996), Kraeuter (1991; 1993), Sorge (1987), Hooper (1986), and Osbeck (1961). Also note the proliferation of magazines aimed at worship leaders and participants (e.g. *Worship Leader*, *Worship Together*).

10. For a useful analysis of Wesley's lyric in this hymn, see Marshall and Todd (1982: 72–73).

11. For various stories concerning experiences that prompted C. Wesley to write 'Jesus, Lover Of My Soul', see Osbeck (1982: 130).

12. 'How Deep The Father's Love For Us', by Stuart Townend © 1995 Thankyou Music.

Chapter 5

1. Dianne Gome's (1997) investigation of colonial hymnody reveals that, despite evidence of some distinctly Australian themes, most worship music was in fact from European sources.

2. It was not, however, until the *NSW Church Act 1836* that equality between the main denominations was established. The four groups recognised in the Act were the Catholics, Anglicans, Presbyterians and Methodists. For further discussion, see Blombery (1996: 12–15).

3. For the Scottish theological basis of Presbyterianism in the nineteenth century, see Burke and Hughes (1996: 1–12).

4. The St Andrews Cathedral Choir School opened in 1885.

5. Many of Sankey's tunes, though present in the *English Hymnal*, appear in a section entitled 'Not Suitable For Ordinary Use'. Although firmly grounded in theology, and closely tied to revivalist missions, an apparent danger was perceived in replacing traditional hymns with Sankey's tunes. Then, as now, contemporary musical stylings

were alienated from the general corpus of Christian song, as something to be very carefully considered.

6. Denominations include the Assemblies of God, the Apostolic Church (Australia), the Full Gospel Church, Christian City Church, Christian Outreach Centre, Christian Life Centre, Christian Revival Crusade, and many others.

7. Glossolalia also refers to non-meaningful speech, often associated with schizophrenic disorders.

8. It is the place of Baptism in the Spirit, and glossolalia, that delineates different Pentecostal denominations. 'Charismatic' Pentecostals believe in a discrete baptism in the Spirit; however, it need not be accompanied by glossolalia. 'Third Wave' Pentecostals believe in the gifts of the Spirit, but not necessarily a distinct baptism of the Spirit (Chant, 2000: 42 n. 25). This latter teaching is one that applies to most evangelical churches as well. Chant concludes that should Pentecostalism ever renege its 'insistence on constituents receiving the Spirit with the sign of tongues ... Pentecostalism would finish up becoming just another Protestant denomination' (ibid.: 545).

9. A movement named after Alexander Dowie, an Australian Congregationalist minister who believed that healing through faith was still possible in the modern church. He eventually moved to the US in 1886 and in 1896 formed his own denomination called the Christian Catholic Church. While much of his theology was tenuous (he began his own city on the shores of Lake Michigan and made special claims for himself as a resurrected Elijah), it was his interest in healing through faith and other gifts of the Spirit that would most influence the Pentecostal Church. For further discussion on Dowie's influence see Hughes (1996: 9–10).

10. Chant rightfully points out that not all such behaviour is strictly 'Pentecostal', but is however representative of the Pentecostal ethos (2000: 47).

11. More recently Planet Shakers Church has also become an important influence in contemporary congregational song.

12. CLC Darlinghurst, Sydney, which was founded by Frank Houston, grew from nine people in 1977 to more than 1300 by 1982 (Breward, 1993: 178). In 1999 it was subsumed into Hillsong Church as a 'city congregation'.

13. 'Assembly' is the Pentecostal word for congregation.

14. Though it is rare for Pentecostal churches to band together, each usually preferring to have its own vision, in February 2000 Houston sought to institutionally cement the significance of the Pentecostal movement within the Australian church by forming an alliance of Pentecostal churches called Australian Christian Churches. This alliance represents over one thousand churches and 170,000 members – by no means all Pentecostals but a major proportion of them. By heading up this alliance Houston has also cemented the significance of Hillsong Church, as well as his personal prominence, within the denomination.

15. In 1986 CCC was officially recognised as a denomination, and by 1995 had over 1500 weekly attendees. Part of the church's vision is to see a CCC in all the major cities of the world. In 1995 there were fifty-four CCCs throughout Australia and the world; in 2006 there are over 150.

16. Later the band became almost exclusively Hillsong based, and Youth Alive morphed into a ministry of Hillsong Church.

17. For examples, see Psalm 105:15 and Isaiah 45:1.

18. It should be acknowledged that not all Pentecostals view musical involvement as essential. Many believe that the anointing can only fall on a group of believers who have achieved a spirit of unity (as opposed to divisiveness). It may be repelled by hardness of heart in various persons present (i.e. the absence of anointing has little to do with lack of expertise or devotion on the part of the music group).

19. For more detailed exegesis of this interpretation see also www.worshipmap.com/compassnf\cl-psalm22.html.

20. A point reinforced by Reinhardt Bonnke to the delegates at Hillsong conference, 8 July 2005.

21. While many of the generalisations presented here are true of many mainstream churches, North American Bruce Johnson makes the valid point that:

> the term 'worship leaders' as used in churches today is not used consistently of ONE role/office. Rather, those given such a label may vary widely in their gifts, function – and hence authority – from church to church. It is a big mistake to think that everyone given such a label fulfils, or SHOULD fulfil, precisely the same role (Worship List posting, 5 June 2002).

22. Some argue that passages from 1 Chronicles (namely 15:22, 27) indicate roles for leaders of worship in the OT sacrificial system. Yet the fact that there are some parallels does not mean the role and office are precisely the same, since the system in which each functions is inherently different. It can also be noted that *groups* of Levites often serve to assist in running the temple and its services – quite independent of any musical involvement.

23. Matt Redman (an internationally acclaimed worship leader and songwriter from the UK) feels that instead of the title 'worship leader', the person should rather be known as 'lead worshipper'. This, he believes, would negate some of the fame attached to the role, and more accurately reflect the worship leader's participation *in* the group of worshippers. (See www.heartofworship.com/articles/)

24. Hillsong Conference was an early Hills CLC initiative, with 150 delegates registering for the conference in 1986. The original conference was modelled on the Australian Christian Music Seminars held annually in Cooma (NSW). Geoff Bullock attended the Cooma seminars prior to inaugurating Hillsong conference. In 2005, Hillsong conference attracted more than 28,000 registrants from fifty-five countries, representing twenty-one different denominations. The free night-time rallies held during the week attracted over 110,000 people. Held at multiple venues throughout Sydney, the conference offers training and programs for pastors, singers and musicians, creative ministries, children's work, media specialists, worship leaders, business people and much more. The conference coincides with the launch of the new Hillsong album every year, and in 1999 the first *United Live* album was recorded live during the conference. The immense popularity of the conference has spawned touring conferences, held in New Zealand and North America each year.

25. The album featured several original Zschech compositions and collaborations, including 'The Only One', 'Dance And Shout' and 'He Loves You'. Geoff Bullock also contributed a song to the album.

26. 'Shout To The Lord' has been labelled the 'Amazing Grace of the modern era' (O'Donnell quoted in Bagnall, 2001: n.p.).
27. Based on a survey of worship websites and the Worship List, other prominent worship leaders include Ron Kenoly (USA), Matt Redman (UK), Robin Mark (Ireland), Tim Hughes (UK), Darrell Evans (USA) and Don Moen (USA). Remarkably, Zschech is the only female amongst this list; in fact she is one of very few internationally recognised female worship leaders.

Chapter 6

1. Adaptations will be clear throughout, many resulting from the lack of fine music instrumentation and structures within popular music. Many terms come directly from traditional musicology, though some ('riff', 'hook', etc.) have developed within popular music studies to reflect and examine more acutely the texts under consideration.
2. For further discussion on the notion of the 'groove', see Feld (1994).
3. Spatial preferencing is a term used to describe the placement of sounds within the sound mix. Such delineation allows for spatial mapping that traces the movement of various sounds, and their hierarchical structure, throughout the course of a work. Spatial preferencing is usually noted in terms of a three-dimensional 'sound box', representing the entirety of the sound mix. It is normally conceived and effected at the mixing stage of production, marking it as the ideal poietic operation. For further discussion, see Hayward (1998) and Moore (1993).
4. In his own classification of contemporary church hymnody, Gieschen follows generic stereotypes to arrive at the following list: Contemporary Esoteric, Church Modern, Neo-Romantic, Pop Chord Romantic, A Touch of Broadway, Popular Triumphalism, Holy Pop, Pseudo-Folk, Clever Casual, and Trivial (cited in Dawn, 1995: 167). Such a categorisation appears altogether useless for the purpose of understanding current variations within congregational song.
5. Corbitt (1998: 195–96) also provides a helpful model for theomusicological analysis, though his model applies more to the comparison and analysis of intercultural church music.
6. Many thanks to Christine Carroll for assisting in the delineation of these categories.
7. Songs with God speaking in the first person appear more prevalent in the 1970s and 1980s, for example, 'I Am The Bread Of Life' (1971), 'And You Shall Seek Me' (1972), 'Be Not Afraid' (1975) and 'This Is My Body' (1980).
8. As found on the Watershed Music release, *Deeper and Deeper* (1999).
9. © 2002 Thankyou Music.
10. According to the 2005 CCLI reporting lists, 'Lord I Lift Your Name On High' was the third most popular song in Australia, South Africa and the USA, and fifth most used in New Zealand and the UK.
11. Released in 1994, 'Shout To The Lord' was the most sung congregational song in Australia and New Zealand according to the 1997 CCLI top 25. It was not until 1998, however, that it took hold outside of Oceania, reaching number thirteen in the UK, number nineteen in the USA, and number one in Canada. The 2001 CCLI lists had the song at number one in Australia and Sweden, number two in the US and Canada, number four in Finland and New Zealand, and number fourteen in South Africa.

According to the 2005 survey, 'Shout To The Lord' had shot to number one in South Africa and the UK, remained at one in Sweden and four in New Zealand, and landed at number two in Australia and number four in the USA. These figures showcase the extraordinary popularity of the song in churches throughout the Western world.

12. In the 1997 CCLI survey, 'This Kingdom' was the eighth most popular congregational song in Australia. By the 2001 listing it had only dropped to thirteenth. This is largely due to its adoption in more traditional mainline churches. It has also been part of the song-list for Katoomba Christian Conventions (KCC), the largest evangelical conferences held in Australia.

13. Given that the Holy Spirit is numerously referred to in Scripture as a masculine, personal being (Ezekiel 3:24; 8:3; 11:5; Acts 11:15; 28:25), the intention or accuracy of the word 'it' is questionable.

14. Most biblical references to 'consuming fire' refer to God's anger and wrath (e.g. Deuteronomy 4:24; Isaiah 30:27); however, Exodus 24:17 describes the glory of the Lord settling on Mount Sinai 'like a consuming fire'.

15. For more on non-traditional church spaces, see Frost and Hirsch, 2003.

16. See, for example, Psalm 100:

> *A psalm. For giving thanks. Shout for joy to the LORD, all the earth. Worship the LORD with gladness;* come before him *with joyful songs. Know that the LORD is God. It is he who made us, and* we are his; we are his people, *the sheep of his pasture.* Enter his gates *with thanksgiving* and his courts with praise; *give thanks to him and praise his name. For the LORD is good and his love endures forever; his faithfulness continues through all generations* (Psalms 100:1-5, emphasis added).

In the psalm the people are collectively called to meet before God, in the unity of their belief and place before him. Once assembled – in like purpose – they move through the gates and into the outer courts of the temple. A progression through the various courts of the temple ensues, until they ultimately meet the priest who has entered the Holies of Holies, the presence of God, on their behalf.

17. Concessionally, it must be noted that renditions of all congregational songs may utilise varying tempi in different settings. For this study the album of release has been the definer of tempo.

18. Appropriately enough, the word 'Toronto' is derived from a term for meeting place in the language of the original indigenous North Americans of the region.

19. The blessing originated at the Toronto Airport Vineyard Church and was subsequently 'transferred' to other churches.

20. See also Deuteronomy 11:14 for a similar linguistic use.

21. Bullock noted how he had desired to use another word, rather than 'worship', in order to avoid such connotations and stereotypes (interview with the author, 2000).

Chapter 7

1. The survey of song-types in Australian congregational song covered a selection of albums between 1992–1999.

2. See full lyrical exposition of this song in Chapter 4.

3. In an international survey of popular congregational song conducted by the Worship Resources Centre website (http://www.praise.net/worship/survey/), 'The Power Of Your Love' was placed twelfth. The official copyright collecting agency for Christian music (CCLI) placed 'Power Of Your Love' second on the Australian list and New Zealand list in August 1997, each time bettered by 'Shout To The Lord'. In the February 2001 list, 'Power Of Your Love' was placed fifth in Australia, fourteenth in New Zealand, eighteenth in Canada and twenty-fourth in the United Kingdom. By the 2005 survey this had improved to seventh in New Zealand, fifteenth in South Africa, twenty-first in the UK, seventeenth in Canada, and remained unchanged at fifth in Australia. Given that 'Power Of Your Love' was written in 1991 and released in 1992, these figures highlight the popularity and relative longevity of the song within churches worldwide.

4. For references concerning the ramifications of seeing the Lord 'face to face' see Judges 6:21-24. Note in contrast, however, the psalmist's cry to 'seek the face of the Lord' (Psalm 27:8).

5. © 2002 Thankyou Music.

6. Altars are only symbolically represented in most Pentecostal churches, unlike many Anglican and Catholic churches which house physical altars.

7. This technique, however, was common within the revivals and evangelistic crusades of the nineteenth and twentieth centuries, where solo items were often performed after the delivery of the sermon, allowing people to meditate on the message and respond appropriately (Mansfield, 1994).

Chapter 8

1. Transcribed from an in-house video interview posted on the Hillsong website (www.hillsong.com.au, accessed 4 June 2001).

2. Taken from www.worshiptogether.com/magazine/default.asp?id=14, accessed 15 November 2002.

3. 'Heart of Worship' by Matt Redman © 1997 Thankyou Music.

Bibliography

Bagnall, D
   2000   'The New Believers'. *The Bulletin* 11/4.
   2001   'Upon This Rock'. *The Bulletin* 26/9.
Balmer, R.
   1999   'Hymns on MTV'. *Christianity Today* 15/11: 32–39.
Banks, R.
   1992   *God the Worker*. Sydney: Albatross Books.
Barker, K. *et al.*
   1985   *The NIV Study Bible*. Michigan: Zondervan.
Barthes, R.
   1977   *Image, Music, Text*. London: Fontana/Collins.
Basden, P.
   1999   *The Worship Maze: Finding a Style to Fit Your Church*. Downers Grove: Inter-Varsity Press.
Begbie, J.
   2000   *Theology, Music and Time*. Cambridge: Cambridge University Press.
Bibby, R.
   2004   *Restless Churches: How Canada's Churches Can Contribute to the Emerging Religious Renaissance*. Toronto: Novalis.
Blombery, T.
   1996   *The Anglicans in Australia*. Canberra: Australian Government Printing Service.
Blume, F.
   1974   *Protestant Church Music: A History*. New York: W.W. Norton.
Boschman, L.
   1999   *Future Worship*. Ventura, CA: Renew.
Breward, I.
   1993   *A History of the Australian Churches*. Sydney: Allen & Unwin.
Bullock, G.
   1998   *Hands of Grace*. Sydney: Strand Publishing.
   2000   *The Power of Your Love*. Sydney: Strand Publishing.
Burke, D., and P. Hughes
   1996   *The Presbyterians in Australia*. Canberra: Australian Government Printing Service.
Careless, S.
   1999   'Former Pentecostal Leader Becomes Anglican'. *Anglican Journal* (April).
Carey, H.
   1996   *Believing in Australia: A Cultural History of Religions*. Sydney: Allen & Unwin.
Carson, D. (ed.)
   1992   *Worship: Adoration and Action*. Grand Rapids: Baker Books.
   2002   *Worship by the Book*. Grand Rapids: Zondervan.

Chant, B.
    2000   'The Spirit of Pentecost: Origins and Development of the Pentecostal Movement in Australia, 1870–1939'. Unpublished PhD dissertation, Macquarie University, Sydney.

Citron, M.
    2000   *Gender and the Musical Canon*. Chicago: University of Illinois Press.

Clarke, E.
    2002   'Jazz Band in Church for Pentecost 2002'. *Music in the Air: Song and Spirituality*. Winter 14.

Clowney, E.
    1992   'Presbyterian Worship', in D. Carson (ed.), *Worship: Adoration and Action*. Grand Rapids: Baker Books.

Cohen, S.
    1997   'Men Making a Scene: Rock Music and the Production of Gender', in S. Whiteley (ed.), *Sexing the Groove: Popular Music and Gender*. London and New York: Routledge.

Corbitt, N.
    1998   *The Sound of the Harvest: Music's Mission in Church and Culture*. Grand Rapids: Baker Books.

Corbitt, N., and V. Nix-Early
    2003   *Taking it to the Streets*. Grand Rapids: Baker Books.

Cox, H.
    1996   *Fire from Heaven: The Rise of Pentecostal Spirituality and the Reshaping of Religion in the Twenty-first Century*. London: Cassell.

Crabtree, J.
    2006   'Instrumental Music in Corporate Worship: The Place of Prayerworks'. Unpublished PhD dissertation, Macquarie University.

Csikszentmihalyi, M.
    1996   *Creativity: Flow and the Psychology of Discovery and Invention*. New York: Harper Collins.

Cullmann, O.
    1953   *Early Christian Worship*. London: SCM Press.

Dawn, M.
    1995   *Reaching Out Without Dumbing Down: A Theology of Worship for the Turn-of-the-Century Culture*. Grand Rapids: Eerdmans.

Dearborn, T., and S. Coil (eds.)
    2004   *Worship at the Next Level*. Grand Rapids: Baker Books.

DeNora, T.
    2000   *Music in Everyday Life*. Cambridge: Cambridge University Press.

Dickson, J.
    1996   'Worship and the Didgeridoo'. *The Briefing* 20/2.

Douglas, J. *et al.*
    1980   *The Illustrated Bible Dictionary*. Sydney: Hodder and Stoughton.

Drinker, S.
    1995   *Music and Women: The Story of Women in Their Relation to Music*. New York: The Feminist Press at The City University New York, 2nd edn 1948.

Etherington, C.
1962   *Protestant Worship Music*. New York: Holt, Reinhart and Winston.
Evans, M.
1999a   'Be Who You Want to be: Identifying (with) Vernacular Music', in G. Bloustien
         (ed.), *Musical Visions*. Adelaide: Wakefield Press.
1999b   'Geoff Bullock Changes his Mind on Worship'. *The Briefing* 29/4.
2000   'Beyond Fear: Taking Christian Music Out of the Safety Zone'. *The Briefing* 18/10.
2001   'The Evolution of Alanis', in T. Mitchell, P. Doyle and B. Johnson (eds.), *Changing
         Sounds: New Directions and Configurations in Popular Music*. IASPM 1999 Interna-
         tional Conference Proceedings. Sydney: University of Technology.
Evans, M., and D. Crowdy
2005   'Wrangling the Figures: Marketing an Industry at the Margins', in M. Evans and
         G. Walden (eds.), *Markets and Margins: Australian Country Music*. Vol. 3. Gym-
         pie: AICM Press.
Faulkner, Q.
1996   *Wiser Than Despair: The Evolution of Ideas in the Relationship of Music and the Chris-
         tian Church*. Westport: Greenwood Press.
Feld, S.
1994   'From Schizophonia to Schismogenesis: On the Discourses and Commodification
         Processes of "World Music" and "World Beat" ', in C. Keil, and S. Feld, *Music
         Grooves*. Chicago: University of Chicago Press.
Ferris, J.
1999   *Music: The Art of Listening*. 5th ed. New York: McGraw-Hill.
Fischer, J.
1994   *On a Hill Too Far Away*. Michigan: Vine Books.
Fischer, M.
1999a   'Jesus, Lover Of My Soul'. *Perspectives* 6.3.
1999b   'Do You Feel Anointed?'. *Perspectives* 5.2.
Flanagan, B.
1995   *U2 at the End of the World*. London: Bantam Press.
Foote, J.
2002   'Cultural Consumption and Participation'. *Canadian Journal of Communication*
         27.2: 209–220.
Frame, J.
1996   *Worship in Spirit and Truth*. Phillipsburg: Presbyterian and Reformed.
Frost, M., and A. Hirsch
2003   *The Shaping of Things to Come: Innovation and Mission for the 21st Century Church*.
         Massachusetts and Erina: Hendrickson Publishers and Strand Publishing.
Gilbert, A.
1980   *The Making of Post-Christian Britain: A History of the Secularization of Modern
         Society*. London: Longman.
Gome, D.
1997   'Australian Colonial Hymnody, 1788–1901: How Australian?', *Australian Music
         Research 2-3*. Melbourne: Centre for Studies in Australian Music.

Goodall, P.
    1995   *High Culture, Popular Culture: The Long Debate*. Sydney: Allen & Unwin.
Grout, D.
    1960   *A History of Western Music*. London: J.M. Dent.
Guthrie, D., and J. Motyer (eds.)
    1970   *The New Bible Commentary Revised*. London: Inter-Varsity Press.
Hallet, P.
    1999   'Praise and Worship: Finding God in all the Hype'. *Alive* (June).
Hamilton, M.
    1999   'The Triumph of the Praise Songs: How Guitars Beat Out the Organ in the Worship Wars'. *Christianity Today* 12/7: 28–33.
Hanning, B.
    2002   *Concise History of Western Music*. 2nd ed. New York: W.W. Norton.
Harding, M.
    1987   'The Biblical Concept of Praise', in B. Webb (ed.), *Church, Worship and the Local Congregation*. Sydney: Lancer Books.
Hayward, P.
    1998   *Music at the Borders: Not Drowning, Waving and their Engagement with Papua New Guinean Culture (1986–1996)*. Sydney: John Libbey & Co.
Hayward, P. (ed.)
    1999   *Widening the Horizon: Exoticism in Post-War Popular Music*. Sydney: John Libbey and Co/Perfect Beat Publications.
Hooper, W.
    1986   *Ministry and Musicians*. Nashville: Broadman Press.
Hughes, P.
    1996   *The Pentecostals in Australia*. Canberra: Australian Government Printing Service.
Hustad, D.
    1981   *Jubilate! Church Music in the Evangelical Tradition*. Des Moines: Hope.
Jensen, P.
    1987   'The Lord and His Church: Implications for Worship', in B. Webb (ed.), *Church, Worship and the Local Congregation*. Sydney: Lancer Books.
Johnson, B.
    1998   'Watching the Watchers: Who do we think we are?'. Web-published IASPM-Australasia seminar paper (http://www.arts.unsw.edu.au/jazz/Arch/BJAR/).
    2000   *The Inaudible Music: Jazz, Gender and Australian Modernity*. Sydney: Currency Press.
Kaldor, P. *et al.*
    1999   *Build My Church: Trends and Possibilities for Australian Churches*. Sydney: Open Book Publishers.
Kaldor, P., R. Dixon and R. Powell
    1999   *Taking Stock: A Profile of Australian Church Attenders*. Sydney: Open Book Publishers.
Kartomi, M.
    1981   'The Processes and Results of Musical Culture Contact: A Discussion of Terminology and Concepts'. *Ethnomusicology* 25: 227–49.

Keck, L.
1992   'Caught in the Act: Praise and Renewal in the Church'. *The Christian Century* 109.37 (December).

Keller, T.
2002   'Reformed Worship in the Global City', in D. Carson (ed.), *Worship by the Book*. Grand Rapids: Zondervan.

Kierkegaard, S.
1958   *Edifying Discourses: A Selection*. London: Collins.

Kraeuter, T.
1991   *Keys to Becoming an Effective Worship Leader*. Hillsboro: Emerald Books.
1993   *Developing an Effective Worship Ministry*. Hillsboro: Emerald Books.

Kynaston, T., and R. Ricci
1978   *Jazz Improvisation*. New Jersey: Prentice-Hall.

Lang, P.
1941   *Music in Western Civilization*. New York: W.W. Norton.

Lawrence, H.
2000   'Mipla preize nem blo Yu': Contemporary Christian Song of Eastern Torres Strait', in T. Mitchell and P. Doyle (eds.), *Changing Sounds: New Directions and Configurations in Popular Music*. IASPM 1999 International Conference Proceedings. Sydney: University of Technology.

LeFever, M.
1997   'Instincts of the Soul'. *Worship Together* 21 (July/August).

Lewis, C.
1961   *Reflections on the Psalms*. London: Fount Paperbacks.
1963   *Letters to Malcolm, Chiefly on Prayer*. New York: Harcourt, Brace and World.
1970   *God in the Dock: Essays on Theology and Ethics*. Grand Rapids: Eerdmans.

Liesch, B.
1996   *The New Worship: Straight Talk on Music and the Church*. Grand Rapids: Baker Books.

Long, K.
1972   *Music of the English Church*. London: Hodder and Stoughton.

Lorenz, E.
1923   *Church Music: What a Minister Should Know About it*. New York: Fleming H. Revell.

Lucas, R.
1980   *Fullness and Freedom: The Message of Colossians and Philemon*. Leicester: Inter-Varsity Press.

Mackinlay, E., and F. Baker
2005   'Singing to Know Baby, Singing to Know Self: Lullaby Singing as a Pedagogical Tool in the Everyday Life of First-time Mothers'. *Perfect Beat* 7.3 (July).

Mansfield, J.
1994   'The Music of Australian Revivalism', in M. Hutchinson, E. Campion and S. Piggin (eds.), *Reviving Australia: Essays on the History and Experience of Revival and Revivalism in Australian Christianity*. Sydney: Centre for the Study of Australian Christianity.

Marshall, M., and J. Todd
  1982   *English Congregational Hymns in the Eighteenth Century*. Lexington: University Press of Kentucky.
Martin, R.
  1964   *Worship in the Early Church*. Grand Rapids: Eerdmans.
Marty, P.
  1998   'Beyond the Polarization: Grace and Surprise in Worship'. *The Christian Century* 115.9 (March).
McClary, S., and R. Walser
  1990   'Start Making Sense! Musicology Wrestles With Rock', in S. Frith and A. Goodwin (eds.), *On Record: Rock, Pop and the Written Word*. London: Routledge.
McIntyre, P.
  2000   'The Domain of Songwriters: Towards a Definition of Song', in T. Mitchell and P. Doyle (eds.), *Changing Sounds: New Directions and Configurations in Popular Music*. IASPM 1999 International Conference Proceedings. Sydney: University of Technology.
Middleton, R.
  1990   *Studying Popular Music*. Milton Keynes: Open University Press.
Midian, A.
  1999   *The Value of Indigenous Music in the Life and Ministry of the Church: The United Church in the Duke of York Islands*. Boroko: Institute of Papua New Guinea Studies.
Moore, Alan
  1993   *Rock: The Primary Text*. Milton Keynes: Open University Press.
Moore, A.
  2002   'Improvisation in the Air – in Jazz and Religion'. *Music in the Air: Song and Spirituality*. Winter 14.
Morgenthaler, S.
  1995   *Worship Evangelism*. Grand Rapids: Zondervan.
Mowinckel, S.
  1967   *The Psalms in Israel's Worship*. New York: Abingdon Press.
Nattiez, J.
  1990   *Music and Discourse: Towards a Semiology of Music*. Princeton: Princeton University Press.
Nehring, N.
  1997   *Popular Music, Gender, and Postmodernism*. Thousand Oaks, CA: Sage Publications.
Nelson, W.
  1989   *1 Samuel*. Colorado Springs: Navpress.
Noll, M.
  1999   'We are what We Sing'. *Christianity Today* 12/7: 37–41.
Osbeck, K.
  1961   *The Ministry of Music*. Grand Rapids: Kregel Publications.
  1982   *101 Hymn Stories*. Grand Rapids: Kregel Publications.
Payne, T.
  1996   'Confessions of a Teenage Praise Junkie'. *The Briefing* 20/2.
Peterson, D.
  1992   *Engaging With God*. Leicester: Apollos.

1996   *Christian Worship*. Sydney: Moore Theological College.
Piggin, S.
1996   *Evangelical Christianity in Australia: Spirit, Word and World*. Melbourne: Oxford University Press.
Price, D.
1998   'Praise & Worship Music Extending its Retail, Radio Reach'. *Billboard* 5/12: 3–6.
Quasten, J.
1983   *Music and Worship in Pagan and Christian Antiquity*. Washington: National Association of Pastoral Musicians.
Redman, M.
2001   *The Unquenchable Worshipper: Coming Back to the Heart of Worship*. Ventura: Regal Books.
Reed, T.
2003   *The Holy Profane: Religion in Black Popular Music*. Lexington: University Press of Kentucky.
Rosar, W.
2001   'The *Dies Irae* in *Citizen Kane*: Musical Hermeneutics Applied to Film Music', in K. Donnelly (ed.), *Film Music: Critical Approaches*. Edinburgh: Edinburgh University Press.
Routley, E.
1967   *The Church and Music*. London: Gerald Duckworth.
1977   *A Short History of English Church Music*. Oxford: Mowbrays.
Rowley, H.
1967   *Worship in Ancient Israel*. Philadelphia: Fortress.
Sadie, S. (ed.)
1980   *The New Grove Dictionary of Music and Musicians*. London: Grove.
Scribner, R.
1986   *The German Reformation*. Basingstoke: Macmillan Press.
Shelley, B.
1995   *Church History in Plain Language*. Dallas: Word Publishing.
Shepherd, J.
1991   *Music as Social Text*. Cambridge: Polity Press.
Shuker, R.
1994   *Understanding Popular Music*. London and New York: Routledge.
Smith, J.
2000   'Think Globally Act Locally'. *Care Communication Concern* (June).
Smith, R.
2000   'Music to Gather by'. *Perspectives* 8.2.
Sorge, B.
1987   *Exploring Worship: A Practical Guide to Praise and Worship*. New York: Oasis House.
Stek, J.
1985   'Psalms: Introduction', in K. Barker *et al.* (eds).
Stott, J.
1979   *The Message of Ephesians*. Leicester: Inter-Varsity Press.
Taylor, T.
1997   *Global Pop: World Music, World Markets*. New York: Routledge.

Thiessen, D.

1994   *Psalms, Hymns and Spiritual Songs: What the Bible Says About Music*. Chicago: Cornerstone Press.

Volf, M.

1992   'Reflections on a Christian Way of Being-in-the-World', in D. Carson (ed.), *Worship: Adoration and Action*. Grand Rapids: Baker Books.

Webber, R.

1998   *Planning Blended Worship: The Creative Mixture of Old and New*. Nashville: Abingdon.

White, J.

1993   *A Brief History of Christian Worship*. Nashville: Abingdon.

Whiteley, S. (ed)

1997   *Sexing the Groove: Popular Music and Gender*. London and New York: Routledge.

Wilson-Dickson, A.

1992   *The Story of Christian Music*. Oxford: Lion Publishing.

Woodhouse, J.

1994   'The key to Church Music', in S. Trethewey, and R. Milne (eds.), *Church Musicians' Handbook*. Sydney: St Matthias Press.

Zahn, H.

1996   *Mission and Music: Jabêm Traditional Music and the Development of Lutheran Hymnody*. Boroko: Institute of Papua New Guinea Studies.

Zschech, D.

1996   *Worship*. Sydney: Hillsong Australia.

2001   *Extravagant Worship*. Sydney: Hillsong Australia.

Index to Bible References

Subject Index

Printed in the United States
78136LV00001B/25-42